PSYCHOTHERAPY
EAST · AND · WEST

A Unifying Paradigm

Swami Ajaya, Ph.D.

Ah-jai-ya

The Himalayan International Institute
of Yoga Science and Philosophy of the U.S.A.
Honesdale, Pennsylvania

*The paper used in this publication meets the minimum requirements of
American National Standard for Information Sciences—Permanence of
Paper for Printed Library Materials, ANSI Z39.48-1984.*

Fourth printing 1992

Library of Congress Cataloging in Publication Data:

Ajaya, Swami, 1940-
    Psychotherapy East and West: A Unifying Paradigm
    Includes bibliographical references.
    I. Psychotherapy— Cross-cultural studies.
    I. Title. [DNLM: 1. Psychotherapy. 2. Yoga. 3. Cross-cultural comparison. WM 420 A312p]
    RC480.5.A38 1984   616.89'14   83-22608
    ISBN 0-89389-087-1

PSYCHOTHERAPY
EAST · AND · WEST

A Unifying Paradigm

Contents

v

Foreword

Yoga psychotherapy is more ancient than any other form of psychotherapy. Its aim is to help one to understand himself on all levels and to realize the source of consciousness within. The psychology of the yogic sages is based on the profound philosophy described in the Upanishads, the Bhagavad Gita, the Veda, and the Yoga Sutras. The yogic sages were lovers of truth, and the psychology that flows from their philosophy leads one to realize his true nature. Yoga psychology dispels the darkness of ignorance and lifts the veil of illusion created by the mind. It allows one to see life as it really is.

The sages studied the psyche scientifically and developed methods for leading their students safely through the barriers of the mind to the reality dwelling beyond it. The students learned by the example and instruction of their teachers and from direct experience attained through practicing the methods described by their teachers. Gradually they came to see the nature of reality and were then able to instruct students of their own. The tradition has been carried on in this way for thousands of years and will continue to be carried on as long as individuals seek to know the ultimate reality.

Modern psychotherapy also aims at helping the individual to know himself, but it is a very young science, and it only goes part of the way. There are many modern schools of psychotherapy, each investigating a different aspect of the human being. Although these psychotherapies provide many useful techniques and have verified many interesting theories concerning human behavior and thinking, their philosophical foundations are frequently not explained. Modern psychology studies the individual's thoughts, emotions, speech, and actions, but it does not reach to the depths beyond the psyche—the spirit. In the modern world, the spirit is generally considered to be the realm of the philosopher, but the yogic sages did not separate philosophy and psychology in this way; rather their psychology was an expression of their philosophy, which was clearly stated and taught. Modern psychology is not built on the firm foundation of a philosophy derived through direct experience. Modern psychotherapy can deal with the surface issues that make people unhappy, but it is not able to deal with the underlying causes of those issues. Without focusing on one's cosmology as well as his behavior, the individual remains unhappy and confused. By placing their psychology within the context of philosophy, the yogic sages were able to deal with the source of human suffering, which is ignorance of the ultimate reality. Emotional maturity can be attained by letting go of the fear and desires that arise within. Everyone has the capacity to do this if he chooses to, and the means are available to those who search and are prepared to practice. Gradually, as one expands his awareness, his perspective changes so that he can enjoy the grand vista of life in its entirety.

This book is unique. It describes the world view and methods of the yogic sages and compares them to those of modern psychotherapists. Of these two systems, one is ancient, comprehensive, and proven, and the other is modern, experimental, and still in an evolving state. By introducing the sophisticated science of Eastern psychology and psychotherapy, the author provides the Western student with a unique opportunity to learn, compare, and apply the methods and knowledge found in both systems.

This book will also be of great benefit to those who are struggling to let go of confining concepts and are seeking to experience life from a more realistic perspective. The author relates the teachings of yoga psychotherapy to the process of self-transformation in a clear and practical manner. Each chapter has been written with such clarity and simplicity that even beginning students will have no difficulty in understanding the Eastern and Western approaches. I have not found any other book that explains the therapeutic paradigms of East and West with such understanding, insight, and clarity. The book will prove to be of immense value to those who apply the concepts and methods with sincerity and consistency.

Swami Ajaya is well qualified in both the Eastern and Western traditions. It is clear that his knowledge of the Upanishads and yoga psychology is profound. Swami Ajaya, formerly known as Dr. Allan Weinstock, was initiated in the ancient lineage of the yogic tradition of the Shankara order. He has lived in India in the Himalayas, studying and practicing all the methods of yoga psychotherapy and Vedanta philosophy. He is also a Ph.D. clinical psychologist with many years of counseling experience. His experience and training has given him great understanding of the difficulties that are frequently encountered on the path of self-understanding and self-realization. I am confident that this book will be widely appreciated and useful to all.

Swami Rama

Acknowledgments

Many associates, students, and clients have contributed their understanding and efforts to make this book possible. I thank the staff of the Himalayan Institute who helped in the preparation of this manuscript. Herb Koplowitz was kind enough to read the chapter on general systems theory and make valuable suggestions. Arpita diligently assisted in editing the final draft of the manuscript; Connie Trombley, Nancy Stunkard, and Janet Zima worked on the design of the book's front cover; Julio Colon prepared the index.

I am especially grateful to Aparna Bharati, who lent herself to the various phases of this project. She not only typed several preliminary drafts of the manuscript but made many valuable suggestions and contributed her editorial skill throughout.

I am also indebted to my clients, who allowed me to tape and transcribe our meetings. I cannot adequately convey how much I have learned as a result of their willingness to share their growth process. If they received half as much from me as I have from them, I would be more than pleased.

Finally I would like to thank those who have imparted their wisdom, that it may filter through this vehicle to you, the reader. During my postdoctoral training, Carl Whitaker, through his example and acceptance, taught me a great deal about the therapeutic process that I have assimilated into my own work.

My Gurudev, Swami Rama, has given me abundantly of his wisdom and love and has patiently guided me through the process of untangling the self-created snares within my own mind and personality. Many of the insights presented in this book came to me as I sat at Swamiji's feet. He imparted his knowledge of how to live practically in the world with joy and generosity for all while remaining above the turmoils of the world and realizing one's unity with the universal Self. He convinced me of the importance of undertaking this project and urged me to complete it.

What is of value in this book flows from the inspiration of the tradition that I seek to serve. Often in the course of writing, I was surprised by the insights flowing forth from a source more profound than my conscious understanding. To the long chain of enlightened masters who guide and nourish me, despite my obstinacy and inattentiveness, I bow in respect and reverence. Any distortions or misunderstandings that may be passed on through this book are the result of my as yet meager knowledge. I ask the reader's patience with any confusion that he may encounter in these pages.

Swami Ajaya

Part I

PSYCHOTHERAPY
EAST AND WEST

Introduction to Part I

Confusion and Conflict in Modern Psychology

There has been a proliferation of theories and methods of psychotherapy, with an ever-increasing variety of approaches. The person who wishes to enter therapy must choose between such strikingly different procedures as psychoanalysis, person-centered therapy, rational-emotive therapy, psychosynthesis, bioenergetics, transactional analysis, gestalt, neurolinguistic programming, primal scream therapy, Jungian analysis, hypnotherapy, family therapy, provocative therapy, and numerous other approaches to alleviating human suffering. Each of these methods may lead not only to a different result, but to a different realm of experience for the person traveling through the therapeutic process. Although many psychotherapists consider themselves to be eclectic and draw from more than one theory and set of techniques, no comprehensive paradigm has yet been presented for understanding how these diverse therapies relate to one another, and there has been no systematic integration or synthesis of these varied approaches. Instead, the practitioners devoted to each school have focused their energy on developing their own particular model, and often there is bitter rivalry over which is the most effective method for inducing change.

One young man who was in therapy with me and also in training to be a therapist himself told me of his confusion: "You know, there's a dictionary of therapies, a consumer's guide, with over a hundred different types and to me that's been a source of anxiety. Are those therapists all different in what they're doing? And if they are, how can I possibly decide which one is right for me as either therapist or client? Which is the most effective? How can I balance the claims of the various approaches and make any sense of the whole business? Do I just spend my time going from one to another, trying each one until it works?"

3

This book considers the assumptions that underlie our current psychologies and the value and limitations that result from building a psychological model from particular assumptions. It also explores new territory that lies beyond the boundaries created by the assumptions that typically characterize modern psychology and describes the way in which the various fragmented, partial, yet insightful perspectives for understanding human experience can be synthesized in a more comprehensive model of human functioning. This broader perspective is based on yoga psychology.

One often hears that psychology is still a young science and that at this stage it is too early to judge which model most accurately describes human functioning and which is the most effective in alleviating suffering. But yoga psychology offers another vantage point that can help one resolve this uncertainty. While modern psychology has emerged as a distinct science in only the last one hundred years, the systematic study of psychology in the East has been evolving over the past few thousand years. The approaches to self-transformation that have developed in yoga have been filtered and integrated into a systematic science. A comprehensive paradigm has been established that includes many of the methods being rediscovered in modern psychology.

Modern psychologists are for the most part unaware of yoga science as a systematic and comprehensive theoretical and applied psychology. However, if one were to study both modern psychology and yoga psychology, he would find that many of the psychological processes described in modern psychology are strikingly similar to conceptions found in yoga texts dating back more than a thousand years. For instance, such concepts as identification, projection, and transference are found in ancient yoga treatises as well as in modern depth psychology. But yoga psychology has extended the implications of these concepts far beyond modern psychology's comprehension of their scope.

Yoga psychology has also achieved considerable integration of seemingly divergent principles expounded by the various systems of modern psychology. Thus it is not unusual to find a behaviorist and a psychoanalyst each asserting that yoga psychology has a great deal in common with his own theory and method. A theorist, comparing modern behavioral psychology with yoga psychology, noted that "the language of the Yoga Sutras [a basic text of yoga psychology] is surprisingly similar to that of Skinner."[1] He concluded that "behavioral psychology can be usefully understood by placing it within the broad context of classical yoga psychology."[2] On the other hand, a psychoanalyst who also studied yoga wrote:

> I saw [the correspondence] between yoga ideas and psychoanalysis. . . . I told one of my colleagues of this observation. He seemed to think that I was saying that Freud had stolen his ideas from yoga. . . .
>
> Rather than doing a disservice to psychoanalysis in noting how many of its ideas are to be found thousands of years earlier in yoga, such observations simply lend weight to these ideas. . . .
>
> For me it was inspiring and instructive to find many psychoanalytic ideas in yoga. . . .
>
> The similarities are to me more striking than the differences.[3]

It may seem astounding that practitioners of two such divergent schools of thought could each claim a strong correspondence between their approach and yoga psychology. This is possible because yoga psychology offers a more comprehensive system that includes more circumscribed models within its scope. Yoga psychology enables one to have a more encompassing purview from which he can see that it is not necessary to choose between the concepts and methods from different systems of modern psychology. From this vista, one realizes that each psychological model has uncovered valid and useful principles applicable within a limited domain. The various models complement each other by focusing on different aspects of human functioning. These approaches, when considered together and integrated, lead to a more complete and accurate understanding of the total human being.

The well-known Indian story of the blind men and the elephant illustrates the relationship between modern theories of psychology. Once a group of blind men wanted to know what an elephant is like. So they went to a circus and stood before a tame elephant. One felt the elephant's leg and said, "An elephant is like a tree trunk." Another felt the trunk and said, "An elephant is like a very thick snake with an opening on the end but no teeth." A third caught hold of its tail and said, "You're both wrong! An elephant is thin, long, and flexible like a rope with a brush on its end."

The fourth grasped a tusk and argued vehemently that an elephant is like a smooth, cylindrical, curved bone which comes to a dull point at one end. The last blind man in the party held the elephant's ear and compared the elephant to a large, flat, broad leaf which waves in the wind.

Of course, each of the blind men was correct in describing some aspect of the elephant, but confusion developed because each believed that the part of the elephant he had experienced was representative of the whole elephant. Instead of working together to develop a more comprehensive view, each man tried to prove that his position was the most correct, and thus added to the confusion. In a similar way, each of the current psychological models meaningfully describes certain aspects of psychical functioning. But all too often the proponents of a particular theory are blind to other aspects of the human being and overextend their model so that its truth becomes a caricature, presenting a skewed and distorted picture of the human being. To those who view the theory objectively, it eventually becomes evident that these limitations prevent the complete truth in all its aspects from being embraced.

We might liken the human being to a gem with many facets. Each current psychological model has explored one or a few of these facets, but none knows the whole. Some of the facets explored by various schools of psychology include:

Facet	School of Psychology
Personal unconscious	Psychoanalysis
Collective unconscious	Jungian analysis
Habits	Behaviorism
Body	Reichian, Bioenergetics
Breath	Bioenergetics
Interpersonal behavior	Family therapists, Neo-Freudians
Self-worth	Person-centered therapy
Will	Psychosynthesis, Existential psychologies
Transference	Psychoanalysis, Jungian analysis
Spiritual	Pastoral counseling, Psychosynthesis

In contrast to the almost exclusive focus on one or a few facets of human functioning found in modern psychologies, yoga psychology gives considerable attention to all aspects of human functioning. Furthermore, yoga psychology provides a comprehensive model; it offers a means of recognizing how and where the truths uncovered by each school of modern psychology fit together in the puzzle that comprises the total human being. In contrast to the fragmentation of the human being that results from disparate views of competing psychological systems, yoga psychology offers a holistic model that respects each dimension of psychological functioning. As a result, the therapeutic approach that has evolved from yoga psychology is a complete system that works with aspects of functioning dealt with separately in different schools of modern therapy.

The word "holistic" is very much in vogue these days, particularly in modern medicine. Many people are beginning to recognize the one-sidedness of particular treatment approaches; patients and physicians alike are seeking to supplement pharmacological and surgical treatments with diet, exercise, biofeedback, and other ancillary treatments. But all too often the term "holistic" is used incorrectly to refer to a patchwork of diverse appendages to the traditional treatment methods. Properly understood, the holistic approach to healing is also an organic approach that considers the way the individual components cooperate together to make a new and synthetic whole.

Early models in modern psychology and those that continue to predominate today are not based on a holistic perspective; rather they are atomistic and mechanistic in outlook. This has resulted in part from the well-documented influence of classical physics in shaping the theories and methods of psychology and other sciences. In the last fifty years, physics and biology have gone through revolutions replacing the traditional mechanistic model with models more in accord with the holistic outlook. However, it takes time for a new world view to become assimilated, and psychology has not yet integrated the new discoveries and perspectives in physics and biology. We are just beginning to develop new models of psychology that are more in harmony with the discoveries in sister sciences. Some authorities have noted certain parallels between the new scientific paradigms and ancient Eastern thought.[4] Eastern psychology offers a perspective more in accord with the new conceptions of modern science and gives an indication of the direction in which modern psychology is likely to develop.

Underlying Assumptions

Geometry offers a clear example of how one may begin with a few assumptions or axioms and, using them as a foundation, logically derive a coherent system of thought with a host of practical benefits. The ancient Greeks followed the logical consequences of their axioms and unfolded the system of plane geometry that provided a grid for understanding and measuring the world of form. For two thousand years, the postulates from which the system was constructed were thought to be self-evident truths. Although they were actually accepted on faith from the very beginning, mathematicians and the educated populace believed until the nineteenth century that these initial assumptions were beyond doubt.

In the nineteenth century, mathematicians began to question the necessity of one of the fundamental axioms of Euclidean geometry concerning the definition of parallel lines. Alternative axioms were introduced in its place, and mathematicians found that equally logical and coherent systems emerged. But these new systems seemed to define a fantasy realm and apparently had little relevance to the "real world" of practical sensory experience. In describing his own work, Johann Bolyai, a famous mathematician of this time, wrote, "I have created a strange new universe." Out of this openminded experimentation, a new attitude emerged. The axioms were now understood to be creations of the human mind rather than absolute givens. These new geometries helped Einstein develop his theories in theoretical physics. He said: "To this interpretation of geometry I attach great importance for should I not have been acquainted with it, I would never have been able to develop the theory of relativity."[5]

One hundred years after Bolyai, when Einstein's theories gained prominence, one of these new geometries actually proved to be more accurate than Euclidean geometry in accounting for astronomical and atomic space. Euclidean geometry is now considered to be an approximate geometry applicable only to intermediate distances at low velocities. It can be usefully applied to the limited range of phenomena perceived by the senses unaided by scientific instruments. But Euclidean geometry cannot be used in dealing with vast distances or with objects moving at a very high velocity.

The assumptions with which one starts are extremely important in determining the sort of structure that will subsequently be created. When one begins any scientific or logical system of thought with certain initial assumptions, the system that unfolds is inevitable. In fact, if two theorists were to begin with the same axioms and work completely independently, the two systems that evolved would be essentially the same. There might be superficial differences in the order of development; the proof of a new theorem might be worked out along different lines; or one theorist might progress further than another; but the systems would parallel one another. However, if a single starting assumption were different, entirely disparate systems with contrasting consequences and applications would emerge.

All that has been said until now is directly relevant to psychological theories and their practical applications. Each psychological system is founded on one or a few basic postulates. Beginning with a few initial assumptions, a psychological theory inevitably unfolds along particular lines. The relationship between psychological theories, their groupings into families, their principal points of agreement and disagreement, and their range of applicability can best be understood by knowing the basic assumptions that underlie each of the theories.

This brief excursion into geometry is important to highlight the central theme around which this book is constructed. For over two thousand years, we did not have the perspective to question our assumptions in geometry. We regarded them as truths rather than assumptions. And we were unwilling to explore the system that might evolve if we experimented with alternative initial assumptions. Today we find a similar investment in the assumptions underlying our modern psychologies. These assumptions are often taken as "truths" rather than hypotheses. The value of starting with alternative assumptions and exploring the systems that can evolve from different assumptions is just beginning to be appreciated.

We are at an especially pivotal time when an alternative psychological vantage point is gaining attention in the West, a perspective that opens up new possibilities in psychology in much the same way that non-Euclidean geometry affected the traditional Western conception of the world of form. The psychologies of the East begin with different assumptions from those of modern psychologies. By juxtaposing the systems of East and West, the hidden assumptions in each emerge, along with their implications for developing therapeutic processes.

Chapter One

Paradigms of Psychotherapy

Four Psychological Paradigms

When we study the psychologies that exist today and classify them according to differences in their fundamental assumptions, four major paradigms emerge: (1) the reductionist paradigm, in which all complex psychological phenomena are understood in terms of something more elemental; (2) the humanistic paradigm, which emphasizes and values those qualities which are unique to human beings; (3) the dualistic paradigm, which interprets experience as an interaction between two complementary principles; and (4) the monistic paradigm, which considers all phenomena to be the illusory manifestation of one unified consciousness.

These four paradigms reflect distinct philosophical positions regarding the fundamental nature of existence. Throughout recorded history, philosophers have debated over which of these positions is valid. During different historical periods, one or another of the first three paradigms has held sway. Today the reductionist paradigm pervades modern thought, while humanistic psychology has gained increasing recognition, particularly in the non-academic environment. The dualistic and monistic paradigms are not given serious consideration within the mainstream of modern psychology as viable alternative foundations for a science of psychology. Psychology based on the monistic paradigm remains almost unknown in the West.* Despite their relative exclusion

---

*The reductionist paradigm has also been termed "monistic" by modern thinkers because it reduces all phenomena, including psychical events, to one basic substratum—material phenomena. However, this is not monism in its strictest sense, since there is a plurality of kinds of material objects. Throughout the course of this book, the term "monistic" will be used in its more traditional sense to refer to the position that considers all phenomena to be illusory expressions of one unitary consciousness.

11

from modern thought, the latter two paradigms have generated rich and detailed psychologies that explain significant portions of human functioning not adequately considered by reductionist and humanistic psychologies. In order to help correct this bias and render the dualistic and monistic paradigms more understandable and accessible to modern humanity, throughout this book these paradigms will be considered in greater depth than will the reductionist and humanistic psychologies.

The Reductionist Paradigm

The fundamental assumptions upon which the reductionist paradigm is constructed are:

That which is, is fundamentally of a material nature.

A. A complex phenomenon is to be understood by breaking it down into its more basic material components (e.g., psychological phenomena can be understood in terms of biology, and biological occurrences can be understood in terms of chemical and physical events).
B. Consciousness is not primary; rather, it is the result of the interaction of material entities. It may be considered an epiphenomenon.²
C. The methods developed in the classical physical sciences are the most useful for studying psychological phenomena. These include:
    1. Sensory observation
    2. Isolation of component parts for analytic study
    3. The study of antecedent causes

Behaviorism, psychoanalysis, general psychiatry, primal therapy, modern (allopathic) medicine, and the mainstream of academic psychology in the United States are based on this reductionist paradigm. Although these approaches to psychology and medicine differ from one another in certain respects, the basic assumptions they share distinguish them from theories within the humanistic, dualistic, and monistic systems.

Schools of psychology that fall within the same paradigm may diverge from one another in certain secondary assumptions and thus appear to be significantly different from one another in major respects.

For example, psychoanalysis and behaviorism are both reductive psychologies, but there are such fundamental differences between these schools that they are often contrasted with one another. Behaviorism is more rigorously materialistic. Behaviorists hold that only behavior and not consciousness can be studied by the scientific method. Psychoanalysis, on the other hand, focuses on the study of the conscious and unconscious mind, but it attempts to understand consciousness in terms of the principles of the reductionist-materialistic paradigm. "Freud's philosophy of nature was a conventional nineteenth-century mechanistic materialism predisposing him to an equally conventional preference for physiological explanations of the mind."[1]

The Humanistic Paradigm

The humanistic paradigm is based on the following assumptions:

The individual human experience is unique and must be studied and valued in its own right rather than reducing it to any sort of components, or regarding it as inferior to any other phenomena or mode of experience.

A. The experience of the individual is primary. The psychologist must relate to the unique world and experience of each individual rather than impose a general theory upon an individual which devalues his personal experience.
B. Each human being is motivated toward actualizing his latent potentials for uniquely human experiences.

Both Freud and the behaviorists were considerably influenced by the physical and biological sciences of their time. They attempted to use mechanistic conceptions and methods from physics to study and explain human functioning. Both psychologies were also influenced by Darwin's theory of evolution. This led to the view that human behavior and experience emerged from animal behavior and to the attempt to understand human beings in terms of more primitive modes of functioning. The humanistic psychologists rallied against this limited perspective and established a "third force," which focuses on those uniquely human qualities that are ignored, denied, or devalued in reductionist psychologies. Humanistic psychology has become a major movement with many enthusiastic followers. The founders of this movement include such renowned theorists and therapists as Kurt Goldstein, Abraham Maslow, Carl Rogers, Erich Fromm, and Rollo May.

Humanism had a long tradition before the rise of humanistic psychology in the middle of this century. It awakened in the Renaissance to give man a new sense of freedom from the medieval order. It has awakened in modern psychology to free man from the reductive conceptions about the nature of human beings. Humanism "recognizes the value or dignity of man and makes him the measure of all things."[2] The humanistic orientation in psychology has contributed considerably to an enhanced view of the nature and potentials of the human being by focusing on experiences that are uniquely human and cannot be adequately explained in terms of more primitive levels of organization.

Humanistic psychology occupies a position between the reductionist paradigm, with its emphasis on prehuman functioning, and the dualistic paradigm, with its interest in transcendent consciousness. Albert Ellis succinctly summarizes the humanistic position: "The essence of humanism . . . is that man is fully acknowledged to be human . . . and that in no way whatever is he superhuman or subhuman."[3] While the humanistic perspective contributes immensely to the understanding of important aspects of psychological functioning neglected in reductionist psychologies, it is nevertheless a very circumscribed point of view, ignoring what lies both below and above this level of awareness. While humanistic psychologies emphasize such qualities as self-actualization and seek to bring out the best in human beings, they do not fully reach upward toward a transcendent or universal consciousness, for they fail to recognize the existence of such a mode of consciousness.

The Dualistic Paradigm

In contrast to the humanistic perspective, dualistic psychologies, both ancient and modern, conceive of a consciousness that transcends human experience. The dualistic models are based on the following basic assumptions:

The universe is fundamentally made up of interacting complementary qualities. *

Both material phenomena and consciousness exist as the fundamental duality.

A. Human existence is that of an individualized, delimited consciousness involved with material phenomena.

B. A transcendent consciousness also exists, which is unidentified with material phenomena.

C. The individualized consciousness is evolving toward a more complete experience of transcendent consciousness.

D. The individualized consciousness can never fully experience the comprehensive or transcendent consciousness.

E. To the extent that the individualized consciousness involves itself with the material phenomena, it will experience a mixture of pleasure and pain; to the extent that a human being realizes or positively relates to a more transcendent state of consciousness, he experiences such qualities as joy, contentment, knowledge, and truth.

To speak of consciousness at all is foreign to most academic psychologists today and to speak of transcendent consciousness, which is basic to the dualistic paradigm, is foreign to most psychotherapists as well. The dualistic position is thus not appreciated or considered valid by most practitioners of modern psychology. But we must keep in mind that modern psychology is not an objective standard by which to evaluate the correctness of these assumptions. Though its perspective may be the most familiar and is usually taken as authoritative, modern psychology is still in its infancy and is only one of several vantage points.

The well-elaborated, though not always explicit, esoteric psychologies embedded in the theistic religious traditions are essentially

---

*There are actually two major types of dualistic psychology. This axiom defines a "dualism of complementary terms," as contrasted with a "dualism of antithetical terms." Antithetical dualism has been more familiar in Western thought, but this form of dualism does not involve a radical break with the type of thinking characteristic of the reductionist paradigm, whereas complementary dualism involves a completely different mode of thought. These two forms of dualism will be further contrasted in the following chapter.

dualistic. Among the moderns, Carl Jung stands apart in offering a comprehensive psychology explicitly founded on the dualistic paradigm. As a consequence of starting with similar premises, Jung's psychology is much closer to the esoteric spiritual psychologies than it is to any other modern psychology. A third major school of dualistic thinking that has recently come into being is general systems theory. In the writings of those in the forefront of this field, we find science and spirituality achieving a reconciliation based on a common dualistic perspective. A similar reconciliation is evident in the writings of Pierre Teilard de Chardin. He creates a bridge between discoveries in the biological sciences and Catholic theology.

The Sankhya system of philosophy and psychology established the dualistic perspective in India as early as the seventh century B.C. The yoga system subsequently codified by Patanjali in his Yoga Sutras evolved out of Sankhya philosophy. In the Far East, Taoist sages have elaborated a psychological model based on the dualistic paradigm since the fifth century B.C.

The dualist perspective involves more than merely an introduction of new concepts that elaborate, extend, or modify the materialistic model. It is a radical change in perspective that involves an entirely new orientation to one's experience, a very different thinking process, even a different logic. Many have difficulty in making the transition from one orientation to the other. When theorists such as Gregory Bateson have taught from this more comprehensive framework, they find that many of their students are unable to make the shift in perspective necessary to understand dualistic thinking.

> I used to teach an informal course for psychiatric residents. . . They would attend dutifully and even with intense interest to what I was saying, but every year the question would arise after three or four sessions of the class: "What is this course all about?". . .
> Gradually I discovered that what made it difficult to tell the class what the course was about was the fact that my way of thinking was different from theirs.[4]

The shift to the dualistic orientation and way of thinking involves a step in the evolution of consciousness. Much of what occurs in therapies based on the dualistic paradigm involves the therapist's attempt to help clients make this transition in their mode of thinking.

The Monistic Paradigm

While dualistic psychology posits two fundamental principles that interact to create the universe, the fourth system to be studied—the monistic paradigm—begins with the assumption that there is only one fundamental principle, consciousness. The monistic paradigm rests on the following premises:

Unitary consciousness is all that exists. *

A. The phenomenal world appears to exist, but it is merely an illusory manifestation of unitary consciousness. The phenomenal world is insubstantial. It may be thought of as a mirage or a dream existence.

B. When one ignores the universal consciousness, the phenomenal world appears to be substantial and is taken as a something rather than the negation which it is.

C. Manifestations of universal consciousness have identified with the phenomenal world, but are engaged in the process of recognizing themselves as the universal consciousness.

To further contrast the dualistic and monistic paradigms, it is useful to distinguish between the terms "monotheism" and "monism." Theism refers to the belief in a god and "mono" of course means *one;* monotheism refers to the conception that there is only one universal consciousness, God. In a monotheistic belief system, God remains separate from the individual whom He has created. The individual worships God and remains subservient to God. But monism does not refer to belief in a god. Rather it is the conception that there is only one existence, one consciousness that is universal. In this system, there is neither the worshiper nor the worshiped, for what may have appeared to be two is actually one. There is only one.

This fourth paradigm is the least commonsensical yet most

---

*Shankara stated: "The existence of pure consciousness is . . . an axiom . . . ; for upon that is based all other proofs."[5]

profound, and so it must be, since it takes its stand in non-sensory experience and considers sensory data to be of little value in conveying knowledge of the fundamental reality. This view is quite foreign and even unnerving both to the materialists, who consider even the theist's world view wishful thinking, and to the theists, who cry "heresy," "delusion," and "danger" whenever anyone asserts that a human being can attain a transcendent or universal consciousness.

Though monistic philosophy and psychology has been expounded by a small number of highly evolved sages in both the East and West during the past several thousand years, it has not been appreciated or understood by the masses, but has been revered as a fountain of wisdom by a select few. This monistic position has been most clearly expressed in the Vedantic philosophical tradition, especially as it is interpreted by the Advaita school established by Shankara in the eighth century A.D. The word *advaita* literally means "no-division" or "no-two." Advaita philosophy is based on the thesis that there is only one consciousness—all manifestation and multiplicity are illusory. This perspective has important practical implications for psychology and psychotherapy. It provides the clearest statement of the way in which human suffering may be completely eradicated. It is time for this view, together with its practical and psychological implications, to be clearly offered to modern humanity as an alternative basis for a comprehensive psychological system.

Having briefly examined the premises upon which each of the paradigms is based, a more in-depth consideration of each paradigm follows.

The Reductionist Paradigm

As students of the history of science have noted, the philosophy of Descartes together with the success of classical physics has led to the reductive-mechanistic conception of the universe that has colored all of scientific thought until now.

> The Cartesian division allowed scientists to treat matter as dead and completely separate from themselves, and to see the material world as a multitude of different objects assembled into a huge machine.

> Such a mechanistic world view was held by Newton, who con-
> structed his mechanics on its basis and made it the foundation of
> classical physics. . . .
>
> The mechanical models of biology had a strong influence on
> medicine, which has come to regard the human body as a machine
> that can be analyzed in terms of its parts.[6]

Today in physics a new scientific construct has replaced the
Newtonian conception of the universe. However, the influence of the
mechanistic perspective has left a deep imprint that continues to affect
current psychological thought. Early in this century, the behaviorists
based their psychology on mechanistic conceptions, and Freud attempted
to construct a scientific psychology based on mechanistic assumptions. In
J. B. Watson's behaviorism, as in classical biology, "living organisms were
seen as machines that react to external stimuli, and this stimulus-response
mechanism was modelled after Newtonian physics."[7]

> Behaviorism, like all other schools, has a long past. It goes back
> directly to Descartes, who viewed the body of man as a complex
> machine. Watson's real contribution was the consistency and
> extremity of his basic viewpoint; he simplified and made objective
> the study of psychology by denying the scientific usefulness of mind
> and consciousness. He espoused a metaphysics to go with his
> methodology and felt it necessary to deny the existence as well as the
> utility of consciousness. . . . His methodological point today is
> accepted, either wittingly or unwittingly, by nearly all experimental
> psychologists. Most other psychologists also are methodological
> behaviorists.[8]

The overwhelming influence that Watson's behaviorism had on
academic psychology is paralleled by Freud's influence on therapeutic
psychology. While Freud affirmed the existence of consciousness, he also
tried to build his theory on the mechanistic metaphor, which was the
current scientific vogue of his day. In certain aspects of Freud's theories,
the influence of mechanistic conceptions stands out most clearly. For
instance, his conception of psychic energy and its transformation was
essentially derived from Newtonian thermodynamics. According to this
conception, if a sufficient amount of energy is not dissipated along the
nervous pathways, it may build up, creating tension. "Unpleasure is seen

as mechanically equivalent to a sudden rise in the level of excitation within the nervous system, and pleasure as mechanically equivalent to its discharge."[9] Freud's early theory asserted that in hysterical symptoms, the energy is not properly dissipated along the nervous pathways but "succeeds in becoming pathologically 'converted' into inappropriate somatic channels."[10] Cathartic therapy was employed so that the bottled energy could be discharged through the nervous system.

If a human being is thought of as a complex machine, he will be treated in a certain way. The inevitable mode of treatment becomes clear if we examine the way one deals with a machine when it breaks down. Consider what happens when your automobile engine is not functioning properly. Suppose it intermittently loses power as you step on the gas pedal. You will probably take it to a mechanic who will attempt to isolate the part that is causing this effect by examining each component separately. He may remove some of the spark plugs to determine whether they are worn. He may then check to see if the carburetor is opening and closing properly to provide the right proportion of air and fuel for the engine. He may examine whether the wires are properly connected. If all of these components are in good working order, he may look more deeply within the engine, checking the compression of the pistons.

The mechanic has certain preconceptions and relates to the machine in a particular way:

1. He starts with an effect and looks for the cause.
2. He isolates the components and examines them separately, seeking the component that is functioning abnormally. Finding it, he returns it to normal functioning.
3. If the problem is in a component that he is not an expert in correcting, e.g., the car's computer or a bent frame, the mechanic may turn the task over to a specialist.
4. The mechanic works on the machine while the machine remains at rest or while it goes on functioning as it has been. The machine is the passive recipient of "being fixed"; it does not participate in the reparative process except to go on running and give off information about how it is operating correctly or incorrectly.
5. The machine does not grow or change itself during this process. It may be returned to normal functioning by the mechanic or modified

by him, but the machine is unable to modify its own structure, organization, or functioning.

The mechanic's assumptions and procedures here seem common-sensical in dealing with the automobile engine. To suggest that this machine could fix itself or redesign itself would court the absurd. But unfortunately these same assumptions and procedures are also followed by many physicians and psychotherapists in treating human disorders. In this case, the validity of the assumptions is open to serious question. Treating a human being as a machine does him a serious injustice and is deleterious to his well-being.

The mechanistic orientation in physics, biology, and psychology had a considerable influence on Freud during his medical and psychiatric training and had a similar influence on those studying in other branches of medicine. As a result, modern medical treatment reflects this mechanistic perspective. The way a physician "fixes" a patient parallels the way a mechanic fixes an automobile. In modern medical treatment, the patient consults a specialist who analyzes the cause of his symptoms in terms of biochemical imbalances. The patient remains passive while he is diagnosed and treated or operated on; his participation in his treatment is minimal or nonexistent. In psychoanalysis the patient must participate more actively in exposing his unconscious to the analyst, but the orientation remains the same. "Psychoanalysis regards the patient as ruled by 'mechanisms,' and it conceives of the therapist as the one who knows how to handle these mechanisms. He is the one who knows the technique by which disturbed mechanisms may be repaired."[11]

Modern medicine and psychiatry have focused their attention on disease or pathology. Their concern is with the breakdown of typical or normative functioning. They have studied deficit functioning in great depth, classifying and categorizing the variety of pathological states. They attempt to return the system to a state of equilibrium. Health is vaguely considered to be the absence of illness, but almost no attention has been given to the other end of the spectrum. Our medical and psychological models, for the most part, lack a clear conception of optimal functioning. Normative functioning is taken for granted as the desirable state of being. In mainstream medicine, psychiatry, and reductive psychology, there is almost no attention given to the possibility of becoming healthy beyond what is considered to be normal.

To find a contrasting perspective that might serve in place of the traditional medical model, we need only turn our attention toward the arena of sports. The athlete is interested in functioning far beyond what is considered normal. He devotes himself to a self-transformation process in which he continually works to extend the limits of his capacity in a given area. A coach may guide him in this process, but the athlete must take responsibility for transforming himself. This approach can be extended to medicine and psychotherapy.

Is there an inherent tendency in the organism to expand its capacity, not only on the physical level, but in the mental and spiritual spheres as well? Those adhering to the more mechanistic-reductive metaphor of how the universe and people function are likely to assert that people change as a result of external influences; there is no inherent tendency to change. One merely seeks equilibrium or homeostasis. A machine does not grow or evolve. Except for wear, it functions in essentially the same manner on its first day of operation as it does five years later.

In the first half of this century, a handful of organismic psychologists put forth a contrasting model of human functioning. One of its spokesmen, Kurt Goldstein, asserted that "the tendency to maintain the existent state is characteristic for sick people and is a sign of . . . decay of life. The tendency of normal life is toward activity and progress. For the sick, the only form of self-actualization which remains is the maintenance of the existent state. That, however, is not the tendency of the normal."[12]

From Reductionism to Humanism

In his "Project for a Scientific Psychology," Freud repeatedly tried to establish a mechanical-physiological model, but he was not successful. In his later years, he retreated from purely mechanical explanations and turned to a new scientific metaphor that arose out of evolutionary theory; he increasingly embraced the evolutionary perspective. In doing so, he substituted one form of reductionism for another.

The term "reductionism" was initially used to refer to understanding complex phenomena in terms of more elementary components—for example, understanding psychological states in terms of biochemical processes occurring within the body. In addition to this physicalistic reductionism, there is also a historical-evolutionary form of reductionism. In this form, a complex psychological experience is understood in terms of the more elementary form of that experience that preceded it in the development of the individual or in the evolution of life forms. For instance, a man smoking a cigar might be understood as expressing a need to suck that was unfulfilled in childhood. Even the childhood need to suck might be interpreted as the expression of a still more primitive experience further back in the scale of evolution. This form of reductionism continues to pervade psychoanalytic theory and has influenced much of psychological thinking. In this conception, what some have thought to be humankind's finest accomplishments are reduced to and understood in terms of reflexes, habits, sexual impulses, and the like. Even religious attitudes and artistic expression are seen as mere elaborations of basic urges. Freud's analyses of the works of Leonardo da Vinci and Michelangelo are based on this way of thinking, as are the writings of many psychoanalysts who have followed in Freud's footsteps. For example, a review in a leading journal of a famous psychoanalyst's two-volume study of Goethe and his works notes that "in the 1,538 pages, the author portrays to us a genius with the earmarks of a manic-depressive, paranoid, and epileptoid disorder, of homosexuality, incest, voyeurism, exhibitionism, fetishism, impotence, narcissism, obsessive-compulsive neurosis, hysteria, megalomania, etc. He seems to focus almost exclusively upon the instinctual dynamic forces that underlie the artistic product. We are led to believe that Goethe's work is but the result of pregenital fixations. His struggle does not really aim for an ideal, for beauty, for values, but for the overcoming of an embarrassing problem of premature ejaculation."[13]

Freud helped awaken modern humanity to the workings of the unconscious mind. His insights encouraged and stimulated others and attracted some of the most brilliant and innovative professionals to study and work with him. However, his theories became dogma and, thus, obstacles to further understanding. For instance, Robert W. White, a leading exponent of psychoanalytic ego psychology, has noted that Freud's theory of psychosexual stages "will stand in the history of thought as an astonishing first approximation to a theory of growth in its dynamic aspects. Nevertheless, . . . the time has come when its continued use will only block further insights. The theory that illuminated us all as a first approximation may only hinder us in reaching those closer approximations that always mark the forward steps in a scientific pilgrimage."[14]

Freud's limited perspective eventually led many prominent analysts, including Alfred Adler, Carl Jung, Otto Rank, Wilhelm Reich, Karen Horney, and Fritz Perls, to disaffiliate themselves with psychoanalysis and establish alternative schools of thought and models of psychotherapy. And it was in reaction to the reductionism of both behaviorism and psychoanalysis that humanistic psychology was born. Gordon Allport, one of the leaders of this movement, described a visit he made to Freud shortly after Allport graduated from college.

> I told him of an episode on the tram car on my way to his office. A small boy about four years of age had displayed a conspicuous dirt phobia. He kept saying to his mother, "I don't want to sit there . . . don't let that dirty man sit next to me." . . .
> When I finished my story Freud fixed his kindly therapeutic eyes upon me and said, "And was that little boy you?" Flabbergasted and feeling a bit guilty, I contrived to change the subject. While Freud's misunderstanding of my motivation was amusing, it also started a deep train of thought.[15]

This incident remained embedded in Allport's mind and influenced him to develop a psychology that emphasized conscious motives, the process of becoming, and the development of mastery and competence. He refused "to accept the Freudian thesis that all motives could be reduced to a few basic unconscious drives."[16]

Allport, Carl Rogers, and other leaders in the humanistic movement accepted a person's report of his own experience rather than attributing to him unconscious or hidden motives. Instead of superimposing an external frame of reference upon an individual in order to better understand him or to correct "distortions" in the way he perceives or experiences, humanistic psychologists are interested in accepting and relating to a person as the person experiences himself. The humanistic psychotherapist appreciates the client's frame of reference rather than making interpretations about the client's behavior in terms of a theory about how people generally function. Carl Rogers says, "I have tried to live understandingly in the experiences of my clients."[17] This phenomenological emphasis is characteristic of humanistic psychology.

The humanists, in general, seem to share this orientation. They tend to show a greater interest in the client's picture of his world or to attach a greater importance and validity to it. For Rogers, adopting the client's frame of reference in an empathic way was the client-centered therapists' primary approach. . . . The Freudians attach less significance to the patient's conscious phenomenal field, often trying to bypass it through free associations and dreams or deal only with one small part of it, that is, the patient's attitudes toward the therapist and therapy (and even these attitudes are viewed primarily as a transference from earlier relationships).[18]

This respect for the conscious experience of the client is both a strength and a constraint of the humanistic paradigm. It has led to an appreciation of the uniqueness, worth, and dignity of each human being's search for meaning and his ability to choose consciously. At the same time, this approach dissuades humanistic psychologists from interpreting behavior in terms of unconscious processes, from developing a general theory of the way the unconscious and conscious mind interact, and from considering that the person's conscious experience of himself does not represent his reality.

Humanists emphasize the "real" relationship between the therapist and client, "the reality of their intimacy, sharing, and common effort, of the mutual respect and appreciation they come to develop for each other as real persons."[19] This perspective helps to correct for the disregard and devaluing of the shared experience between therapist and client that occurs in reductive psychologies, but at the same time it engenders new distortions. As important as it is to value the immediate relationship between therapist and client and the conscious experience shared between the two, can one objectively assert that the person's ordinary conscious experience is fundamentally real and ultimate? Psychologists from the other three paradigms would clearly disagree with the humanistic position on this point. They would assert that the reality of a person is not found in his experience of himself in waking consciousness. This distinction sets humanistic psychology apart from the other paradigms. If one remains completely within the humanistic framework, he is not likely to use concepts referring to unconscious motivation. Such concepts as projection and transference play a central role in the other paradigms, but have no place in humanistic models, where the therapist takes the person at face value.*

Another emphasis in the humanistic approach that sharply distinguishes it from the reductionist paradigm is its focus on health rather than on pathological and abnormal functioning. Freud and the psychiatrists who have subscribed to the medical model developed their theories by studying patients in pathological states. Then they inappropriately extended their conclusions to apply to everyone, never suspecting that their view of human functioning might be distorted in favor of pathological processes. For instance, those who are disturbed or neurotic may respond in habitual and compulsive ways, exhibiting little ingenuity, creativity, or freedom of choice. If one were to develop a general theory of human functioning based on observations of such people, it would be a very biased and limited view of the human being and his capacities. The humanists recognized this bias in the psychological theories that were generated from observations of patients. So they chose to study normal functioning, and in some cases studied those who were unusually productive, creative, resourceful, or self-actualized, and they developed a psychology of optimal human functioning. The human potential movement evolved out of such interests.

> The humanistic thrust led to the group dynamics work of the late forties and fifties and the "human potential movement"—human relations and sensitivity training, encounter groups, body awareness, meditation, and so on—of the sixties. All of these approaches tended to expand our conception of human potential and to explore questions like: What are human beings capable of? How can normally functioning individuals most fully realize their capacities? To what extent can daily living become a peak experience? This meaning of the term "humanistic" stands in marked contrast to the other forces in psychology, which have focused on helping people solve their problems so they can make an "adjustment" to living. The humanists have said, "We don't even know yet what real living is."[20]

Leaders of the humanistic movement have sought to foster the awareness and cultivation of a wide variety of qualities they believe to be

---

*Humanistic psychology will not be considered in much depth throughout the following chapters since it neither deals with the issues stressed in the other paradigms nor does it represent a distinct mode of cognitive development as do the other paradigms.

important for a satisfying and meaningful life. These qualities include creativity, self-regard, empathy, trust in human nature, assertiveness, openness to experience (including sensory pleasure and emotional states), will, and sensitivity to interpersonal relations. Some theorists have focused on only one or a few such qualities, and theorists differ as to which they choose to emphasize. With this wide variety of focuses, the field of humanistic psychology has become a hodgepodge with little consensus regarding the most important qualities to be cultivated. One theorist notes that "humanistic psychology has become a rallying point for those who have been dissatisfied with what they felt were the stifling constraints of the behaviorists or the institutionalized dogma of classical psychoanalysis. In many ways the third force is most clear about what it opposes and least in harmony about what it supports."[21]

Humanistic psychology provides a bridge between the reductionist and the dualistic paradigms. Between these two viewpoints, there is actually a whole spectrum of orientations, each emphasizing different human potentials. At the end of the spectrum closest to the reductive view are those psychological orientations that focus on the material realm. Here we find therapeutic approaches that emphasize the release of physical blocks and the enhancement of sensory gratification. Bioenergetics is one such approach. Alexander Lowen, the co-founder of bioenergetics, states:

> Bioenergetics is a therapeutic technique to help a person get back together with his body and to help him enjoy to the fullest degree possible the life of the body.[22]

> The therapeutic goal is to integrate the ego with the body and its striving for pleasure and sexual fulfillment.[23]

The work of Reich and Lowen is clearly an important contribution to psychotherapy. However, Lowen makes sensory pleasure the measure of man and fails to appreciate the value of therapies that focus on the enhancement of other human potentials.

Albert Ellis criticizes certain approaches within the humanistic paradigm for their excessive emphasis on the enhancement of emotional life.

Humanistic psychotherapy . . . has often gone off in its own idiosyncratic realms and has been particularly preoccupied, in recent years, with experiential, nonverbal, and physical approaches to personality change. It has assumed that modern man has become too intellectualized, technologized, and unemotional, hence alienated and dehumanized, and it has therefore proposed itself as a corrective experiential force to make up for the lapses of classic behaviorism and orthodox psychoanalysis. In this respect, it has made notable contributions to psychotherapy and to the actualizing of human potential.

However, man does not live by emotional . . . bread alone. . . . Of his main traits, his high-level ability to think—and especially his ability to think about his thinking—is probably his most unique and most "human" quality.[24]

While Ellis emphasizes the development of cognitive abilities, other humanistic approaches, such as that of Eric Fromm, stress the metamorphosis of human beings from a competitive, possessive, and consuming orientation to that of being at one with life and developing the capacity to love others. Abraham Maslow, who developed the most inclusive view of human potentials, emphasized studying such qualities as self-actualization, peak experiences, and the "farther reaches of human nature." Maslow studied those qualities that are at the far end of the spectrum, approaching a consideration of transcendent consciousness integral to the dualistic paradigm. As humanistic psychology turned increasingly to the consideration of man's highest potentials, it moved beyond humanism to a consideration of that which transcends ordinary human consciousness. It eventually became clear to leaders of the humanistic movement that the humanistic paradigm is limited in its scope. "As more data became available on the farther reaches of well-being, the absence of relevant guidelines in traditional Western psychology became even more apparent. Indeed, the humanistic model itself began to show gaps and even the concept of self-actualization proved unable to encompass the newly recognized farther reaches of experience."[25] In his later work, Maslow increasingly recognized these limitations. He wrote: "I consider Humanistic . . . Psychology to be transitional, a preparation for a still 'higher' . . . Psychology, transpersonal, transhuman, centered in the cosmos rather than in human needs and interest, going beyond humanness, identity, self-actualization, and the like."[26] In the late 1960s, Maslow and other prominent leaders of the humanistic movement went on to found the Association for Transpersonal Psychology in order to collaborate in exploring man's attempt to reach beyond the human.

The Dualistic Paradigm

Dualism in Western Spiritual Traditions

Spiritual leaders in various cultures and times examined man's relationship with the transcendent long before humanistic psychology began to grow in this direction. Embedded in the teachings of the great religions of the world are psychologies that describe human nature and the human being's quest to experience the transpersonal. Within the teachings contained in the Old and New Testaments and within the spiritual traditions based upon these teachings there is a profound and practical psychology for understanding human experience, the means for dealing with problems of living, the goal and purpose of human life, and the means of overcoming symptoms and suffering. However, this psychology has come to be associated with the religious dogmas and institutionalization that have grown up around the spiritual traditions. Today these dogmas and institutions have come into disrepute among the educated members of society. In the last centuries, the reductionist perspective has largely replaced the religious. As a result, spiritually oriented dualistic psychology has not been treated with the same consideration and respect as the materialistic psychologies.

Modern psychology has sought to disassociate from religious beliefs in order to show itself to have a scientific attitude. However, it is possible to objectively study the teachings and experiences of spiritual leaders and their followers as systems of psychology and therapy without embracing any religious dogma that may be associated with those psychological systems. A comparative study of spiritually based psychologies can be extremely fruitful; it can delineate a psychological view of human beings that contrasts with that of the reductionist and humanistic positions and can bring to light alternative therapeutic models. Though religions differ from one another in dogmas and rituals, the esoteric psychologies embedded within their teachings share certain commonalities that are inevitable since the various esoteric spiritual traditions embrace most of the assumptions of the dualistic paradigm. It is useful to draw out the common psychology that lies behind the apparent diversity of spiritual beliefs and practices.

Throughout recorded history, long before psychology existed as a distinct science, a dualistic form of psychology was elaborated in the context of various spiritual teachings. In the Old and New Testaments, for example, existence is understood in terms of the interaction of two principles, the egoistic consciousness of the human being and the supreme or universal consciousness, God. In this dualistic model, human suffering increases to the degree that one is alienated from the sustenance and guidance of the supreme consciousness, and suffering diminishes to the extent that one establishes a conscious relationship to the universal consciousness, God. The stories and myths of the Bible beginning with Adam and Eve and running through the lives of Abraham, David, Job, Jesus, Judas, Paul, and others describe the various dramas that can unfold as the individual either becomes alienated from or aligned with the transcendent consciousness. Throughout these dramas, the two principles, individual consciousness and universal consciousness, remain distinct. They can never completely merge into one another, for then the dramas would come to an end. Those few who have suggested the possibility of an individual attaining unitary consciousness have been labeled heretical, have been excommunicated, and have had their writings burned.

In the more popular or exoteric religious teachings, fundamental principles such as good and evil or God and devil are seen as antithetical to one another. A dualistic psychology developed that emphasized the conflict between good and evil and the consequent sin, guilt, punishment, and redemption that are experienced as one enacts the dramas of life created out of this model of the universe. However, in the more mystical or esoteric traditions there is a deeper understanding of the way opposites interact. In these traditions, the two sides of a polarity are understood as complementing and supporting one another. A profoundly different form of dualistic psychology from that found in popular religions has resulted from this understanding of polarities. This form of dualistic psychology can be found in mystical teachings within the spiritual traditions. It emphasizes the synthesis of opposites and the transcendence of polar identifications. The comprehension of two sides of a polarity as complementary and mutually supportive is a step forward in the development of consciousness.

These two forms of dualism are strikingly different from one another. The first is a dualism of antithetical terms and is not really a part of the dualistic paradigm, for this form of dualism is actually an expression of the mechanistic mode of thinking. Dualistic models that consider the two poles to be complementary involve an entirely different form of cognition. This cognitive mode, which will be described in some depth in the following chapters, characterizes the dualistic paradigm in psychology.

The Psychology of C. G. Jung

Although aspects of dualistic psychology can be found in the esoteric traditions throughout Western history, it was not until this century, with the work of C. G. Jung, that a comprehensive dualistic psychology was established in the West outside of a religious context. The son of a Protestant minister, Jung was well acquainted with the writings of theologians, Christian mystics, Eastern sages, and Western philosophers who preceded him. In order to comprehend Jung's uniquely dualistic position among modern psychological theories, it is necessary to understand the way he synthesized the conceptions of the great thinkers who came before him.

In the development of Christian thought, theologians had speculated on the qualities and attributes of God. St. Augustine and other theologians assimilated Plato's idealism into Christian theology and constructed a metaphysics in which they conceived of the Platonic ideals as prototypic ideas within the mind of God. The term "archetype" is associated with Jung's psychology, but Jung acknowledged that "'archetype,' far from being a modern term, was already in use before the time of St. Augustine, and was synonymous with 'Idea' in the Platonic usage."[27] Jung acknowledged that in certain respects he was a follower of Plato. In contrast to other modern psychologists, Jung believed that the Platonic Idea was supraordinate to and preexistent to matter. In discussing the origin of the experience of being mothered, for instance, a materialist might say that one's repeated childhood experiences with a nurturing woman leads to the abstract concept "mother." The conception of mother is secondary and derived from sensory experience. In contrast, Jung asserted that the ideal is primary. He wrote: "Were I a philosopher, I should continue in this Platonic strain and say: Somewhere, in a place beyond the skies, there is a prototype or primordial image of the mother that is pre-existent and supraordinate to all phenomena in which the 'maternal,' in the broadest sense of the term, is manifest."[28]

Jung's psychology stands alone among the moderns in being constructed from the philosophy of idealism. For this reason, its conclusions are quite different from those of other modern systems, and Jung is not understood by those who have a materialistic bias. The distinction between these two paradigms is not new. Those familiar with our philosophical heritage have noted that "the opposition between Freudian and Jungian psychology has provided a parallel to the classical distinction between the Aristotelians and the Platonists."[29]

Jung was also strongly influenced by the eighteenth century German philosopher Immanuel Kant. Kant had put forth cogent arguments criticizing metaphysical speculation about that which transcends nature. He had logically demonstrated that because of limitations inherent within human mental functions, it is not possible for human beings to reach any demonstrably valid conclusions about the nature of ultimate reality. Kant's arguments were convincing and have been widely accepted by philosophers and intellectuals who came after him. His thesis has had an enormous influence on the intellectual community. Since Kant, speculation on questions that cannot be answered by scientific experimentation and observation have not been accepted. Qualities that had been ascribed to transcendent consciousness or God, and even the very existence of such a universal consciousness, were called into question.

It is clear throughout Jung's writings that he was very interested in spiritual matters, but Kant's influence and the scientific genre of his time led Jung to avoid religious terminology and metaphysical speculation. It seemed as though there was no longer a solid foundation for an idealistic psychology, as though both Platonic idealism and spiritual psychology no longer had a place in modern thought. Indeed, materialistic psychologies have predominated ever since Kant's time. Jung wrote: "Anyone who continues to think as Plato did must pay for his anachronism by seeing the 'supracelestial,' i.e., metaphysical, essence of the Idea relegated to the unverifiable realm of faith and superstition, or charitably left to the poet."[30]

Jung, however, accomplished an astounding feat, reminiscent of the brilliant strategist who snatches victory from the jaws of defeat. He reestablished a spiritual psychology based on the Platonic Idea by turning Kant's thesis outside-in. He used Kant's conclusions as the very foundation for reestablishing in a new form the idealistic position that Kant's thesis seemed to negate: "Significantly enough, it is Kant's doctrine of categories, more than anything else, that destroys in embryo every attempt to revive metaphysics in the old sense of the word, but at the same time paves the way for a rebirth of the Platonic spirit. If it be true that there can be no metaphysics transcending human reason, it is no less true that there can be no empirical knowledge that is not already caught and limited by the *a priori* structure of cognition."[31]

Jung was able to reestablish the Platonic Ideas by moving them inward. Instead of conceiving of these archetypal ideals as metaphysical givens or as ideas in the mind of God, Jung conceived them to be images within the human psyche from which psychological phenomena are manifest. He took ideal forms that had always been regarded as external and asserted that they were part of the very structure of the psyche. Jung asserted that "there are present in every psyche forms which are unconscious but nonetheless active—living dispositions, ideas in the Platonic sense, that preform and continually influence our thoughts and feelings and actions."[32]

Jung resurrected the gods by showing that they existed as universal forms within the psyche. He thereby overcame the conception predominant in Western religion that God is "out there," forever separate from human consciousness. In this respect, Jung brought an Eastern spiritual perspective to the West, for the Eastern spiritual traditions have always asserted that divinity exists within, that the Self or center of consciousness within is not different from that which has been called God and has been externalized in Western thought.

Many mistakenly believe that Jung's position is identical with that of Eastern psychology, but this is far from the truth, for Eastern psychology in its most profound form is uniquely monistic, while Jung's psychology is dualistic. Although Jung brought divinity into the human psyche, he did not transcend the dualistic perspective. Like the proponents of Vedanta psychology, Jung conceived of a universal center or self within. However, he believed that the self can never be experienced directly, that it always remains in the unconscious and can be known only through symbols. In other words, the duality that formerly existed in Western thought between man and God now existed within the psyche as the duality between the ego as the seat of consciousness and the self as the comprehensive center of the psyche.

General Systems Theory

General systems theory is another form of dualistic thought that is becoming increasingly influential. Although most people have never heard of general systems theory, its impact on our lives is enormous. Along with revolutionizing many of the sciences, it led to the development of computers; it plays an important role in business and management; and it provides insights into the process of change in psychotherapy. General systems theory has this wide variety of applications precisely because it is a general theory explaining the way things are organized, whatever these "things" may be: the parts of a machine, the molecules of a chemical compound, the functioning of the human body or of a business. This theory came into being in the 1920s as an alternative to the reductive scientific method in which something complex is analyzed by studying its parts in isolation. Systems theory studies components in relation to one another and examines the way they function as a whole.

General systems theory points out that there are different types of systems. It distinguishes between mechanical systems, biological systems, ecological systems, and social systems. It has helped scientists to become aware of the inappropriateness of explaining human systems in terms of the way in which mechanical systems are organized. As this science has evolved, it has led to an increasing understanding of how systems maintain stability and how they develop or evolve. The insights developed from this science have helped psychologists to understand disturbed functioning, the process of development, and effective ways for inducing change in interpersonal relations. General systems theory has played an important part in the development of paradoxical psychotherapy and family therapy.

Systems theory deals with the way polarities interact with one another and with the underlying unity in any polarity. It has helped modern science move toward an understanding of polarities as complementary rather than antithetical. This view leads to a psychology that is strikingly different from the reductionist-mechanistic orientation. The psychology that evolves from systems theory is in many respects parallel to that of Jung and certain Eastern psychologies.

Sankhya Philosophy

Sankhya, a major school of Indian philosophy, is also based upon a dualistic conception of the universe. Sankhya literally means *samyak akhyayate*—"that which explains the whole." Sankhya is one of the oldest of philosophical traditions. Traces of Sankhya philosophy are found as far back as 2000 B.C., and some historians believe that it was systematized in the eighth century B.C. Patanjali, who compiled and organized the teachings of yoga in the second century B.C. and who is considered to be the codifier of yoga psychology, based his teachings on the Sankhya system.

Sankhya postulates two ultimate principles underlying all that exists in the manifest universe. The interplay of these two principles leads to the manifestation of the universe, with its innumerable activities and forms. These two principles are *prakriti,* the primordial substance from which all material forms evolve, and *purusha,* the principle of consciousness, intelligence, or Spirit. According to Sankhya, everything that exists is made up of both consciousness and the material principle.

Sankhya philosophy and psychology analyzes the way the universe evolves out of these two principles. It developed a theory of evolution ages before any such conception was established in the West. This evolutionary view was applied to the human being and methods were developed to assist in a person's evolutionary unfoldment. These methods are known as yoga. A major concern of Sankhya philosophy is freeing the human being from the experience of suffering. It provides the means for eliminating misery in one's life. Many of the methods of yoga therapy have evolved out of the Sankhya system.

The Monistic Paradigm

Monistic philosophy and psychology is founded on the assumption that there is an underlying unity in all existence. When one experiences a world of multiplicity and apparently separate existences, it is as though he is living under an enchantment. He experiences forms that have no more substantiality than that of an apparition, but he takes them to be real and substantial. The illusory world of diverse forms creates sensations of pleasure and pain and experiences of happiness and sorrow, attainment and disappointment. It is a world of melodramatic entanglements. Caught up in these entanglements, a person remains confused about the nature and purpose of his existence. His pleasures are fleeting, and he knows not whence he came nor whither he is going. In a hypnotic-like spell, one lives in the bondage of time, space, and causality.

Monistic psychology asserts that one may release himself from this enchantment and awaken to the experience of unity. Then he will find that what seemed to be seeker and goal are one and the same, that all differences and distinctions emanate from and have their existence in the same ultimate source, and that he himself is not distinct from that source. Upon awakening to the underlying reality, one realizes that he had been playing a game of hide and seek with himself, but the game is now over. In this awakened state, all distinctions, even those that lead to the experience of time, space, and causality, are transcended; one knows a state of being that is free from all boundaries and fetters.

This conception of unitary consciousness is almost completely lacking in the Western philosophical and religious traditions. A few rare sages such as Plotinus, Meister Eckhart, and Franklin Merrell-Wolff have given us glimpses into this mode of consciousness and into the understanding that emanates from this consciousness. These men represent rare and isolated instances in the Western hemisphere of immeasurable attainment. Their teachings are read and partially understood by only the minutest fraction of a fraction of humanity.

The most outstanding and influential expression of the monistic view is found in Vedanta philosophy and psychology. The latter and finest part of the Veda, the Upanishadic wisdom, is called Vedanta. The Upanishads are a series of philosophical treatises on the nature of ultimate reality and the way to attain it. In the eighth century A.D., the great sage Shankara wrote commentaries on the Upanishads and on other fundamental texts of Vedanta to further clarify and illumine this nondual philosophy and psychology.

According to Vedanta, the illusory world of form emanates from pure consciousness, just as a dream with its characters and scenario emanates from the dreamer. While dreaming, one may experience a nightmare. He becomes absorbed in and identified with the drama that is taking place. But when he awakens, he realizes that those experiences were not based on anything substantial. In the waking state, one also experiences physical and emotional pain and conflict, incompleteness, and dissatisfaction. One is never fully unified, fully whole. According to Vedanta, the individual must also awaken from this so-called waking state. To accomplish this, one must go through a process of giving up his identification with the melodramas that surround him. Then he will awaken to his true nature. When he comes to realize the unity that lies behind all multiplicity, he will be free from all the hindrances and restrictions of the world of forms and names.

Monistic psychology posits a center within each being that is a center of universal consciousness. The individual ego has split off and established itself in apparent independence of this universal consciousness. As a result, the ego experiences alienation and is ridden with insecurity and anxiety. Ultimately, the ego must recognize its relationship to the unitary consciousness that exists both within and without. The final phase of a person's evolutionary process consists of recognizing his true identity as the Self or unitary consciousness. Monistic psychology describes the means for becoming aware of one's essential nature. The practice of yoga leads toward this awakening.

Relationship Between Paradigms

The reductionist, humanistic, dualistic, and monistic paradigms need not be considered opposed to one another. Instead they can be understood as progressively more comprehensive frames of reference. We find a similar relationship between paradigms in physics, where relativity theory provides a more comprehensive and accurate model of the physical universe than does classical physics, yet classical physics remains extremely useful for understanding and manipulating a certain area within the total spectrum of physical phenomena. Similarly, the monistic view embraces the dualistic, humanistic, and reductionist paradigms as circumscribed models with useful applications within its more comprehensive umbrella.

Although the phenomenal universe is illusory according to the monistic model, the illusory universe has a particular form, order, and lawfulness. This lawfulness has been partially uncovered and described by the various sciences that study aspects of the material universe and the interior world of the psyche. Since one is living in and dealing with the phenomenal universe, the more he understands its underlying principles and laws, the more effective he will be. Thus it is perfectly possible for one to embrace the monistic position that the universe is an illusion and to also accept and use the dualistic perspective for understanding the structure, form, and dynamics of this illusion. When operating within the phenomenal world, the monistic psychologist recognizes the usefulness of the dualistic perspective and incorporates this perspective in his applied psychology. The dualistic perspective similarly incorporates the still less comprehensive humanistic and reductionist paradigms. Each paradigm can be used within its limited range of applicability.

Yoga psychology can be fruitfully approached as an integration of the monistic system of Vedanta and the dualistic system of Sankhya philosophy and psychology. The humanistic and reductionist positions have a more circumscribed application within the scope of the Sankhya system. For understanding the ultimate truth that is beyond the phenomenal world and leading to the experience of nondual consciousness, the monistic paradigm is essential. However, for understanding the world of form, including the functioning of the psyche and the process of disentangling oneself from the forms and the suffering they create, the dualistic psychology of Sankhya has also been used by the yogic tradition. Still another school of Indian philosophy and psychology—tantra—unifies the monistic and dualistic perspectives within its scope.

The more comprehensive paradigm contains the more limited within itself and thus embraces it and uses it as well. But the more circumscribed paradigm cannot comprehend, incorporate, or apply the laws uncovered in the more comprehensive paradigm. For example, classical physics cannot accommodate relativity theory, and the reductionist paradigm in psychology cannot comprehend, appreciate, or apply what has been discovered in the dualistic paradigm. Nor can those who embrace the dualistic paradigm assimilate, understand, or make use of the recognitions from the monistic paradigm. To the extent that modern man is able to envision a more comprehensive perspective in psychology, the range and depth of his understanding will expand dramatically.

Chapter Two

Polarities East and West

Everything that exists is part of a polarity and thus has its counterpart. The world of ordinary experience is made up of innumerable polar qualities, such as inside/outside, hot/cold, near/far, light/dark, high/low, stop/go, and so on. The reductionist, dualistic, and monistic paradigms each understand and deal with polarities in a distinct way.

Throughout the history of Western civilization there has been a strong and pervasive tendency to regard the two sides of a polarity as antithetical to or opposing one another. Hence the term "opposite." The conception of opposition is ingrained in the Western mind and reveals itself in all aspects of one's life. One typically tries to ally himself with one side of an antithesis and to disown the other. A person may seek to be

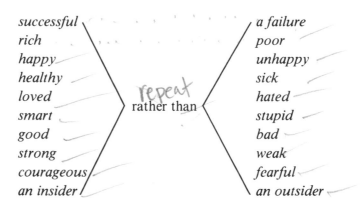

successful		a failure
rich		poor
happy		unhappy
healthy		sick
loved	repeat	hated
smart	rather than	stupid
good		bad
strong		weak
courageous		fearful
an insider		an outsider

and so on through an unending list of contrary qualities. People differ in respect to the side of a polarity with which they identify. One person may identify with liberal and another with conservative; one with aggressive, another with passive. But no matter which side of an antithesis one chooses as his own, he regards the other side as opposing and threatening. Whenever one finds himself opposed to something, whether it be to a quality, a person, a group, an ism, or to something within himself, he is basing his opposition on a preconception that the two sides of a polarity are antithetical to one another.

The conception that polarities are made up of opposing forces is also expressed in shared belief systems. For example, the polarity "us and them" (where "them" may refer to believers in another religion or members of another political party who are regarded as antagonists) exemplifies this type of thinking. The assumption that the two ends of a polarity are antithetical to one another is particularly evident in Western religion, in which good and evil are set against one another and regarded as clashing and irreconcilable forces.

The Reductive View of Polarities

The conception that the two ends of a polarity are antithetical is integral to the reductive mode of thought. Instead of beginning with a study of a system as a whole, reductionists use analysis to separate and isolate its qua ties and then try to put the pieces together. The reductionist approach has led to the conception that the two sides of a polarity are independent forces, diametrically opposed, with each attempting to assert itself over its antithesis. The conception that the two sides of a polarity are antithetical is most prominent at the stage of cognitive development that comes into ascendancy in adolescence. Jean Piaget described this level of cognitive development as the stage of formal operations.

However, there is another way of experiencing polarities that is found in more primitive thinking, in myths and dreams, in mystical thought, in a few schools of modern psychology, and in Eastern philosophy. Here the two sides of a polarity are regarded as complementary and mutually supportive. According to this view, complementary qualities may transpose themselves, that is, transform themselves into one another. For example, in myths and fairy tales, we frequently encounter the transformation of a being into his counterpart. A frog becomes a prince; Cinderella is transformed from a lowly servant into a princess; a good fairy turns out to be a witch in disguise. Access to this way of experiencing polarities is found in both more elementary and more evolved stages of cognitive development than in the stage of formal operations, which characterizes Western reductive thought. Formal operations thinking, in fact, seems to be an intermediate stage in which the view that polarities are antithetical reigns supreme. But at both less evolved and more evolved stages of cognitive development, one experiences the two sides of a polarity as complementary, interchangeable, and mutually sustaining.

Carl Abel, a nineteenth century German philologist, used the study of language to corroborate that in the distant past man viewed polarities in this complementary way. He showed that many words originally encompassed and denoted both sides of a polarity. For example, the ancient Egyptian word *ken* means strong/weak. In Latin *altus* means both high and deep, and *sacer* means holy and accused. The English *cleave* means to cling to and to divide. Abel stated: "Since every conception is thus the twin of its opposite, how could it be thought of first, how could it be communicated to others who tried to think it, except by being measured against its opposite? . . . Since any conception of strength was impossible except in contrast with weakness, the word which denoted 'strong' contained a simultaneous reminder of 'weak', as of that by means of which it first came into existence. In reality this word indicated neither 'strong' nor 'weak', but the relation between the two, and also the difference between them which created both in equal proportion."[1]

Freud came upon a similar interdependence of opposites in the content of dreams. He noted: "Dreams show a special tendency to reduce two opposites to a unity or to represent them as one thing. Dreams even take the liberty, moreover, of representing any element whatever as the opposite wish, so that it is at first impossible to ascertain . . . whether it is to be taken negatively or positively."[2] Freud at first did not have a conceptual framework for understanding these observations. He later became familiar with the work of Carl Abel and concluded that the way polarities interact in dreams exemplifies the primitive functioning of the unconscious mind. Freud quoted Abel's conclusion that this is a more primitive way of experiencing polarities that is left behind as man develops his capacity for rationality: "Man has not been able to acquire even his oldest and simplest conceptions otherwise than in contrast with their opposite; he only gradually learnt to separate the two sides of the antithesis and think of the one without conscious comparison with the other."[3] Though realizing that opposites have an interdependence and stem from an underlying unity, Freud did not regard this way of experiencing opposites as appropriate or useful in scientific thinking. This mode of experience was something to be transcended rather than used as the basis for building a psychology.

Except for interpretations of unconscious material, Freud dealt with polarity in the same way it is treated by other forms of reductionist thinking: isolating the components of a polarity for individual study and understanding the interaction between the two sides of a polarity as one of opposition. The id and the superego, the pleasure principle and the reality principle, primary and secondary process, the life instinct and the death instinct, conscious and unconscious, and the individual and society were seen to be opposing forces. According to Freud, the tragedies of human life result from conflicts between these antagonistic forces.

The Antithetical View of Polarities Versus the Complementary View

Dualistic psychologies share a common approach to the study of polarities that differs from that of reductionism. In contrast to Freud, various proponents of the dualistic paradigm—including Jung, general systems theorists, some Western mystics, and certain schools of Eastern psychology—consider the two sides of a polarity to be complementary rather than antithetical. Their conceptions of the way polar qualities interact are astoundingly similar one to another, given the wide separation of time and place in which these theories developed. These schools of thought take their perspective from within the nonrational world—the unconscious mode of experience that Freud called primary process—and use this mode of experience as the basis of their psychological models of human existence. The transformation of something into its opposite is considered to be not merely a primitive mode of experience, but a basic quality of the phenomenal world.

In dualistic psychologies, the pairs of opposites are seen to be supporting one another. Each side of a polarity makes the existence of the other side possible. The notion that good and evil support one another is quite foreign and illogical to the reductive way of thinking, but it is the very foundation of the dualistic point of view.

The dualistic conception of polarities as complementary has been most consistently espoused in ancient Chinese philosophy, particularly in Taoism. The revered Chinese sage Lao-tzu tells us:

> It is because we single out something and treat it as distinct from other things that we get the idea of its opposite. Beauty, for example, once distinguished, suggests its opposite, ugliness.
>
> And goodness, when we think of it, is naturally opposite to badness.
>
> In fact, all distinctions naturally appear as opposites. And opposites get their meaning from each other and find their completion only through each other.[4]

In Taoism it is believed that when one is unaware that the two sides of a polarity support one another to form a whole, he identifies with only one side of the polarity. This in turn leads to suffering and self-destruction. But understanding how the two poles support one another leads to a peaceful and integrated life.

Chuang-tzu, a Taoist master of the second century B.C., wrote:

> Those who would have right without its correlative, wrong; or good government without its correlative, misrule,—they do not comprehend the great principles of the universe nor the conditions to which all creation is subject. One might as well talk of the existence of heaven without that of earth, or of the negative principle without the positive, which is clearly absurd. Such people, if they do not yield to argument, must be either fools or knaves.[5]

The *I Ching* or *Book of Changes* is an ancient Chinese predictive manual that helps one understand and live in harmonious accord with the mutually supportive interplay of polarities. In the *I Ching*, "change is conceived of partly as the continuous transformation of the one force into the other and partly as a cycle of complexes of phenomena . . . such as day and night, summer and winter."[6]

In Chinese thought, one learns to live in harmony with the interplay of the two forces in a polarity. "The sage no more seeks to obliterate the negative—darkness, death, etc.—than to get rid of autumn and winter from the cycle of the seasons. There emerges, then, a view of life which sees its worth and point not as a struggle for constant ascent but as a dance. Virtue and harmony consist, not in accentuating the positive, but in maintaining a dynamic balance."[7] In sharp contrast to this point of view, in most Western thought one seeks to identify with what he considers to be the positive side of a polarity and to obliterate the negative. "By and large Western culture is a celebration of the illusion that good may exist without evil, light without darkness, and pleasure without pain, and this is true of both its Christian and secular, technological phases."[8]

There are of course a few notable exceptions to the rigid compartmentalization of polarities that has characterized Western thought throughout history. We find such exceptions in the writings of alchemy, gnosticism, and the ancient Greek philosopher Heraclitus, who espoused a philosophy based on the unity of opposites. Heraclitus recognized that opposites support one another, but he went a step further, asserting that one side of a polarity inevitably becomes transformed into its opposite. He called this transformation "enantiodromia." His observation appears to be similar to what Freud observed in dream experience. However, Heraclitus believed that this nonrational mode of experience permeates all aspects of one's life. He wrote:

> It is by disease that health is pleasant; by evil that good is pleasant; by hunger, satiety. . . .
> It is one and the same thing to be living or dead, awake or asleep, young or old. The former aspect in each case becomes the latter, and the latter again the former, by sudden unexpected reversal.[9]

Gnosticism, which flourished in the first century A.D., was interested in helping one transcend his identification with polarities within the world of form. The Gospel of Thomas, a scripture from this gnostic tradition within early Christianity, stated:

> When you make the inner as the outer
> and the outer as the inner and the above
> as the below, and when
> you make the male and the female into a single one,
> then you shall enter the Kingdom.[10]

The alchemical traditions of both the East and West have also focused on the interplay of polar opposites and their synthesis. However, insights of alchemy into psychological functioning have been couched in the language of chemical transformations. In part, this was necessitated in the West by the fear of reprisal from those in the religious traditions who were strongly identified with antithetical dualism. Carl Jung devoted the latter years of his life to discerning the rich insights of the alchemists and translating their findings into psychological terminology. He wrote, "In alchemy there lies concealed a Western system of yoga meditation, but it was kept a carefully guarded secret from fear of heresy and its painful consequences."[11]

The popular or exoteric religions of the West have dogmatically maintained that such polar qualities as matter and spirit and good and evil are in never-ending opposition to one another. They have vehemently asserted that the polarity between man and God cannot be fully transcended. Those who viewed polarities as supportive of one another were not understood. As a result, they and their teachings were banished from the orthodoxies, but their teachings continued to live as the mystical or esoteric traditions. In the West, the mystical or esoteric lore has been considered a threat to the common understanding and has been repeatedly cast out and ignored. The conception that opposites are complementary, mutually supportive, and necessary for one another's existence has been beyond the scope of the Western mind, except for isolated individuals. The views of the mystic threaten the tenuous security that the orthodox find in rationality and in formal operations thinking. Mystical insights also threaten to expose as illusory the melodramas that people create by identifying with one side of a polarity and casting out its opposite. The esoteric aspect of religion "is always guarded and is always mystical or 'closed'. . . because of the danger that the opposites will be confused if their unity is made explicit. It is thus that mysticism is never quite orthodox, never wholly respectable. 'Inside knowledge' of this kind is taboo in somewhat the same way as the exposure of the sexual organs. For as the latter is reserved for special occasions between special people, the former is reserved to an elite minority—to those who can be trusted not to spoil. . . . the cosmic game of hide-and-seek."[12]

But it is just this game of hide and seek that creates human melodramas with their consequent suffering and misery, for if one views the two sides of a polarity as opposed to each other, he then identifies with one and banishes the other, attempting to deny its existence. Nonetheless the opposite remains, hidden, waiting to surprise him. Unconsciously one seeks out his antithesis in order to become complete. He struggles in seeking to recover that which he has hidden from himself, and this is the source of his conflicts in life.

Polarities in Gestalt Psychology, in Jungian Psychology, and in General Systems Theory

Gestalt psychology recognizes the complementary interplay of polarities. Gestalt theorists point out that we do not perceive objects in isolation, but in relationship. A figure stands out in relief against a background; there is no background without a foreground. These two depend on one another and may quickly shift so that what was background becomes foreground. Edgar Rubin's famous example of a chalice and two faces that easily alternate as figure and ground illustrates this principle (fig. 1). According to gestalt psychology, the primary unit of perception consists of a reversible, mutually supportive relationship between figure and ground.

Figure 1

Fritz Perls was a psychoanalyst for many years until he became disillusioned with Freudian psychology and developed an approach to psychotherapy based on gestalt psychology. Perls described the way complementary qualities interact within the person. He emphasized the fluid interchange of figure and ground in many aspects of one's life, and he explained how a rhythmic alternation takes place in the organism's contact and withdrawal from the environment.

In his therapeutic work, Perls often focused on the particular polarizations that emerged in a client. When he discovered that someone was identifying with one side of a polarity and leaving the other side in the background, he would encourage the person to carry on an internal dialogue. The person would alternately play one part and then the other until the two sides became more integrated. Two prominent gestalt therapists have noted:

> There is nothing new about looking at polarities in man. What *is* new is the gestalt perspective that each individual is himself a never-ending sequence of polarities. Whenever an individual recognizes one aspect of himself, the presence of its antithesis, or polar quality, is implicit. There it rests as background, giving dimension to present experience and yet powerful enough to emerge as figure in its own right if it gathers enough force. When this force is supported, integration can develop between whatever polarities emerge in opposition to each other, frozen into a posture of mutual alienation. . . .
>
> The task in resolving the polarity is to aid each part to live to its fullest while at the same time making contact with its polar counterpart.[13]

Perls studied Eastern spiritual traditions, especially Zen and Taoism, and these disciplines strongly influenced gestalt therapy from its inception.[14] These teachings played a significant part in shaping Perls' understanding of the complementary nature of polarities. Although Perls' theories have many characteristics of dualistic psychology, he did not fully elaborate a comprehensive dualistic psychology. He did not extend his dualistic conceptions to a consideration of the relationship between individual consciousness and transcendent consciousness. In this respect and in his emphasis on the enhancement of sensory experience, Perls is more closely allied with the humanistic schools than with the dualistic paradigm.

Despite basic differences in their personalities and in their thera-peutic techniques, the ways in which Perls and Jung regarded polarities are parallel in many respects. But Jung was more thorough in con-structing a psychology around the conception of opposites interacting in a complementary way. Jung was familiar with the writings of Lao-tsu and referred to his teachings. Jung wrote: "If we carefully scrutinize our own character we shall inevitably find that, as Lao-tzu says, 'high stands on low,' which means that the opposites condition one another, that they are really one and the same thing."[15]

Jung considered not only the personality but the entire phenomenal world as well to be created out of the pairs of opposites. He stated:

> The world exists only because opposing forces are held in equi-librium.[16]

> Everything requires for its existence its own opposite, or else it fades into nothingness.[17]

Jung's entire psychology focuses on understanding polarities and the way they function. His magnum opus is subtitled "The Separation and Synthesis of Psychic Opposites in Alchemy." Jung dealt with a range of polarities far beyond those considered by Freud. The polarities that Jung studied most closely included conscious and unconscious, persona and shadow (good and evil), animus and anima (male and female), and introvert and extrovert. In contrast to Freud, Jung consistently regarded the two poles as complementary parts of a whole, essentially supportive of each other rather than conflictual. The other side in any polarity was regarded as balancing the one-sidedness of a position taken toward one pole.

Jung believed that if one consciously identified with one side and ignored or rejected the other, the rejected side would assert itself in the unconscious. In this way, the conscious and unconscious mind, them-selves a pair of opposites, balance one another. Together, they form a whole. Jung said that when

> the complementary opposite is lost sight of, and the blackness of the whiteness, the evil of the good, the depth of the heights, and so on, is no longer seen, the result is one-sidedness which is then compensated from the unconscious. . . .[18]

Every process that goes too far immediately and inevitably calls forth compensations, and without these there would be neither a normal metabolism nor a normal psyche. In this sense we can take the theory of compensation as a basic law of psychic behavior. Too little on one side results in too much on the other. Similarly, the relation between conscious and unconscious is compensatory.[19]

If one consciously takes a position toward one pole, the unconscious will take a position toward the other end. The more extreme the conscious position toward one end of the polarity, the stronger and more exaggerated will be the unconscious tendency in the opposite direction. "This . . . practically always occurs when an extreme, one-sided tendency dominates conscious life; in time an equally powerful counterposition is built up. . . . "[20]

Jung asserted that separating the two sides of a polarity gives that polarity increased energy and power over the individual. The power of opposites "increases the more one tries to separate them."[21] When one identifies with one pole and attempts to get rid of the other, the denied aspect takes on a vitality of its own. An unwanted and unaccepted aspect of oneself has an energy which is equivalent to the conscious mind's investment in its antithesis. If the conscious mind is strongly invested in identifying with being a good person, the qualities of devilishness, mischievousness, rebelliousness, destructiveness, and so forth, will carry an equal charge of motivating force, but this force will be alien to waking consciousness and will exert power over it. This occurs not only on an individual basis but collectively as well. The tendency in Western societies to ignore the interdependence of opposites has created collective belief systems that give life and energy to the very qualities they seek to stamp out. In the religious and moral sphere "the opposition between light and good on the one hand and darkness and evil on the other is left in a state of open conflict, since Christ simply represents good, and his counterpart the devil, evil. This opposition is the real world problem, which at present is still unsolved."[22] The compensating position of the unconscious is expressed individually in dreams and collectively in myths. If these expressions are understood, they can point the way to the needed correction of the one-sidedness of the conscious mind.

Jung's model implies a central balancing or neutral point about which the personality and the dramas of life revolve. "The tragic counterplay . . . represents, at bottom, the energetics of the life process, the polar tension that is necessary for self-regulation. However different, to all intents and purposes, these opposing forces may be, their fundamental meaning and desire is the life of the individual: they always fluctuate round this centre of balance. Just because they are inseparably related through opposition, they also unite in a mediatory meaning. . . ."[23]

The conception that opposites balance around a center, leading to a state of equilibrium, is characteristic of complementary dualistic models. As a result, the dualistic theories are strikingly similar to one another in many respects. For example, in yoga psychology the law of karma is based on the conception that a person is always growing toward increased recognition and synthesis of the polarities within. According to yoga psychology, whenever an individual acts in an imbalanced manner by identifying with one side of a polarity, the other pole is inevitably strengthened in the unconscious. There is an inherent tendency for the unconscious to express the side neglected by the conscious mind, so that both sides can be known and integrated within the conscious mind. In order to achieve this synthesis, the individual unconsciously creates situations that cause him to confront the opposite or ignored pole so that he can assimilate it. A similar conception is also found in gestalt therapy, where the need to achieve closure in one's actions by completing the unfinished business of the past is emphasized.

General systems theory extends the conception of opposites balancing one another around a center to the interpersonal sphere. Systems theorists who work with families in therapy have pointed out that members of a family often adopt behaviors that are polar opposites and therefore balance one another. For example, an unstable family member may be counterbalanced by another member who is unusually stable. Here the center of balance is the life of the family. When one member changes, the equilibrium is disturbed, and the family members attempt to return the "deviating" member to his "usual" way of being. If this fails, the other members of the family must also change in order to establish a new equilibrium.

This interdependence between a group member and its reciprocal is well borne out by the peculiar crisis that occurs when for one reason or another the one is no longer counterbalanced by the other, desirable as this may seem at first glance. Only then can the stabilizing function of this interdependence be appreciated, a fact that can again and again be observed in family therapy. If and when the condition of the identified patient (the family member who carries the official label of a psychiatric diagnosis) improves, there usually is no great rejoicing; either the family system attempts to lead the "patient" back into his scapegoat function (most frequently by defining any improvement as new evidence of his craziness), or another family member may become the identified patient.[24]

Family therapists have noticed a tendency for family members to interchange their positions around a point of balance. For example, a wife may be characteristically warm and affectionate, while her husband remains characteristically cool and aloof. If the husband shifts his behavior and becomes affectionate, instead of being pleased and returning the affection, the wife may well adopt the husband's previous position, responding in an aloof manner. Partners in a marriage may shift back and forth in this way across various polarities, including active/passive, persecutor/victim, and parent/child.

Jung focused on a similar process within the individual in the partnership between the conscious and unconscious mind. He believed that in many instances the conscious and unconscious positions reverse themselves.

The Monistic Conception of Polarities

Yoga philosophy and psychology can be understood as a hierarchical system, with the most comprehensive and encompassing understanding at its apex. More limited conceptions are subsystems within that framework, each with an appropriate range of application. The most encompassing perspective, which is found in Vedanta philosophy, accepts polarity as the very basis of life in the phenomenal world. The distinction is made, however, that polarity exists only in the apparent reality. One can transcend the apparent reality and can experience the absolute reality which is beyond all polarity. Vedanta asserts that the ultimate reality is an indivisible formless oneness of being, without time, space, causation, or any division whatsoever. There is a single consciousness without a second. It is neither eternal nor noneternal, for it transcends all polarization.

According to the Vedantic conception, this unitary consciousness manifests an illusion of division. Vedanta accepts dualistic conceptions as appropriate and necessary for understanding and describing this illusory world of names and forms. In the manifestation of form, there is an initial bifurcation, a primary polarity. Once that illusion of splitting occurs, the process branches out and repeats itself in a series of bifurcations and trifurcations into progressively more material forms until we have the apparently multifarious world that our senses experience.

In various schools of Indian philosophy, the initial polarization in the process of manifestation is sometimes described as the division into male and female. This bifurcation parallels the concept of yin/yang in Chinese philosophy. The difference between these two approaches is that Advaita Vedanta asserts that there is a formless unity out of which this bifurcation comes, while Chinese and Buddhist philosophies remain silent on this point. In their analysis of the world of form, however, the Vedantic, Chinese, and Buddhist perspectives have much in common.

The division male/female is stressed in tantra, a particular branch of yoga philosophy. Tantra teaches that the male and female principles are essentially one. They come from the same source, and the goal of life is to reunite them. The play and drama of life with its apparent tragedies and comedies emerges from the dancing and interweaving of these two principles in their various forms and postures.

> In the essentially dualistic cosmic vision of tantrism the kinetic verve of the primordial female energy (Sakti) is supported by an indispensable correlative principle, Śiva . . . or the male principle. . . . The whole universe lies extended between these two opposite yet complementary principles, and all creation is held to be a result of the creative play (līlā) between them. In our own sphere of existence these two cosmic principles appear as opposed (male/female, static/dynamic, plus/minus), but in conceptual terms their contrariety is the basis of synthesis—unity is the foundation of duality. . . .
>
> Though the universe is an expansion of the mystic combination in the Śiva-Śakti equation and though the two principles diametrically opposed, they are "essentially" identical. Their mutual dependence is so great that they remain inseparable, since each requires the other in order to manifest its total nature.[25]

In both the tantric system and the yogic system of Patanjali, which is based on Sankhya philosophy and psychology, a developmental process is described in which the individual becomes aware of and resolves the splits within himself. At less evolved stages of development, a person identifies with one side of a polarity and discards the other, participating in a dance and drama with the discarded other. In the process of personal evolution, one gradually learns to assimilate his discarded half and to attain a more encompassing perspective that embraces both. When this is achieved with respect to each and every polarity, the individual has completed the developmental process. He has realized that there is only one unity in all apparent diversity.

The process of assimilating the rejected opposite and thereby becoming free of entanglement within a polarity has been described in the yogic tradition for ages and is essentially the same process that is now being fostered in modern therapies based on the dualistic paradigm. Analytic therapy, gestalt therapy, and therapies based on general systems theory each lead to a similar process: learning to transcend one's identification with one pole and to assimilate the other. Through this process, one can achieve a metaperspective with regard to the polarity in question.

Yoga psychology differs from these modern approaches primarily in that it extends this process to the resolution of all polarities, with the result that all conflict and suffering are transcended. In the Bhagavad Gita (chapter 2, verses 14-15), Krishna, the spiritual guide, advises his disciple Arjuna: "Contacts with the material world give rise to cold and heat, pleasure and pain. These come and go; they are impermanent and unreal. . . . He who is not disturbed by these polarities . . . is wise and fit for immortality." Likewise, Shankara has said that the illumined person is he "who is . . . able to remain unmoved by either pleasure or pain and all life's other pairs of opposites."[26]

Jung also believed that the aim of psychotherapy is the transcendence of identification with the pairs of opposites. According to Jung, in the process of individuation, one transcends his polarized identifications and arrives at a more comprehensive awareness. Jung wrote: "I have . . . called the union of opposites the 'transcendent function.' This rounding out of the personality into a whole may well be the goal of any psychotherapy that claims to be more than a mere cure of symptoms."[27]

But modern dualistic psychologies do not recognize that the dissolution of *all* polarities is possible. This is precisely why they are dualistic, whereas Vedanta psychology is nondual. Although Jung claimed that the transcendence of involvement with polarities is the goal of psychotherapy, he also asserted that this goal is unattainable. He stated: "Like the alchemical end-product, which always betrays its essential duality, the united personality will never quite lose the painful sense of innate discord. Complete redemption from the sufferings of this world is and must remain an illusion."[28]

Yoga psychology, on the other hand, seeks to dissolve all polarities in the sense that they have no hold or determining influence on the individual. This does not mean that the polarity is necessarily destroyed; rather, its domination over the person is ended as he achieves an equilibrium with respect to that polarity. Once this is accomplished, the individual may continue to function in the world of polarities, but he experiences polarities as illusory manifestations rather than regarding them to be real in any fundamental sense. The polarities then take on a playful quality rather than being perceived as the compelling and inevitable divisions of reality.

The spiritual traditions of the East point out that the pairs of opposites are creations of the mind. The *Lankavatara Sutra* of the Mahayana Buddhist tradition states: "False-imagination teaches that such things as light and shade, long and short, black and white are different and are to be discriminated; but they are not independent of each other; they are only different aspects of the same thing, they are terms of relation, not of reality. Conditions of existence are not of a mutually exclusive character; in essence things are not two but one."[29] And the *Tao Te Ching* concludes that "the intelligent man accepts what is. . . . He does not devote himself to the making of distinctions which are then mistaken to be separate existences."[30]

Jung, in a rare statement written while in a trance and that he refused to have published during his lifetime, temporarily transcended the dualistic paradigm and agreed with this perspective. He stated:

> We labor to attain to the good and the beautiful, yet at the same time we also lay hold of the evil and the ugly, since . . . these are one with

the good and the beautiful. When, however, we remain true to our own nature . . . , we distinguih ourselves from the good and the beautiful, and, therefore, at the same time, from the evil and the ugly. . . .

Ye must not forget that the pleroma hath no qualities. We create them through thinking.[31]

This insight is of fundamental importance, for it is through rigidifying such distinctions, treating them as if they were fundamentally real, and identifying with one pole of a pair of opposites that one becomes drawn into the melodrama of life with all its suffering. It is by ceasing to identify with that pole that one is able to loosen the grip that polarity has over him, moving closer to a state of equilibrium and unitary consciousness.

Chapter Three

Projection

Contrasting Concepts of Projection

When a person identifies with a particular quality, he rejects or disowns its antithesis. He tries to get rid of the opposite, to throw it away. But one may ask, How can a person expel his opposite if it exists with and supports the very quality with which he identifies? Wouldn't it stick to him like his shadow? Indeed, the unwanted opposite always remains with a person despite his repeated attempts to get rid of it.

One can pretend that the unacceptable quality does not exist or that he has gotten rid of it. If something is unwanted, one can lock it in the cellar and forget about it, expecting never to see or hear from it again. This method of dealing with unacceptable sexual drives was analyzed in depth by Freud and his followers. Locking these impulses in the unconscious mind was termed "repression." But that which is hidden in the basement does not wither and die: it begins creating havoc by making frightening noises or messing up the plumbing, heating, or electrical systems—in other words, it begins producing symptoms. It was through studying these symptoms and tracing them to their origin that Freud was led to the feared monster in the basement. He took a major step forward in modern psychology by describing the process by which unacceptable contents are thrown into the unconscious. He devised a method to recover these rejected parts of oneself and to bring them into the light of consciousness.

Freud found that in addition to denying the existence of an unwanted aspect of oneself by throwing it into the unconscious (repression), one can also expel what is unacceptable out into the world. This process he termed "projection." The word "projection" comes from the Latin *projectus,* which means "to cast forward." Though the origin of this concept in modern psychology is generally attributed to Freud, the concept had precursors in Western thought as far back as the Middle Ages. Thomas a Kempis, the fifteenth century mystic, wrote, "What a man is inwardly that he will see outwardly."[1]

Projection involves a casting forward or externalization of that which is within. A movie projector casts onto a blank screen the image on the film. A person may similarly project his own qualities onto another person and perceive them as though they are a part of that person, not realizing that the qualities he is observing in the other are actually his own unwanted qualities. For example, if a person's anger is unacceptable to him, he may pretend to himself and others that he is sweet and loving all the time. He may unconsciously get rid of his angry feelings by projecting them onto other people, who will then appear to him to be very angry without any reason.

Despite Freud's major advance in understanding depth psychology, his work remains quite circumscribed by the biophysical model of his time. Freud's perspective was also limited by his personal preoccupations and those of his culture. He lived in the Victorian era, a time when most people in society assumed a prim and proper demeanor. They denied and attempted to eliminate anything within themselves that was not in accord with this persona. They locked their sexual and aggressive drives in the unconscious, where they wreaked havoc and produced various sorts of symptoms. When Freud traced the symptoms back to their source, he discovered these repressed aggressive urges and sexual desires.

According to psychoanalytic theory, repression is the chief means of dealing with unacceptable impulses. This is the primary means of defense. In some cases, the individual may also use secondary defense mechanisms, such as intellectualization or reaction formation, to help in the process of disowning unacceptable impulses. In psychoanalytic theory, projection is but one of several mechanisms a person may use to defend himself against desires that he tries to disclaim.

As a result of his discoveries, Freud attracted some of the most brilliant and open-minded psychiatrists of his time to study and work with him. Among these, C. G. Jung stood out as the most perspicacious, and for a time Freud considered Jung to be his successor. But Jung was so well versed in archaeology, anthropology, mythology, religion, and

Western and Eastern philosophy that he could not long remain within the scope of Freud's limited view.

Jung believed that projection plays a much more significant role in psychical functioning. He viewed projection as the inevitable complement to the process of repression. According to Jung, each time one denies an unacceptable quality, it is both cast into the unconscious (repression) and thrown out onto the world (projection). Jung said, "Everything unconscious is projected; i.e., it appears as a property or activity of an object."[2] Furthermore, according to Jung, it is not only one's sexual and aggressive drives that are projected onto the world, but any quality contrary to the quality with which one consciously identifies. For example, if one believes himself to be good, he encounters the evil side of himself as it is projected onto others. Jung called the unacceptable aspect of oneself "the shadow." A person's reaction to encountering his shadow in a projected form is aversion or even repulsion, but at the same time there is an equally strong fascination. In fact, it is just this aversion/ fascination for one's antithesis that gives the unwanted quality its vitality and power.

Jung believed that in the past, mythological beings served as a receptacle for one's undesirable qualities but that more recently we have come to project these qualities onto our fellow man.

> The meeting with ourselves is one of the more unpleasant things that may be avoided as long as we possess living symbolic figures into which everything unknown in ourselves is projected. The figure of the devil, in particular, is a most valuable possession and a great convenience, for as long as he goes about outside . . . we know where the evil lurks. . . . With the rise of consciousness since the Middle Ages he has been considerably reduced in stature, but in his stead there are human beings to whom we gratefully surrender our shadows. With what pleasure, for instance, we read newspaper reports of crime! A bona fide criminal becomes a popular figure because he unburdens in no small degree the conscience of his fellow men, for now they know once more where the evil is to be found.[3]

Projecting one's unwanted qualities upon another is useful and even necessary for those who are at less evolved stages of development. The projective process leads one to function according to the polarity I/not-I (subject/object) and to fill in the content of each so that one knows what he is and what is other than himself. This process establishes ego boundaries, enabling one to take responsibility for that which he defines as "I."

In the early stages of the development of self-consciousness, projection enables one to feel good about himself—to feel adequate, capable, and lovable. If one does not project the qualities that he considers to be negative, he will experience considerable conflict in trying to reconcile the contrary qualities within himself. Thus, as Jung observed, "This line of division serves a purpose, which is why the normal person feels under no obligation to make these projections conscious, although they are dangerously illusory. War psychology has made this abundantly clear: everything my country does is good, everything the others do is bad. The centre of all iniquity is invariably found to lie a few miles behind the enemy lines."[4] It is only at a later, more mature stage of development that one can again loosen the boundary between I and not-I, subject and object, and reassimilate his projections.

According to Jung, every unacceptable quality is projected outward. The world one encounters is made up of those aspects of oneself that have been rejected. "Projections change the world into the replica of one's own unknown face."[5] A similar perspective is found in gestalt therapy: Fritz Perls tells us that we think our eyes are windows which look out at the world, though actually we have only mirrors. One believes that he is meeting others when he is actually meeting himself, at least those aspects of himself that he has not yet assimilated. Since the other person serves as the vehicle for one's projections, the relationships one has are based more on fantasy than on one's experience of the person as he really is. Jung wrote, "Everyone creates for himself a series of more or less imaginary relationships based essentially on projection."[6]

Jung's view of the process of projection goes far beyond the Freudian conception in several respects. This is typical when a dualistic model considers concepts that were originally put forth within a reductionist framework. Time and again, we find that Jung vastly expanded Freud's concepts. For instance, Jung believed that a person projects not only what he considers to be negative qualities, but also the best and most positive qualities in himself that he is not yet able to assimilate within his personality. A person projects positive qualities onto an idealized figure such as a religious leader, a movie star, or someone with whom he falls in love, rather than recognizing and experiencing those qualities within himself. Through the projection of his ideals, he meets that which he loves in others and in the world. The shy person adores the charismatic, and male and female seek each other so that they may find their missing halves. Beyond this, there is a level of projection that represents the noblest and most ideal qualities which one is not yet ready to embody. These ideals may be projected onto other people or onto divine figures. One's predominant attitude toward these projections is adoration.

In the psychologies based on the dualistic paradigm, projection is not viewed as a defensive process; it is considered to have a positive function, to be helpful in the process of unfoldment. In fact, it is characteristic of dualistic psychologies to reinterpret various experiences that are viewed as negative by reductionists in a more positive and purposeful light. Jung's understanding of projection exemplifies this. He believed that projection is the necessary means for reassimilating that which the individual has rejected and expelled. By repeatedly coming into contact with the unacceptable quality as it appears to exist outside of himself, one gradually learns to accept that quality within himself. This process is necessary for the development of a comprehensive consciousness. Without the process of projection and reassimilation, one would not be able to integrate the qualities that are contrary to those with which the ego identifies. One could not become whole. As Jung pointed out, the unconscious content "can never be found and integrated directly, but only by the circuitous route of projection. For as a rule the unconscious first appears in projected form."[7]

By projecting unintegrated qualities onto others and drawing oneself into repeated contact with those qualities, they become more tolerable and begin to be assimilated. In this process, one develops intensely ambivalent feelings toward those who are the receptacle of his projections. He is drawn to and fascinated by those foreign qualities and at the same time is repelled by them, experiencing a mixture of attraction and aversion. This process leads him into intense relationship with the person, object, or situation that carries his projections. The person or object seems to hold a spell over him.

A clear example of the way this process functions is seen in the relationship between the police officer and the criminal. The officer identifies with law and order; he cannot tolerate its contrary—lawlessness—and thus seeks to stamp it out. The criminal or outlaw, who represents the other end of the polarity, has a similar aversion for the law officer. Despite their mutual aversion, the lawman spends most of his time chasing after and trying to catch the criminal. And if he is successful, the law officer and criminal may spend years interacting in close proximity with only a curtain of steel bars between them. As a result of their continued interaction, perhaps each will gain greater understanding of the other, weakening his identification with one side of this polarity and becoming more complete. This will occur only to the extent that one is receptive and open to growth. If one's identification with a polar quality is strong and his boundaries impermeable, this transformation will be postponed until he is more secure and more open to that which appears foreign.

Relationships between male and female and between intellectual and emotional types may be understood in a similar way. In such cases, each of the pair is both drawn toward and taken aback by the other, so they begin chasing one another around in a most fascinating ritualized dance. If they happen to catch each other, they each must deal with their opposite intensely on a day-to-day basis. If one's aversion to the other comes to the fore, the couple may end up in marital counseling on the brink of divorce.

In therapy it is not uncommon for an intellectual man to complain that his wife is unpredictable and extremely emotional and for her to demean his incessant logic and orderliness. With some guidance from the therapist, they may begin to realize that they each chose the other as a partner because they were attracted by the very qualities that they now find aversive. Because they each experience themselves as incomplete, as representing only one side of the polarity, they chose one another so that they could come into intimate contact with the qualities they had been denying in themselves. If the therapy process proceeds satisfactorily, they each will come to recognize the projected qualities as they exist within themselves. Perhaps the man will experience his feminine side and the woman her masculine side. On the other hand, if the partners cling tightly to their identifications, little growth will take place, and they each may repeatedly run from their opposite rather than learning to assimilate it.

Dualistic theories point out that one does not merely happen upon or chance to meet his opposite: he actively seeks out an appropriate vehicle to carry his projection. Furthermore, of all the characteristics that the other has, one brings out or amplifies those particular qualities with which he has the most difficulty, whether they be negative or positive. For example, a man searches after a female and responds to and thereby enhances those very qualities in her that he has the most difficulty facing in himself. Although another person may have some inherent quality or potential that makes him or her a fit vehicle for one's projections, the person as experienced is more a reflection of oneself than a person in his or her own right.

Projecting unassimilated qualities onto others and then becoming entranced with those projections is the central dynamic of ordinary human interaction, and it occurs in all of one's relationships. Most people are blind to this process, so they are held within its grip. Only by becoming aware of projection in each relationship can one become free. Jung observed that "unless we prefer to be made fools of by our illusions, we shall, by carefully analyzing every fascination, extract from it a portion of our own personality, like a quintessence, and slowly come to recognize that we meet ourselves time and again in a thousand disguises on the path of life."[8]

Here Jung comes very close to agreement with the Vedantic conception that the phenomenal world is an illusion (*maya*). The seemingly objective world is not so objective after all. The external world is essentially a means of reaching awareness of oneself. This conception is made explicit in the Yoga Sutras. There Patanjali states, "The universe exists in order that the experiencer may experience it, and thus become liberated."[9] According to yoga psychology, liberation from the bondage of the external world is attained when one realizes that the "objective" world he experiences is actually a projection from within.

Jung summarized this view when he explained that striving after selfhood first involves the creation of egoistic consciousness, which "is merely the creation of a *subject,* who, in order to find fulfilment, has still to be confronted by an *object*. This, at first sight, would appear to be the world, which is swelled out with projections for that very purpose. . . . There are, and always have been, those who cannot help but see that the world and its experiences are in the nature of a symbol, and that it really reflects something that lies hidden in the subject himself, in his own transsubjective reality."[10]

Jung here approaches an understanding that transcends the polarity inside/outside. He echoes the yogic conception that inside and outside are one, that the microcosm (the world within the human being) and the macrocosm (the universe) are one and the same. The Katha Upanishad states:

> What is within us is also without. What is without is also within. He who sees difference between what is within and what is without remains trapped in the drama of struggling unceasingly to find that which is already within.[11]

The Chandogya Upanishad also informs us that

> as large as the universe outside, even so large is the universe within the lotus of the heart. Within it are heaven and earth, the sun, the moon, the lightning, and all the stars. What is in the macrocosm is in this microcosm.[12]

How similar is Jung's assertion that

> all the mythologized processes of nature, such as summer and winter, the phases of the moon, the rainy seasons, and so forth, are . . . symbolic expressions of the inner, unconscious drama of the psyche which becomes accessible to man's consciousness by way of projection—that is, mirrored in the events of nature.[13]

If one were to embrace this view that one's experience of the entire universe, including all of one's relationships, is the projected experience of one's inner being, what would the consequences be for that person? Jung leaves us with this query:

> What if I should discover that . . . the poorest of all the beggars, the most impudent of all the offenders, the very fiend himself—that these are within me, and that I myself stand in need of the alms of my own kindness—that I myself am the enemy who must be loved—what then?[14]

Perhaps this was the very perspective of Jesus in the following dialogue:

> "For when I was hungry, you gave me food; when thirsty, you gave me drink; when I was a stranger you took me into your home, when naked you clothed me; when I was ill you came to my help, when in prison you visited me." Then the righteous will reply, "Lord, when was it that we saw you hungry and fed you, or thirsty and gave you drink, a stranger and took you home, or naked and clothed you? When did we see you ill or in prison, and come to visit you?" And the king will answer, "I tell you this: anything you did for one of my brothers here, however humble, you did for me."[15]

Karma

Since both Jungian and yoga psychology start with the premises of the dualistic paradigm, their conclusions about the way cause and effect operate in human life are inevitably similar. Jung's conception of how projection functions is essentially a reformulation and explication of the law of karma in yoga psychology. The principle of karma extends the conception of projection beyond the perceptual sphere to the realm of behavior. The Sanskrit word *karma* means "action," and the law of karma is the law of action and reaction. This law posits that every imbalanced action—that is, action which springs from identification with one side of a polarity—creates an equal and opposite reaction.

In yoga psychology, the term *samskara* refers to a latent tendency within the unconscious mind that is the result of previous actions. Samskaras are units of experience. There are many recesses of the unconscious; some samskaras remain known, some unknown, and some dormant. Samskaras can cluster together and become active, either in response to an external situation or as a result of their own ripening. When they become active, they motivate actions and create external circumstances, so that what is unfinished and important can be completed and thereby transcended. Samskaras are the bits or units of experience that activate the karmic process. They are like tiny seeds that can sprout and create a painful melodrama.

In modern depth psychology, the term "complex" has a similar meaning to that of a grouping of related samskaras in yoga psychology.

The term "complex" refers to a cluster of concerns that leads an individual to behave in a biased and often ineffective way. Jung said that complexes

> are "vulnerable points" which we do not like to remember and still less to be reminded of by others, but which frequently come back to mind unbidden and in the most unwelcome fashion. They always contain memories, wishes, fears, duties, needs, or views, with which we have never really come to terms, and for this reason they constantly interfere with our conscious life in a disturbing and usually a harmful way.
>   . . . they indicate the unresolved problems of the individual, . . . his weak spots in every sense of the word.[16]

One's complexes are thought to be dissolved in successful psychotherapy. Similarly, in the process of self-realization through yoga, the samskaras are metaphorically described as being "roasted." They become like burnt seeds that can no longer sprout; they can then no longer lead to impelled and unregulated action through unconscious motivation.

It is the latent impressions, the samskaras, in the unconscious mind that lead one to create experiences in the external world that will help him integrate the previously unaccepted side of a polarity. At various times, one finds himself in a situation that he experiences as difficult. One ordinarily does not believe that he has created the situation, but assumes it to be the result of circumstances in the external world. The conception of karma, however, leads one to understand that the situations in which he finds himself are in fact created by his latent impressions from previous thoughts, emotions, and actions. One unconsciously becomes involved in, or creates, those experiences that will bring him in touch with, and help him to assimilate, his "other side."

One projects onto other people and the external world the very qualities that he has rejected in himself. For example, consider the person who is very dominant and cannot stand weakness in anyone. He attacks weakness and attempts to eliminate it. Such a person finds weakness wherever he goes, in many circumstances where a neutral person would not even be aware of weakness. To the dominant person, it will seem as though it is his unhappy fate to be encountering weak people everywhere. He will not be aware of the part he plays in creating his experience. As another instance of projection, I have met a person who is extremely afraid of snakes. She finds snakes everywhere, even in areas where no one else has seen any snakes for years.

Every situation is pregnant with an immense variety of possibilities for what may be experienced in that situation. Each individual amplifies exactly that aspect of a situation that will teach him the lesson he needs in order to transcend his limited identification with one side of a polarity and to become whole. He amplifies a certain aspect of a situation by projecting his unaccepted quality onto it and then reacts to his projection so that that quality comes into the foreground for him.

The unconscious may also lead one to become the obverse of his present self in order to eventually reach a state of conscious integration with respect to a particular polarity. For example, the dominant person may create circumstances in which he feels weak and helpless. This reversal of the pole with which one identifies is an example of the process described by Heraclitus as enantiodromia. The tendency in this reversal is to change from one extreme to the other rather than experiencing integration of the two aspects of the polarity. One undergoes a conversion of one sort or another and becomes his heretofore rejected opposite: the liberal politician suddenly becomes an arch-conservative; the high-spirited extrovert becomes withdrawn and depressed; the atheist, a believer in God. However, through a series of progressively less extreme oscillations between the two sides of a polarity, one gradually attains a more balanced and integrated state, a state in which he accepts both sides but identifies with neither one nor the other.

The principle of karma is misunderstood by many. If a person dislikes something that is happening to him, he calls it "bad karma." If someone gets a traffic ticket or if his house catches fire, he may say "That's my bad karma." He may believe that he has done something bad in the past and is now being punished by an external agent. This is a completely distorted conception. According to the theory of karma, none of the situations one encounters are created by anyone or anything external, but result from one's subconscious mind. Furthermore, the circumstances one faces have nothing to do with reward or punishment. Each experience that one encounters is manifest solely to help one become more balanced and more complete.

In yoga psychology, the important question is: How do I respond to these self-created predicaments and melodramas? Do I identify with a limited and imbalanced way of being, or do I use each situation to gain a more integrated perspective? If one reacts to a situation in an imbalanced way, his unconscious will create additional predicaments until he learns the lesson of that circumstance.

According to this principle, one's life consists entirely of the circumstances that he needs in order to transcend the limited perspective and suffering created by identifying with one side of various antitheses. A person will unconsciously place himself in a seemingly unending chain of circumstances until he resolves his one-sided polarized identification with respect to each and every polarity. When he achieves this integration, he will no longer be bound by the law of cause and effect, the rope of karma. He will be free from the pain and suffering created by his imbalanced reactions to the circumstances he created.

The ordinary person reacts to getting a traffic ticket by feeling like a victim, by feeling guilty, by becoming angry at the police officer, or in some other imbalanced way. But one who practices the principles of yoga science would ask, "How can I use this and every situation as a training ground to teach me equilibrium?" I had the following interchange during a therapy session with a client who was well acquainted with these principles.

CLIENT: I had some great experiences this week. I crashed up my car, and it was good to see how I was with that.

THERAPIST (*surprised at this comment*): It was good?

C: Yes, to see how I dealt with that experience. It didn't do anything to me. That was really easy; that was nothing. Today my five-year-old had the worst temper tantrum in his whole life, and that was more difficult than the wreck. It was a good week; I had some really intense things happening. I'm beginning to sit back and watch people that I'm dealing with. Sometimes I get rewarded: I'll meet someone who is really crabby.

T: That's a reward?

C: Of course. Or I may be with someone who is really talkative, and he is the most boring person. I get to sit there and deal with my own boredom and learn from that. Being able to do that with circumstances is really great.

This person is obviously an exception to the typical client in psycho-therapy who is very reactive and unable to learn from the "negative" circumstances he encounters.

In the yogic model of cause and effect, the individual is considered to be completely responsible for his experiences. The yogic conception contrasts markedly with the conception of cause and effect in reductionist psychology, where the basic cause of one's behavior is usually considered to be external. The social environment or the internal biochemical environment are cited by reductionists as the causative agents for a person's current condition. In psychoanalytic theory, conscious and unconscious motives are considered important in determining one's behavior, but tracing these motives to their apparent source leads the psychoanalyst to conclude that childhood family environment is a primary cause of one's adult behavior. In modern psychiatry and medicine, biochemical imbalances are considered to be the source of one's symptoms. If one believes that the social or material environment is the primary cause of his current situation, he makes himself helpless. All too often, this perspective is used to avoid taking responsibility for one's life. Even the process of therapy can become a means of rationalizing why one is the way he is rather than a means of self-transformation.

Yoga psychology acknowledges the important effects of environ-ment, reward and punishment, and biochemistry, but it understands the causative process in the reverse order from that of reductionist psy-chology. In yoga psychology, the conscious and unconscious choices are primary, and these determinants lead one to experience particular internal and external environments that in turn affect behavior and subsequent circumstances. In the yogic model, one's environmental circumstances—such as the influence of one's family in childhood and one's biochemistry—are seen as the means of affecting the outcomes determined by the conscious and unconscious mind. Modern psycho-somatic medicine, with its emphasis on the way in which one's state of mind creates biochemical disturbances, is more closely allied with the yogic perspective.

Reductionist psychologies, with their focus on externals, consider external interventions to be the means of change, while yoga psychology focuses on providing one with the tools to alter his own life. The yoga therapist helps one to become conscious of his personal responsibility in creating his particular situation. To the extent that one acknowledges his responsibility in manifesting his present situation, he is able to take control and change his circumstances. As one matures psychologically, he takes ever-increasing responsibility for his internal and external environments. As one progresses, he acknowledges that he is entirely responsible for his circumstances.

Reductionist psychologies focus on causality, and this provides only a one-dimensional understanding of a human being. Human beings live in three dimensions of time: past, present, and future. Obvious though this is, there is no modern psychology that gives adequate attention to each component of time. The reductionist psychologies focus almost exclusively on the past as the cause of what is occurring in the present; they take a deterministic stance that diminishes the significance of present and future. Humanistic therapies emphasize the present moment. These therapies help one free himself from the constrictions of the reductionist perspective and to find himself in the present. Dualistic psychologies emphasize the future. They understand a human being as guided by his destiny rather than determined by his past.

Yoga psychology is all-inclusive; it deals with all three aspects of the human being. As one comes to understand karma, the way in which his past actions influence his present circumstances, he begins to accept responsibility for himself, yet he does not dwell on his past actions. Through meditation, he learns how to let go of his involvement with his past and to fully experience the present moment. Yoga psychology also emphasizes that each situation helps one evolve toward unitary consciousness. This model enables one to understand the way in which his destiny is guiding his present experiences. Yoga therapy helps one to take responsibility for his past actions, to live fully in the present, and to understand the purpose and usefulness of each experience as a means for reaching that which he will become.

Chapter Four
Transference

Contrasting Views of Freud and Jung

The reductionist paradigm leads one to look backward for antecedent causes of the present situation. In contrast, the psychologies based on the dualistic paradigm focus on where the current situation is leading the person. Dualistic psychologies share an emphasis on understanding the present, including symptoms and suffering, in terms of the person's growth process and his evolution toward a more comprehensive consciousness. Jung recognized the similarity of his approach to certain schools of yoga psychology in this regard: "Freud's procedure is, in the main, analytical and reductive. To this I add a synthesis which emphasizes the purposiveness of unconscious tendencies with respect to personality development. In this line of research important parallels with yoga have come to light, especially with kundalini yoga and the symbolism of tantric yoga, lamaism, and Taoistic yoga in China. These forms of yoga with their rich symbolism afford me invaluable comparative material for interpreting the collective unconscious."[1]

Dualistic psychologies do not ignore causality—the effect of the past—but consider it to be like one side of a coin, the other being one's orientation toward the future. Thus, in Jung's view, "A man is only half understood when we know how everything in him came into being. If that were all, he could just as well have been dead years ago. As a living being he is not understood, for life does not have only a yesterday, nor is it explained by reducing today to yesterday. Life has also a tomorrow, and today is understood only when we can add to our knowledge of what was yesterday the beginnings of tomorrow. This is true of all life's psychological expressions, even of pathological symptoms."[2]

While reductive psychology inevitably understands human beings in terms of antecedent conditions, idealistic psychologies, such as Jung's, are inevitably prospective, viewing the human being as oriented toward the realization of ideal forms. Even regressive behavior is seen in this light. Jung's understanding of regression contrasts with that of Freud, who viewed it as the return to an earlier level of development as a result of being fixated at that level. Jung asserted that regression is not an end in itself but a means for gaining information that will help the individual to evolve: "Regarded causally, regression is determined, say, by 'mother fixation.' But from the final standpoint the libido regresses to the *imago* of the mother in order to find there the memory associations by means of which further development can take place. . . ."[3]

The contrast between the reductive and dualistic psychologies is most striking in the way they regard the phenomenon of transference. Transference is a key concept in psychoanalytic theory; it is used to explain the origin of symptomatic behavior and distortions in interpersonal relations. It is by becoming aware of transference and resolving it that a "cure" is thought to occur. The concept of transference is also central to both dualistic and monistic psychologies, but transference is viewed in these systems in a completely different light than it is in the reductionist models. In fact, the reductionist and dualistic conceptions of transference are polar opposites. Transference, like projection, is understood in a progressively more comprehensive way as we move from reductive to idealistic and then to monistic thinking. It is interesting to note that as we move to progressively more comprehensive models, the conceptualization of transference undergoes a transformation similar to that found with the concept of projection.

In the reductionist model, transference means that something of the past is being transferred onto the present. A past experience determines one's way of experiencing and acting in the present. As a result, one is not free to respond to the current situation as it really exists. Consider the example of a person who has a chronic fear that he will be criticized by his employer even though his employer is quite friendly and considerate. If the employee is in psychoanalysis, he might recognize that his boss resembles and is in a role similar to that of his father. He might conclude that he is transferring onto his present relationship with his boss the fear of being criticized that developed in childhood from experiences of being criticized by his father. According to this view, the neurotic person is still trying to come to terms with his past in his present situations. Otto

Fenichel, a prominent psychoanalyst, summarizes this conception of transference in the following way: "The patient misunderstands the present in terms of the past; and then instead of remembering the past, he strives, without recognizing the nature of his action, to relive the past and to live it more satisfactorily than he did in childhood. He 'transfers' past attitudes to the present."[4] According to the psychoanalytic model, the recall to consciousness of the past experiences that have been repressed but are now being acted out helps to free the patient from this compulsion.

Freud considered projection and transference to be quite distinct processes. Projection was thought of as the externalization of inner id impulses, while transference referred to the superimposition of a previous relationship upon a current one. However, in dualistic psychologies, transference is not viewed in terms of one's past experiences but is rather understood as a form of projection. Jung conceptualized transference as the projection of an inner archetype either onto a person to whom one is relating or onto the external environment. Transference is a special case of projection, in which the archetype which is being projected is that of soul or spirit.

Jung did not consider the specific event (for example, being criticized by one's father) as significant in forming the transference. In fact, he found that the childhood events described by patients were often not even real occurrences but fantasies created by the child and remembered as if they had actually occurred. According to this view, it is the archetype of the stern, critical, parental figure that is now being transferred onto the employer and that had earlier also been transferred onto the patient's father. And it is by becoming aware of the archetype, rather than becoming conscious of the past, that one is freed from transference. In Jungian therapy, transference is not resolved by interpreting it in terms of the patient's past experiences but rather by helping the patient become conscious of the archetype. Furthermore, the projection of the archetype onto another person, relationship, or situation may be understood in a positive way as a means of growing toward more direct recognition of the archetype.

Jung repeatedly criticized Freud and his followers for their narrow reductive interpretations and the lack of progress that ensued from the application of this view:

The understanding of the transference is to be sought not in its historical antecedents but in its purpose. The one-sided, reductive explanation becomes in the end nonsensical, especially when absolutely nothing new comes out of it except the increased resistances of the patient. The sense of boredom which then appears in the analysis is simply an expression of the monotony and poverty of ideas—not of the unconscious, as is sometimes supposed, but of the analyst, who does not understand that these fantasies should not be taken merely in a concretistic-reductive sense, but rather in a constructive one. When this is realized, the standstill is often overcome at a single stroke.[5]

Is the patient bound to his past, or have the psychoanalysts created the illusion of bondage through their reductionist assumptions and interpretations? If the latter is true, psychoanalysts are in the peculiar position of placing their patients in straitjackets (their past) and then struggling to free them from the confinement that the psychoanalysts themselves have created. In this way, psychoanalytic theory may have the effect of creating a stalemate that inhibits growth and evolution: the analyst defines the patient in terms of his past, and yet at the same time attempts to free him from that past. It is no wonder that so many psychoanalysts remain pessimistic about the possibility of real transformation. Jung recognized that the application of the reductionist view has a debilitating effect on the patient:

Analysis and reduction lead to causal truth; this by itself does not help us to live but only induces resignation and hopelessness.[6]

There is absolutely no point in everlastingly reducing all the finest strivings of the soul back to the womb. It is a gross technical blunder because, instead of promoting, it destroys psychological understanding. . . . The continual reduction of all projections to their origins—and the transference is made up of projections—may be of considerable historical and scientific interest, but it never produces an adapted attitude to life; for it constantly destroys the patient's every attempt to build up a normal human relationship by resolving it back into its elements.[7]

Archetypal Psychology

The reductive explanations of psychoanalytic theory are often used to avoid self-responsibility. For instance, many people use psychoanalytic explanations to feel justified in blaming their parents for their own problems. However, Jung points out that one's feelings and attitudes toward parents come not so much from the way his parents actually behaved toward him as from the ideal images that he has been projecting upon his parents. Each person has an inner image of the ideal mother who will always be there for him, who will look after all his needs, love, accept, and nurture him unconditionally, and forgive him no matter what he may do. One projects this image onto his mother and expects her to live up to the ideal. In a similar way, one has an inner image of an ideal father that he projects onto his natural father.

As one grows, he projects these and other ideals onto friends, teachers, mate, employer, and others in his life. This is not a transfer of something from a past relationship onto a present one, but the projection or transfer of an ideal (archetype) onto human relationships. One does not transfer his response to his parents' behavior onto others; his way of relating to his parents is itself based on transference. Jung said:

> My own view differs from that of other medico-psychological theories principally in that I attribute to the personal mother only a limited aetiological significance. That is to say, all those influences which the literature describes as being exerted on the children do not come from the mother herself, but rather from the archetype projected upon her, which gives her a mythological background and invests her with authority and numinosity.[8]

Jung asserted that one's mother is merely a human being and should come to be regarded as such instead of being weighted down with the archetype that is projected upon her and the consequent expectation that she embody an ideal.

> Why risk saying too much, too much that is false and inadequate and beside the point, about that human being who was our mother, the accidental carrier of that great experience which includes herself and myself and all mankind, and indeed the whole of created nature, the experience of life whose children we are? . . . a sensitive person cannot in all fairness load that enormous burden of meaning, responsibility, duty, heaven and hell, on to the shoulders of one frail and fallible human being—so deserving of love, indulgence, under-standing and forgiveness—who was our mother. He knows that the mother carries for us that inborn image of the *mater natura* and

mater spiritualis, of the totality of life of which we are a small and helpless part.[9]

In the premodern world, one could more readily relate to the archetype "mother" through symbolic expressions and thereby have his needs met for a connection to the ideal. The ideals or archetypes were experienced in one's relationship to gods, goddesses, or what were believed to be human incarnations of God. A connection was made between the inner ideal and an outward symbol that was an apt embodiment of the ideal or archetype within. Transference of the archetype onto an ordinary human being is bound to lead to disappointment because human beings are not capable of living up to and embodying the ideal. When one relates to the symbol that has been offered by myth or a spiritual tradition, the inner need for relating to the ideal and the outer expression of that ideal in the world of form meet and one finds a much higher degree of fulfillment than is possible when one projects the archetype onto a human being. The symbol is able to carry or express the ideal in a way the ordinary person cannot.

Such symbols exist in different degrees of perfection. The parts enacted by movie stars and other performers carry our projections of the archetypes, but give only partial satisfaction, for the portrayal is far from a complete representation of the archetype. We sometimes expect those who portray heroes, heroines, and other ideal types to be the same in real life as they are on the stage, and we often become disappointed when we learn that a famous performer is not in his real life the ideal we took him to be. This confusion is experienced because the performer is mistakenly identified with the archetype he is portraying.

The roles, dramas, and symbolic expressions fashioned by such exceptional artists as Goethe, Shakespeare, Leonardo da Vinci, and J. S. Bach provide outer forms that conjoin with the inner archetypes to a profound degree. We revere such artists and their works because they have been able to experience the ideal forms more directly than is usually possible and to give them an outer expression in form that establishes for others a deep connection to the archetype within.

Finally, there are those transcendental expressions that so fully embody the ideal that focusing one's attention on them can open new vistas and dimensions of unfathomable majesty and lead one to explore the sublime and glorious presence of that ideal. These expressions are found in more or less veiled symbols in spiritual traditions. Mantras and mandalas, which are used as objects of meditation in the East, and the many forms or aspects of divinity depicted in art, dance, music, and myth offer possibilities for coming into direct contact with the ideal. Outer embodiments of the archetype can also be found in the lives and works of divine incarnations and spiritually realized beings.

The religious traditions encourage man to withdraw his projections from the human sphere, where he cannot find satisfaction, and to direct his longing for the ideal toward the divine, where this longing may be fulfilled. The words of Jesus in the Essene Gospel of Peace, an ancient text from the first century A.D., make this point even more directly than most religious writings:

> The Heavenly Father is a hundred times greater than all fathers by seed and by blood, and greater is the Earthly Mother than all mothers by the body. . . . More wise are the words and laws of your Heavenly Father and of your Earthly Mother than the words and the will of all fathers by seed and by blood, and of all mothers by the body. And of more worth also is the inheritance of your Heavenly Father and of your Earthly Mother, the everlasting kingdom of earthly and heavenly life, than all the inheritances of your fathers by seed and by blood, and of your mothers by the body.[10]

Unfortunately, modern man has lost his connection to those expressions that can embody the ideals to a high degree. As a result, he is floundering about looking for outer forms that can fulfill his inner longing. He ends up projecting the inner ideal onto isms, ideologies, heroes and heroines of sport and war, movie stars and rock-and-roll musicians, and religious and political leaders, who portray ideals in the media.[11] One projects his ideal onto one or more of these representatives and becomes a devoted follower until the supposed carrier of the ideal, like the Wizard of Oz, is revealed for what he is. Then the ideal that the devoted follower thought he had within his grasp flutters away free from the cage he thought he had placed around it.

Where is modern man to find forms worthy of fulfilling that inner longing to encounter the ideal? This is the unanswered question for human beings today. As Jung noted:

Only in the age of enlightenment did people discover that the gods . . . were simply projections. Thus the gods were disposed of. But the corresponding psychological function was by no means disposed of; it lapsed into the unconscious, and men were thereupon poisoned by the surplus of libido that had once been laid up in the cult of divine images.[12]

Our "civilization" . . . has turned out to be a very doubtful proposition, a distinct falling away from the lofty ideal of Christianity; and, in consequence, the projections have largely fallen away from the divine figures and have necessarily settled in the human sphere.[13]

James Hillman, a proponent of archetypal psychology, has further described the fall of archetypes into the human sphere, pointing out that we also project the archetypes onto our friends and loved ones:

Persons are no longer just human beings; they have been dehumanized by being divinized. Our weekends of encounter, our group sessions and sensitivity workshops, are religious phenomena: they attest to where the divine persons now reside—in human beings.

. . . we spoil our actual friendships, marriages, loves, and families by looking to people for redemption. We seek salvation in personal encounters, personal relations, personal solutions. Human persons are the contemporary shrines and statues.[14]

My own recognition of the way human beings are expected to fulfill one's ideals came when I was working with a young man in psychotherapy. He described several short-term relationships with women and told me how he repeatedly became disappointed because these women did not turn out to be all that he expected. He wanted someone who would be understanding, nurturing, and comforting, and all of the women he encountered fell short.

C: In the last two years, I've been involved with a lot of different people. It always ends in disappointment. I think I'm looking for an ideal, not another person. When I find that someone is vulnerable, with human weaknesses, it's hard for me to take. I have a misconception that I'll find someone who will give me one hundred percent happiness. But every human being has their share of faults. At first I'm thinking, "Oh! This is so good; this is the perfect person." I'm just fooling myself.

T: You aren't really relating to the person as they are?

C: More to my conception of them, what I want in a person, what I expect as far as happiness goes.

Many therapists would encourage this client to realize that his expectations are unrealistic, that he should give up his fantasies and face the fact that one cannot expect total happiness or perfect understanding, nurturing, and comforting in life. Therapists following the reductive paradigm might interpret his search as being the result of an inadequacy in the way his mother related to him; perhaps she overindulged or underindulged him at a particularly crucial point in his childhood.

At that time I had been studying Eastern spiritual traditions and was familiar with the conception of God as the Mother of the universe. In Eastern cultures, many people relate to God as a Divine Mother who nurtures and sustains all beings, who is all-accepting and all-forgiving, for all living things are her children. Although most people in the West today think of God as masculine, aspects of this Divine Mother are found in the Western conception of Mother Nature, and she has also been worshiped as the Blessed Virgin Mary in the Catholic tradition. It occurred to me that it was not necessary for my client to give up his search for an ideal mother in favor of a more "realistic" attitude; he was simply looking in the wrong place. Since he was Catholic, I asked him if he was familiar with the worship of Mary in the Catholic tradition and encouraged him in this direction. Being a modern person and a psychotherapist to boot, he was not inclined to take my advice.

At that time, I had little acquaintance with Jung, but as I began to read Jung's description of transference, I was surprised to find that what he said was essentially in agreement with what I had "discovered"— namely, that my client was not transferring an attitude that developed in his relationship with his mother onto his girlfriends, but that he was transferring an ideal onto both his mother and his girlfriends. It now seems clear that this similarity in point of view is inevitable since both Jungian and other dualistic psychologies begin with similar assumptions.

The transference of ideals onto the human sphere causes most of the interpersonal catastrophes and soap opera melodramas in our lives. Jung noted that archetypes are complexes of experience that come upon us like fate, and their effects are felt in our most personal life. The anima [feminine ideal] no longer crosses our path as a goddess, but, it may be, as an intimately personal misadventure, or perhaps as our best venture. When, for instance, a highly esteemed professor in his seventies abandons his family and runs off with a young red-headed actress, we know that the gods have claimed another victim. [15]

The male projects or transfers the ideal feminine (anima, soul) onto the female in his life, while the female projects the ideal masculine (animus, mind or spirit) onto the man in her life.*

Every mother and every beloved is forced to become the carrier and embodiment of this omnipresent and ageless image, which corresponds to the deepest reality in a man. It belongs to him, this perilous image of Woman; she stands for the loyalty which in the interests of life he must sometimes forgo; she is the much needed compensation for the risks, struggles, sacrifices that all end in disappointment; she is the solace for all the bitterness of life. And, at the same time, she is the great illusionist, the seductress, who draws him into life with her Maya—and not only into life's reasonable and useful aspects, but into its frightful paradoxes and ambivalences. . . . [16]

It is the deepest unknown counterpole of oneself that is projected onto one's mate.

A man, in his love-choice, is strongly tempted to win the woman who best corresponds to his own unconscious femininity—a woman, in short, who can unhesitatingly receive the projection of his soul. Although such a choice is often regarded and felt as altogether ideal, it may turn out that the man has manifestly married his own worst weakness. This would explain some highly remarkable conjunctions. [17]

Thus, when a man "falls in love," he is not loving the other person so much as being captivated by his own projected anima or soul image. Likewise, the woman is captivated by her projected animus. This is so characteristic of male/female relationships that Jung questioned whether there is really a relationship between conscious human beings or merely the unconscious acting out of instinctual rituals.

---

*"Ideal" here does not necessarily imply a positive valuation, but refers to prototypic qualities. We may, for example, speak of an ideally evil person, such as a witch or a devil.

The language of love is of astonishing uniformity, using the well-worn formulas with the utmost devotion and fidelity, so that once again the two partners find themselves in a banal collective situation. Yet they live in the illusion that they are related to one another in a most individual way.

. . . Very often the relationship runs its course heedless of its human performers, who afterwards do not know what happened to them.[18]

This point of view represents a reversal of the ordinary way of regarding a person's behavior. Usually, the person is regarded as being the foreground. It is he who acts. But here precedence is given to the archetype, and the person is viewed as merely the vehicle for the expression of the archetype, in much the same way that the body may be regarded as a vehicle for the person. The archetype comes to the foreground as the significant source of meaning and motivation. This perspective helps to correct one's egocentric and inflated position. It helps one to realize that ego-consciousness, which regards itself as the be-all and end-all of the world, is actually quite circumscribed. In fact, there is a more comprehensive organization or mode of being that expresses itself through the person.

When a person remains unconscious of the archetype but is taken over by it, he does not act as an individual but in a collective and ritualized way, in just the same manner as do others who are taken over by that archetype. Jung believed that this tendency to react with unconscious ritualism could be overcome by gradually withdrawing the projections and becoming increasingly conscious of the archetypes. He felt that it is important to wrestle with the archetype and thereby bring it into the light of ego-consciousness. Through this process, one becomes free from compulsive bondage to the archetype and acts as an individual. Thus, Jung called this the process of growth individuation. In order to accomplish this, one needs to develop respect and appreciation for myths, perhaps even more than for the personality.

As James Hillman has pointed out, Freud was also aware of a relationship between the psyche and mythology, but he viewed the relationship in the opposite direction from that of archetypal psychology. Freud believed that the pathology he observed was primary and that the myth helped to clarify it, whereas archetypal psychology regards the myth as primary and pathological behaviors the result of acting out the myth. Hillman wrote:

> I began by examining various psychological syndromes as if they were mythical enactments, as if they were ways in which the soul is mimetic of an archetypal pattern. Of course this approach in modern times started with Freud. He imagined psychopathology against a background of the Oedipus myth. But Freud's method of reversion took a positivistic course; it became reduction. Instead of leading events back to their base in myth and seeing that pathologizing was ultimately mythical behavior—the soul's return to myth—Freud tried to base the myths on the actual behavior of actual biological families, ultimately reducing the mythical to the pathological.*[19]

One means of becoming more aware of these archetypal forms is through personally studying their representations in myths, fairy tales, and divine symbols and by developing a conscious relationship with embodiments of the archetype. This method has been used in spiritual traditions throughout the world. In exoteric religions the archetypes are conceived of as divine forms that exist outside of the individual, but in the more esoteric traditions these embodiments are considered to be external representations of that which exists within.

In the Eastern traditions, Shakti, Kali, Quan Yin, and numerous other female embodiments of divinity continue to be regarded as expressions of the anima. Hymns, chants, and prayers glorifying the Divine Mother help one withdraw his projections of the anima from the human sphere and turn to the ideal as it is represented in divine forms. Shankara composed a hymn that makes us aware of the pure and unconditional love of the ideal mother. A portion of the hymn states:

> Here in this world of Thine, O Mother!
> Many are Thy guileless children;
> But restless am I among them all.

---

*Monistic psychology takes this approach a step further and asserts that it is neither the person nor the archetypes that is primary, but unitary consciousness. It considers the person as an individual ego to be essentially an instrument in the service of unitary consciousness. The personality must get out of the way and make room for the universal consciousness to express itself through the individual. According to monistic psychology, to the extent that a person ceases to identify with both the ego and the archetypes, regarding them merely as instruments, to that extent will he experience the unitary center of his being.

And so it is nothing very strange
That I should turn myself from Thee.
Yet surely it were impossible
That Thou shouldst ever turn from me:
A wicked son is sometimes born,
But an unkind mother there cannot be.

Mother of the world! Thou, my own Mother!
Never have I served Thee, never yet
Offered Thee gold or precious gems;
And still Thy love is beyond compare.
A wicked son is sometimes born,
But an unkind mother there cannot be.[20]

Though Shankara was considered to be a sage of unparalleled wisdom and spiritual attainment, we see that his own attitude was that of a humble and inept child before the Mother of the universe.*

In ancient Greece, Athena, Demeter, Artemis, and other goddesses represented various aspects of the anima. In the Christian world, the Blessed Virgin Mary has fulfilled this office, and her many personalities can bring one in touch with various aspects of the anima. Over the past two thousand years, the worship of Mary as the Virgin, the Bride of God, the Queen of Heaven, the Mother of God, the intercessor for sinners, Mater Dolorosa, and in other forms has been one of the primary means of bringing the Westerner into relationship with the anima.[21] These divine expressions of the feminine ideal are able to fulfill one's need for experiencing the archetype in a way that human beings cannot. Instead of finding disappointment, as occurs when the archetype is projected onto the human sphere, one who establishes a relationship with the divine form can come to know the anima in all her glory.

A few highly evolved seekers have gone beyond the forms provided by myth, artistic expression, and conceptual thought to experience the Divine Mother directly in illumined states of consciousness. For example, St. Francis de Sales provided the following description of his mystical

*Although Shankara is regarded as the highest authority on and chief exponent of the monistic position, we see here that he also embraced a dualistic view within the monistic perspective. Shankara is also considered to be the leading authority on tantra in its most pure and evolved form.

experience of receiving divine nurturance: "In this state the soul is like a little child still at the breast whose mother, to caress him while he is still in her arms, makes her milk distill into his mouth without even moving his lips. So it is here . . . our Lord desires that our world should be satisfied with sucking the milk which His Majesty pours into our mouth."[22] And St. Teresa of Avila stated: "From those Divine breasts, where it seems that God is ever sustaining the soul, flow streams of milk, which solace all who dwell in the Castle."[23] St. Bernard explained that the bosom of the Divine Mother swells with beneficent milk and that "if we but persevere, despite our own dryness and tepidity, grace will overpower us, . . . and the milk of sweetness will overflow everywhere in a torrent."[24] It is in fact recorded that when Bernard was reciting a prayer of adoration before a statue of the Virgin and "came to the words Monstra esse Matrem (Show thyself a mother), the Virgin appeared before him, and pressing her breast, let three drops of milk fall onto his lips."[25] Though strange to our ears, the writings of numerous mystics of various times and places indicate that these descriptions are more than metaphor, that they actually depict the experience of receiving a divine nectar, an ambrosia, an experience of total love and comfort from the ideal feminine principle that sustains all beings.

Such experiences are incomprehensible to the person who is experiencing the world from the egoistic mode of consciousness.

> Even if we must recognize that there is a non-ego experience, it is a long way until we realize what it might be. That is the reason why these experiences are secret. They are called mystical because the ordinary world cannot understand them, and what they cannot understand they call "mystical"—that covers everything.
>
> But the point is that what they call mystical is simply not the obvious. Therefore the Yoga way or the Yoga philosophy has always been a secret, but not because people have kept it secret. For as soon as you keep a secret, it is already an open secret: you know about it and other people know about it, and then it is no longer a secret. The real secrets are secrets because nobody understands them. One cannot even talk about them, and of such a kind are the experiences of the Kundalini Yoga.[26]

Sri Ramakrishna, a revered sage who lived in India in the last century, devoted his life to the worship of the Divine Mother. His biographer provided an account of the way in which Ramakrishna experienced the Divine Mother: "Previously, at the time of worship and meditation, he saw that there appeared a wonderful living Presence in the stone image before him. Now he did not see that image at all when he entered the temple; but saw instead, standing there, the living Mother Herself, all consciousness, and with hands that offered boons and freedom from fear."[27] Ramakrishna did indeed experience the Mother in her various forms and aspects, as he himself attested: "'I felt a desire to enjoy the Mother, who is of innumerable forms and is the embodiment of endless relations, in as many forms and relations as She would be pleased to show me. Therefore, whenever I desired to see or enjoy Her in any particular form or relation, I persisted in praying importunately to Her to reveal Herself to me in that form or relation. The compassionate Mother on Her part made me personally do whatever was necessary and supplied me everything required and revealed Herself to me in that form and in that relation.'"[28]

These experiences, whether they are taken as fact or as fancy, give some indication of the way in which the spiritual seeker functioning from the dualistic perspective reorients his relationships. Instead of projecting the ideal onto others, he relates to the ideal itself in its symbolic representation or in his direct experience of that ideal. Relationship to the Divine Mother has been given as an example, but one might also relate to other archetypes in a similar way. For instance, instead of projecting (transferring) the father, child, or hero archetype onto others in one's interpersonal relationships, one can develop relationships to the abundant and overflowing symbolic embodiments of these archetypes that have been offered in myths and by the spiritual traditions.

Yoga psychology leads one to the direct experience of the pure or archetypal forms. In the practice of yoga meditation, one goes through a preliminary stage of concentration *(dharana)*, in which the mind is fixed on a single object for several minutes without wavering. Initially, one may concentrate on an external object such as a candle flame or an icon. As the quality of one's practice deepens, he becomes aware of the subtle essence or the archetype of which that object is a particular adumbrated expression in the world of form. He is then no longer concentrating on, for instance, a particular flame, but on the flame principle. The understanding that an object is significant as an embodiment of the genus rather than as a particular object is reflected in the Sanskrit language, where there are no definite or indefinite articles. "A flame" is not different from "flame" or the flame principle. Concentration on the object leads one to an awareness and understanding of the flame principle, with all its attendant conditions, qualities, times, spaces, causes, sequences, and effects. Here Vedanta psychology goes beyond Jungian psychology and beyond the dualistic perspective. Whereas Jung believed that one cannot fully experience the archetype but only its manifestations, yoga psychology offers a method for realizing the archetype itself. Through this process, the yogi not only experiences the archetype, but gains mastery over that archetypal principle and its various forms of expression.

In advanced yogic practices one does not concentrate on the external object at all, but on the archetype itself. In fact, many of these archetypes ordinarily have no external visible expression in the world of form. There are no objects of the senses for these archetypes; they exist only in thought. The deities depicted in spiritual traditions, as well as icons, mandalas, yantras, and mantras, are symbolic expressions of such archetypes, many of which would otherwise not have a clear expression in the sensory world. These ideal forms are experienced internally by the adept and are reproduced as external images for the advanced student of yoga to aid him in visualizing these forms within. They are a means for achieving an inner direct experience of the archetype itself. Paintings, statues, and other archetypal representations of this sort are not creative expressions of an artist but exact and detailed reproductions of subtle forms experienced in transcendent states of consciousness. As a result of such inner visions, detailed texts on iconography have been handed down that give exact descriptions of the minutest facets of the archetype in order to render it in a form available to the senses.

As the yogi progresses to a deep state of meditation, he experiences the archetype as an object within the mind. He goes on to recognize that he himself projects the archetype onto the screen of his mind, and then onto the external world. The average person believes that he perceives by taking what is outside into him through the senses, but at this stage of awareness the yogi realizes that what is outside is a manifestation of what is already within. In perceiving an object outside, one is recognizing (re-cognizing) in an adumbrated form that which is within. What is within are not inner objects but the principles and essences from which objects are manifest. The yogi learns to consciously gather the subtle essences within and to thereby construct the forms and expressions that the archetypes can take. He is then able to produce the external form at will and is called an adept, one who has mastery over the world of form.

But this is not yet the last stage of one's awakening to his true nature. The practice of yoga involves a movement from identification with the sensory world to an awareness of the subtle realm of archetypes and finally to an awareness of the formlessness from which these realms arise. It is a reversal of the creative process. One goes from the manifest to the unmanifest. One dissolves the world of form to experience the subtle realm of archetypes and then dissolves even the archetypes to realize oneself as pure consciousness unenclosed by form of any sort. Ramakrishna's experience of the Divine Mother is an example of the direct experience of the mother archetype. At this stage in his development, Ramakrishna had not yet reached the heights of Vedantic realization.

The experiences of Sri Ramakrishna and other mystics are likely to seem incredible to the modern reader. Ramakrishna's descriptions of his experiences may seem closer to the ravings of a lunatic than the words of an enlightened master. Indeed, for a time, those acquainted with Ramakrishna were unsure about whether he was insane or enlightened. A large gathering of pandits was assembled to test him and to compare his experiences with the descriptions of enlightenment given in the scriptures. These comparisons, together with his inspired and insightful teachings, his practical guidance, his positive effect on the lives of others, and the vast charitable and educational work of the order he founded, indicate that his experiences were indeed inspired and of a highly spiritual nature, that he did indeed experience the anima directly in her various aspects.

The strangeness and unbelievability of these experiences for the modern reader show how extensively modern man is enmeshed in the reductionist perspective. Reductionist psychologies, such as psychoanalysis and behaviorism, discount the validity of relationships to ideal forms. Such relationships are thought of as irrational fantasies that lead to an escape from the "real" harshness of life. In psychoanalytic theory and in modern thought in general, such experiences as those described above are considered to be hallucinatory. Psychoanalysts believe that mystics such as Sri Ramakrishna, St. Bernard, St. Francis de Sales, and St. Teresa of Avila had regressed to primitive states of consciousness. The following assertion is typical of psychoanalytic writings: "We propose that mystical states represent regressions to very early periods of infancy. The basic characteristic—that of ecstatic union—suggests a regression to early nursing experience."[29]

This conception illustrates the reductionist bias, in which each current experience is understood in terms of the earliest developmental experience that it resembles. Psychologies within the reductionist paradigm conceive of human growth and development in much the same way that one thinks about construction. If one were constructing a building, he would begin with the foundation. Its strength and form would then determine both the limitations and potential of that which is built upon it. The second floor must be built upon the first, the third upon the second, and so on. In each case, what came before determines what can come later. If we want to understand why the fourth floor is formed in a particular way, we can look back to that which supports it. In this model, what comes later is considered to be a kind of imitation or extension of that which came earlier. What came earlier is primary, and what comes later is its elaboration. Most of modern psychology treats human development in this way. Psychoanalysts are likely to look at a person's drinking problem at age thirty as the outcome of the under-indulgence or over-indulgence of oral dependency needs that the person had in his first year of life.

This is the seemingly commonsense approach to understanding human development. The dualistic point of view thus seems quite irrational to one enmeshed in the reductive model, for it proposes that growth occurs in the other direction—that one grows upside-down, as it were. From the dualistic perspective, a person's growth is directed by his future; the present can best be understood by understanding one's future.*

---

*Jung was aware of an interesting symbol in both Christian mysticism and Indian philosophy that expresses and expands this view. He observed that "John of Ruysbroeck makes use of an image which was also known to Indian philosophy, that of the tree whose roots are above and its branches below: 'And he must climb up into the tree of faith, which grows from above downwards, for its roots are in the Godhead.'"[30]

Reductive psychologies reduce the more evolved or complete experiences of being nurtured to the infant's experience of being nurtured by its mother. They view mystical experiences as a regression to a fantasized infantile state. But those psychologies based on the dualistic paradigm take quite the opposite perspective: the more ideal state is taken as the basis for understanding those experiences that occur earlier in the developmental process; the more primitive state is understood in terms of the ideal. From this vantage point, the infantile experience is a prefiguring or an adumbration of the more mature and complete experience that will come later in development. In terms of receiving nurturance, the individual is developing toward an ever more complete or ideal experience that is reached in the mystical state, in which one experiences total nurturance and sustenance. The infant's experience of being nurtured is an incomplete approximation, an adumbration, of the mystic's experience.

If one considers the experiences of children playing, he will see that this notion is not as radical as it may at first appear. For example, a girl playing with her doll imitates the behavior of her mother. When she changes the doll's diaper, dresses it, combs its hair, or cuddles it, she mimics her mother's actions, words, and attitudes. Through this imitative process she rehearses and gradually learns the behaviors, attitudes, and ways of being she will assume as an adult. Similarly, when this girl wears her mother's shoes and purse and plays at being a grown-up, she is again imitating her mother and learning the attitudes and behaviors that will be appropriate later in life. Of course, her imitations are caricatures, distorted and limited by her own level of understanding. But through such simulation she approximates and gradually masters more mature ways of being. Without playful enactment of these roles, the child might never come to learn the behaviors and attitudes of the adult. Through her play, she gradually, year by year, comes to experience ever more closely that which she has been imitating.

Extending this perspective leads to the conclusion that even being a mother or father is an imperfect approximation of a more ideal or archetypal expression of motherhood or fatherhood such as may be found in myths, in religious symbolism, and in highly evolved beings who are models of love and compassion. For example, Jesus, the Blessed

Virgin Mary, Mother Teresa of Calcutta, the guru in the Indian tradition, and God as envisioned in the New Testament may be considered ideal or archetypal parents whose compassion, consistent understanding, guidance, nurturance, patience, and forgiveness far exceed those of the ordinary human parent. The ordinary person's experience of being a parent is an adumbration or imperfect copy of the ideal. In other words, adults who find themselves in the role of mother or father are really playing at, and growing toward, becoming the embodiment of the parental ideal. Through their ongoing play they are approximating the ideal ever more closely. They are gradually learning to refine, understand, and appreciate the experience of parenthood with ever more subtlety; they are slowly learning to embody the archetype in its fullness.

The dualistic paradigm extends this perspective to all areas of one's life. All of one's experiences are seen as part of a developmental process in which one approximates through play a more mature way of being. Of course, one does not ordinarily experience his seemingly consequential activities as play any more than the little girl takes her imitation of mother to be play. Adults like to contrast their "serious" attempts to deal with life situations with what they believe is the carefree play of children. However, the child who is playing at being mother also believes that what she is doing is serious and important. When one has a more encompassing perspective, he sees that what the child is taking so seriously is not real in some deeper sense. In a similar way, the experiences an adult takes to be real, such as getting married or being a parent, though they are considered to be serious from the perspective of the participant, are seen as play through the eyes of someone who has evolved still further toward the experience of the ideal. An activity or undertaking that from a more encompassing perspective looks like play is considered to be work from the perspective of the person who is participating. The participant takes his activity seriously and is usually unable to see its playful aspect.

The developmental process in every area of life involves growth through play toward ever more complete realization of the archetypal forms. One comes to realize his relationship with the ideal through a series of progressively more refined experiences in the course of development. He learns to appreciate ever more subtle aspects of these experiences. His own consciousness becomes enriched, and he moves into closer attunement with the archetype itself. Growth is guided by what one will be.

Whenever one's play falls short of the ideal, he experiences limitation and incompleteness. He remains unfulfilled and so tries again in a new way, incorporating the corrections that became apparent in his very experience of being less than ideal. Parents universally go through this process. How often parents realize, after losing their temper with their children, that they are far less perfect than they would like to be. The realization may be quite upsetting, and parents who expect themselves to be perfect may feel that they have failed. But from the dualistic perspective, there is no failure. The "failure" to embody the ideal is simply an indication of one's position in the growth process and of the corrections that must be made in order to take the next step. Those who expect themselves to be perfect, rather than realizing that each imperfection is a means of gaining information about how to modify oneself in order to reach the ideal, block their growth process and remain mired in self-created suffering. It is by accepting where he is in the developmental process, imperfect though he may be, that one can see clearly where to solidly place his foot in taking the next step forward.

The relationship between husband and wife can also be appreciated in a new way when seen from this perspective. A marriage between two people is considered to be an adumbration of the mystic marriage described in the spiritual traditions. Marriage is an ongoing experience in learning to transcend one's ego and become united with the other. When the partners are still immature, their relationship may be marked by considerable conflict, manipulation, domination, rejection, and so on. But one very gradually learns from the pain of such strife and slowly develops consideration, acceptance, love, and other qualities that lead one out of egoistic concerns. According to this view, marriage is not an end in itself, but a training ground for achieving a still more perfect union.

The experience of union remains incomplete unless it grows still further into a spiritual union between oneself and one's ideal. In esoteric spiritual traditions, the ideal or archetypal marriage is that experienced between the soul and the Divine. In the Hebrew tradition, marriage between a man and a woman is considered to be the means of experiencing a union between the masculine and feminine aspects of God. A leading authority on this subject asserts that the kabbalistic tradition "rejected asceticism and continued to regard marriage . . . as one of the most sacred mysteries. Every true marriage is a symbolic realization of the union of God and the Shekhinah."*[31] Christian mystics, on the other hand, have often advocated the renunciation of marriage to a physical partner. They have asserted that the most evolved form of marriage is attained through direct worship of God. Here the soul, or bride, becomes betrothed to God and evolves toward union with the Divine. St. Teresa describes this relationship: "The soul is now completely determined to take no other spouse; but the Spouse disregards its yearnings for the conclusion of the Betrothal, desiring that they would become deeper and that this greatest of all blessings should be won by the soul."[32] After continued devotion, the soul becomes prepared for mystic union: "When Our Lord is pleased to have pity upon this soul, which suffers and has suffered so much out of desire for Him, and which He has now taken spiritually to be His bride, He brings her into this Mansion of His . . . before consummating the Spiritual Marriage."[33]

This union of feminine and masculine principles has been represented in many traditions as the ultimate resolution of all polarities. Jung called the anima and animus the "supreme opposites." He believed that this polarity underlies all others: "This primordial pair of opposites symbolizes every conceivable pair of opposites that may occur: hot and cold, light and dark, north and south, dry and damp, good and bad, conscious and unconscious."[34] In Jungian psychology, coming to terms with this polarity represents the culmination of the individuation process. In his later years, Jung became increasingly absorbed in the study of alchemy as a system for bringing about the union of the primordial pair. He asserted that in alchemy the ultimate phase of the work is "the union of opposites in the archetypal form of the . . . 'chymical wedding.' Here the supreme opposites, male and female (as in the Chinese *Yang* and *Yin*), are melted into a unity purified of all opposition and therefore incorruptible."[35]

In the more exoteric expressions of these traditions, the spiritual marriage may be thought of as a union with something external to the

---

*In the kabbalistic tradition the Shekinah is considered to be the feminine aspect of God, and also the dwelling place of the soul.

essence of the conscious being who is seeking union. But the more esoteric teachings point toward a union that occurs within. In his discussion of the psychology of transference, Jung pointed toward this inner union: "It is possible that the endogamous urge is not ultimately tending towards projection at all; it may be trying to unite the different components of the personality . . . on a higher plane where 'spiritual marriage' becomes an inner experience that is not projected."[36]

These conceptions in the Hebrew, Christian, and alchemical traditions have their parallels in Indian philosophy and psychology. While the more purely monistic schools of Indian philosophy emphasize the nonreality of the manifest universe, tantra philosophy and psychology recognizes and leads one to mastery over the polarities in the world of form as well as to transcendence of the phenomenal world.* Tantra is a synthesis of dualism and monism. In tantra, the primordial polarity is symbolized by Shiva (the masculine principle representing pure consciousness uninvolved in the world of form) and Shakti (the feminine principle of energy from which the phenomenal universe emerges). According to tantra, all human beings contain both the masculine and feminine principles within themselves, but are not conscious of both. The ultimate goal is to experience the union of these two principles. In this union, all polarities within and without are transcended. One transcends dualistic existence and experiences unitary consciousness.

Tantra encompasses many practices and rituals directed toward mastery of the phenomenal universe and the transcendence of various polarities. Less evolved forms of tantra may involve the ritualistic union of a man and a woman. This is taken as a symbol of the union of the primordial pair and thus of all polarities. However, in higher forms of tantra, the outward projection is withdrawn and no external ritual is used; the yogi recognizes that his complement exists within himself, and through inner worship of and meditation on the primordial pair, he experiences the union of these two principles within.

> She who "shines like a chain of lights" . . . in the centre of his body is the "Inner Woman" to whom reference was made when it was said, "What need have I of any outer woman? I have an Inner Woman

---

*The word *tantra* means "through which knowledge is expanded" *(tantyate vistaryate manam aneneti tantram)*.

within myself."... The ... Yogi unites within himself his own
principles, female and male ... or Sakti ... and Śiva. It is their
union which is the mystic coition (Maithuna) of the Tantras. There
are two forms of union ..., namely the first which is the gross ...,
or the union of the physical embodiments of the Supreme Consciousness; and the second which is the subtle ..., or the union of
the quiescent and active principles in Consciousness itself. It is the
latter which is Liberation.[37]

Tantra philosophy and psychology in its most mature expression is
monistic, for it is based on the recognition that Shiva and Shakti are in
essence united, but only appear to be separate for the purpose of carrying
on the love dance of the illusory universe. Within this monistic
framework, tantra also encompasses a dualistic conception of the
universe. By understanding the subtle laws of the phenomenal universe
and becoming aware of the primordial pair within oneself, one achieves
mastery over the world of form. When one unites these two in his
consciousness, he transcends all identification with and limitations of the
phenomenal world.

The Monistic View: Superimposition

Jung's understanding of transference was far more encompassing
than Freud's. In Freud's conception, one transfers onto others the
unconscious attitudes engendered by the way his parents related to him
when he was a child. In resolving the transference, one must expand his
consciousness to include memories of childhood interactions. From the
perspective of yoga psychology, Freud's view of the origin of transference
is not to be discarded, for it offers valuable insights into the way one
distorts his current experiences as a result of his past. But Freud's
perspective is limited; it does not take into account deeper layers of the
transference phenomenon. Dualistic psychology goes further and asserts
that aspects of the majestic and compelling realm of archetypes or ideal
forms are projected onto others in the transference process. One resolves
the transference by withdrawing these projections and becoming aware of
the archetypes more directly and completely. This conception leads one to
appreciate another dimension in the establishment of transference, but
this understanding too is incomplete. As we move from the dualistic to

the monistic viewpoint, the concept of transference becomes still more comprehensive.

The Vedantic term *adhyasa* has been translated as both "transference" and "superimposition." In the eighth century A.D., Shankara reviewed different conceptions of adhyasa and presented a view of superimposition that remains the best description of the monistic paradigm that has ever been offered. Shankara noted that various definitions "agree in so far as they represent superimposition as the apparent presentation of the attributes of one thing in another thing."[38] The term *adhyasa* is used by the Vedantists to refer to errors in perception. It is believed that rather than perceiving an object as it is, the perceiver superimposes what he recalls from a previous perception onto his current experience so that his current perception becomes distorted. As a result, the thing being perceived appears to be other than what it really is.

> Superimposition takes place . . . when the qualities of one thing not immediately present to consciousness are, through memory, given to, or projected upon, another thing that is present to consciousness and are identified with it.[39]

> Superimposition is nothing more than the qualities of a particular object being imagined as though they are present in something else. These qualities were perceived in a different context and they have remembrance as their basis.[40]

The monistic paradigm extends the conception of transference beyond that considered in modern psychology. It reaches a meta-perspective in which the concept of transference is applied not only to the objects of one's perception but to the perceiver as well. According to this view, one also distorts his perception of himself. The perceiver superimposes upon himself the illusion of being a separate entity. This artificial division engenders the superimposition of further distinctions, and the illusory world of form is established. The person in reality is unitary consciousness, but ignoring the underlying unity, he superimposes limited qualities onto himself as well as onto the external world.

In this process, a second level of superimposition takes place in which the qualities one falsely attributes both to himself and to the world become confused with one another. One superimposes qualities of the world onto himself and inner qualities onto the world. It is this secondary superimposition of inner qualities onto the world that is regarded as transference in dualistic psychology. Fritz Perls described the complementary process of superimposing qualities of the world onto oneself, and he called this process "introjection." "Introjection . . . is the neurotic mechanism whereby we incorporate into ourselves standards, attitudes, ways of acting and thinking, which are not truly ours. . . . When the introjector says, 'I think,' he usually means, 'they think.'"[41] Franklin Merrell-Wolff also refers to this dual process of projection and introjection: "Man . . . constantly projects himself into the objects seen, and complementarily, introjects the object into himself, thereby superimposing upon himself the limitations of those objects. Every human problem grows out of this, and the never-ending stream of unresolved or half-resolved problems cannot be eliminated until this vicious habit is broken."[42]

According to Vedanta, we are in actuality pure consciousness, but we become confused and entangled in the world of names and forms through superimposition.

> We say, as a matter of course, "I am fat," "I am tired," "I am walking," "I am sitting down"—without ever stopping to consider what this "I" really is. We go further. We claim purely external objects and names for our own. We say "I am a Republican," or "This house is mine." As superimpositions multiply, extraordinary statements become possible and normal—such as "We sunk three submarines yesterday" or "I carry a good deal of insurance." We identify our ego, more or less, with every object in the universe.[43]

One can be extricated from this entanglement through the process of yoga. In the first phase of this process, one resolves the secondary superimposition (transference and introjection). He withdraws the inner projections from the world and the introjections of the world from himself. To use Jung's term, one goes through a process of individuation. A similar process occurs in the modern psychologies based on the dualistic paradigm, but these psychologies lead one only part of the way toward disentanglement from the world of names and forms. Vedanta psychology helps one to dissolve all secondary projections and introjections, leading one from the subject-object mode of consciousness to a state of pure subjectivity or nirvanic consciousness. Vedanta psychology then takes one still further to resolve the more primary superimposition in which qualities from the world of form, such as polarization, are superimposed on the unitary consciousness.

Monistic psychology accepts both the Freudian and Jungian conceptions of transference as valid, meaningful, and useful in the development of therapeutic procedures for disentangling one from the web of his self-created illusions. Nevertheless, these are seen as circumscribed conceptions that do not get at the root of the phenomenon. Transference as described by Freud overlays the more basic transference explained by Jung, but the transference of archetypes onto people, institutions, and so forth that Jung delineated is itself an overlay of a still more fundamental transference that is revealed by Vedanta philosophy and psychology. According to the monistic view, these two forms of transference—in which one transfers something of the past onto the present or projects an archetype onto another person—are adumbrations of a more primary transference in which the world of form is projected onto the ultimate Reality, called Brahman, the unitary consciousness.

In the same way that one superimposes qualities, including archetypes, onto a person and then relates to the person he has created rather than to the person as he really is, one superimposes the various qualities from the world of names and forms, including the archetypes, onto the one pure consciousness that is without form and division and that is one's true nature. Through his own projections a person creates for himself the illusion that form and qualities exist. Self-created illusion is a prime characteristic of *maya*.* As Shankara stated: "When one is impelled by the power of projection, one superimposes upon the Atman [unitary consciousness] various kinds of activities and as a result of it experiences the consequences that flow from them such as good and evil. That is how people wander about lost in the sea of samsara [the bondage of life, death, and rebirth]."[44] Superimposition maintains the appearance of the world of names and forms at all levels, from the most subtle to the most material. Not only are material objects created by this process, but the archetypes as well, and all conceptions of God in form. From

---

Ma means "no," *ya* means "that." Maya is that which does not exist in reality, yet seems to be existing. It appears to be real but actually is not.

the monistic perspective, these are all illusions established by super-imposition.

There is yet another side of the process of superimposition to be understood, for superimposition takes place in two directions. Not only are the illusory worldly attributes transferred onto the unified consciousness, but the qualities of the unified consciousness are also transferred onto the world of form. Shankara goes a step further than dualistic psychology and shows that it is not merely the archetypes that are being projected onto one's relationships with people and objects: one also projects onto the sensate world qualities of the unitary consciousness that underlies the archetypes and from which the archetypes arise. Thus, the world of names and forms is perceived as though it possessed the formless qualities of the pure consciousness, such as infinitude, eternality, perfection, purity, substantiality, and unchangeability. One not only relates to others and to objects as though they were embodiments of the archetypes, but one expects these relationships to be unchanging, eternal, perfect, and so on, which are qualities only of the formless unitary consciousness. Instead of recognizing the impermanence and incompleteness inherent in relationships within the world of form, one expects perfection from them and, as a result, is repeatedly disappointed. Patanjali, the codifier of yoga science, calls this confusion between the world of form and the unitary consciousness *avidya* (ignorance) and asserts that avidya is the fundamental cause of all human suffering. According to this view, human suffering can be transcended only when avidya and its consequent sources of pain—egoism, attachment, aversion, and the fear of death—are erased by dissolving one's identifications and superimpositions. Meditation, contemplation, and other practices of yoga are the means that enable one to understand and dissolve these identifications and superimpositions.

Chapter Five

General Systems Theory and Beyond

General Systems Theory As a Dualistic Model

Another psychological model that follows the assumptions of the dualistic paradigm is based on general systems theory, which has developed in the latter half of this century as a general scheme of the way parts interact with one another to function as a whole. For instance, a car's cooling system may consist of a water pump, radiator, fan, thermostat, and other components that function together. Systems are found in all aspects of the phenomenal world. One frequently hears about the nervous system, the legal system, the heating system in a house, the economic system, and many other systems that are found in nature, society, and mechanisms. General systems theory attempts to uncover and understand the lawfulness in relationships that transcends any specific content area. It has found useful application in such diverse fields as biology, computer science, the study of organizations, and family therapy.

General systems theory is inherently dualistic since it is dependent on a relationship between two or more components. In fact, general systems theory may be considered to be the science of dualistic interaction. In contrast to reductionist thinking, which takes things apart and studies them as though they were nothing but the sum of their parts, general systems theory treats the arrangements and organized interaction of those parts as an entity. The logic of systems theory differs from the logic of reductionist thinking. Reductionist thinking is one-directional, competitive, hierarchical, classificational, and atomistic, while the logic upon which systems theory is based is mutualistic, symbiotic, interactionist, rational, and contextual. A leading systems theorist uses a simile that sheds light on the difference between reductionist and dualistic logic: "The mainstream logic in Western cultures has been Aristotelian logic, even though countermovements have occurred at different times in history. This logic . . . has a *monocular vision*. Vision with one eye

101

has no depth perception. On the other hand, vision with two eyes has depth perception . . . because the *differential* between the two images enables the brain to compute the third, not directly visible, dimension. Binocular vision allows us to see space three dimensionally."[1] In a similar way, the dualistic model enables one to achieve a third perspective that comprehends and synthesizes the two sides of any polarity.

Within the field of psychology, systems theory has had its greatest impact in the study of family interaction, in understanding how behavior is generated by interpersonal relationships, and in the development of therapeutic applications directed at changing families and organizations. The application of this dualistic model to understanding human motivation and behavior and the use of therapeutic techniques developed by systems theorists do more than simply add to the repertoire of therapists who function from the reductionist perspective. Systems theory does not merely extend one's understanding in a linear fashion; it leads to a profound shift in orientation. Problems are understood and solved in a radically different way when using this model than they would be from the reductionist perspective. In fact, the solutions offered by systems theorists may be diametrically opposed to those suggested by "common-sense" psychology.

Although general systems theory has developed completely apart from and in different areas of human functioning than Jungian psychology, both are based on the assumptions of the dualistic paradigm. As a result, many similarities can be found between these two models. For example, both focus on the complementary interaction of polar opposites, and both have a teleological view of human functioning.

The monism of Vedanta transcends the systems theory perspective. According to the monistic view, one experiences the dissolution of all systems in unitary consciousness. Systems exist only in the illusory world of form. General systems theory is one way of explaining how the world of form is organized. It uncovers universal principles that apply across content areas of the phenomenal universe and relative principles that differ from one content area to another.

Systems theory has, for example, helped to clarify the way in which simple mechanical systems differ from complex biological systems. Systems theorists have distinguished between systems that tend either toward increasing entropy (uniformity) or toward homeostasis (equilibrium) and systems that evolve toward increased order and complexity. They have shown that it is inappropriate to try to understand complex organic systems in terms of the way simple mechanical systems function, an error that has often been made not only in psychology but in other areas of science as well. Highly complex systems may maintain, repair, reorganize, replicate, and program themselves.

In classical physics, the second law of thermodynamics states that a system, if left alone, will tend to develop toward a state of equilibrium, homogeneity, or randomness. For example, if first hot water and then cold water flow into a bathtub, initially the hot and cold water will not be evenly distributed throughout the tub; there will be warmer and cooler areas. Eventually the molecules of hot and cold water will become randomly distributed and the water will reach a uniform or homogeneous temperature: there will be no thermal distinction between the water in one part of the tub and that in another part.

The second law of thermodynamics has been applied to the universe as a whole, leading to the conception that the entire physical universe is a system tending toward equilibrium or homogeneity. Presently the universe contains stars so hot and dense that atomic fusion occurs; it also contains vast empty spaces at temperatures near absolute zero. According to this theory, through the ineluctable workings of the second law of thermodynamics, there will come a time when this distinction will no longer exist: matter will eventually be evenly distributed throughout every cubic inch of the universe and the entire universe will exist at a uniform temperature. According to this view, the physical universe is running down or moving toward a state of entropy.

Some theorists in the biological sciences, adopting this principle, have asserted that living organisms avoid running down by importing energy from outside and maintaining a steady state of equilibrium within. This equilibrium or homeostasis is accomplished through a process called negative feedback.* The thermostat that regulates a home furnace is an example of a homeostatic mechanism that maintains a more or less steady

---

*The term "negative feedback" is sometimes used in general discourse to indicate criticism. In systems theory, negative feedback is not inherently either good or bad; it is feedback that negates change.

state. If the temperature falls a degree or two below the specified level, the furnace automatically comes on. When the furnace raises the temperature a degree or two above what is desired, the thermostat shuts it off until the temperature again falls below the specified level. In each case, the furnace responds to the negative feedback given by the thermostat which signals that the system is straying too far from the steady state and that correction through a change of state (from on to off, or from off to on) is needed. The steady temperature in human beings is regulated by a similar homeostatic process.

Reductive psychological theories have borrowed from physics and biology, positing that animals and human beings function psychologically in a way similar to that described above: "Psychologists have broadened the principle of homeostasis to mean that any *physiological* or *psychological* imbalance will motivate behavior designed to restore equilibrium. Thus, a hungry, anxious, uncomfortable, or fearful person will be motivated to do something to reduce the tension."[2]

The principle of homeostasis in biology together with the second law of thermodynamics applied to the physical universe leads to the conception that living organisms attempt to maintain themselves against the tendency of the physical universe to run down. According to this view, the best that an organism can do—whether it be a lower form of life, an animal, or a human—is to maintain itself.

> Although the homeostasis model transcends older mechanistic models by acknowledging directiveness in self-regulating circular processes, it still adheres to the machine theory of the organism. . . .
> . . . The organism is essentially considered to be a reactive system. Outside stimuli are answered by proper responses in such a way as to maintain the system. The feedback model is essentially the classical stimulus-response scheme, only the feedback loop being added.[3]

There has not been a generally accepted conception in modern science of organisms enhancing themselves by *purposefully* leaving behind old structures and creating new ones. The mechanistic-reductive model predominates even in the generally accepted theory of evolution, which utilizes such statistical concepts as random mutation or natural selection to explain phylogenetic development, rather than positing any inherent evolutionary potential or purpose within the organism itself. In modern psychology, a similar perspective holds sway. Developmental psychology has focused primarily on normative changes that occur in the course of the life cycle. There is little consideration given to the possibility of an inherent tendency within the person to evolve himself in ways that are innovative and unique.

In early applications of general systems theory to the understanding of family dynamics, the emphasis was on the family's tendency to maintain homeostasis and to minimize deviance from the established pattern of interactions through negative feedback. Systems theorists observed that a family system resists change and will react to stress— either from within the family or from outside—by attempting to maintain the family system with minimal change. According to this view, if one person in the family changes his behavior dramatically (even if that change would be regarded by most people as being in the direction of greater health or normality), the other family members will act in a way that is designed to pull the person back into his former behavior. Systems theorists working with families in psychotherapy found that the families of severely disturbed patients show an exaggerated tendency to maintain the family system intact. These families often devote extraordinary amounts of energy to preserving the family system no matter what the cost in suffering or restriction to its individual members: "Such a model for family interaction was proposed by [Dr. Don D.] Jackson when he introduced the concept of *family homeostasis.* Observing that the families of psychiatric patients often demonstrated drastic repercussions (depression, psychosomatic attacks, and the like) when the patient improved, he postulated that these behaviors and perhaps therefore the patient's illness as well were 'homeostatic mechanisms,' operating to bring the disturbed system back into its delicate balance."[4] In the 1950s, Jackson and other family systems theorists also described the "double bind," a form of self-contradictory communication whereby members of dysfunctional families limit the options of other members and thereby maintain the status quo. Since family systems theorists have worked primarily in clinical settings with families having one or more severely disturbed members, it is natural that they would initially notice and emphasize a family's tendency to maintain a steady state.

As general systems theory has developed further, especially during the last fifteen years, there has been increasing appreciation of a process that complements homeostasis. This process involves positive feedback rather than negative feedback. Positive feedback is also known as deviance-amplifying feedback, for in contrast to negative feedback, it leads to ever-increasing deviance from the norm established in that system.* While negative feedback loops oppose change, positive feedback loops evoke change. They lead to an amplification of change rather than a return to a previous norm.

> The development of the study of feedback systems can be roughly divided into two phases. The dividing line, somewhat oversimplified, is around 1960. In the 1940s and the 1950s engineers and biological scientists focused their attention mainly on deviation-counteracting feedback systems (so-called negative feedback systems), which were useful for automatic control of various engineering devices as well as automatic regulation in biological systems. During the same period, however, a small number of thinkers, for example . . . the cultural psychiatrist Gregory Bateson, began to conceptualize theories of deviation-amplifying mutual causal processes (so-called positive feedback systems.)[5]

A familiar example of the result of positive feedback is the intense noise that occurs when one places an open microphone near a loudspeaker to which the microphone is connected. The minutest sound picked up by the microphone is amplified by the speaker, re-enters the microphone, and is then amplified further. As this feedback loop continues, the sound continues to intensify and a runaway situation occurs. Instead of leading toward stability, this sort of feedback leads to increasing change, to ever-increasing deviation from the original state: "Positive feedback is a deviation-amplifying mechanism that can lead to a breakdown or a so-called runaway in the system. If the wires on a furnace thermostat became crossed so that when the furnace reached 68 a positive

---

*The word "deviance" is used here not in a pejorative sense but merely to indicate change from what is usual. For example, if hostility is the norm in a family, a change toward more acceptance among family members would exemplify deviance from that norm. In a similar way, "positive" refers to the response in the feedback process which is positive with respect to what is being expressed and which thereby amplifies that expression. The term "positive" is not used in a valuative sense, connoting qualities such as good or bad. Thus, if one has the thought "I am disliked," positive feedback amplifies that thought and negative feedback diminishes it.

impulse was sent by the thermostat, the heat would keep climbing until the house (or at least the furnace) burned up."[6]

Positive or deviance-amplifying feedback also occurs in family systems. An argument between a couple is an example of deviance-amplifying feedback functioning in human communications. First the husband's harsh words evoke a biting retort from his spouse. Her sarcasm in turn increases his anger to the point that he calls her a demeaning name. The hostility between husband and wife escalates. She continues to feed this cycle by insulting him, whereupon his anger turns to rage and he strikes her. If this process is not interrupted by a negative feedback loop (for example, an implicit rule that leads one or both of them to back off or to temporarily separate themselves), the argument could lead to a radical change in the system, such as divorce. Positive feedback cycles that are not interrupted by negative feedback will be limited by the energy available to the system (one can scream only so loud) or by the system's strength (a family can take only so much screaming before it will split). Nevertheless, positive feedback can lead to extreme effects: "The spread of a fire, a rumor, a chain letter, or an epidemic disease—all of these are the result of positive feedback, as are all chemical and nuclear chain reactions. What they all have in common is an *explosive* quality, whereby a tiny initial spark can quickly cause enormous results. They are also often dangerous. As a result positive feedback loops are usually kept under very tight control in both natural and social systems."[7]

Families that are flexible and open to modification of their system and desirous of its continuation will integrate negative and positive feedback.

> All families that stay together must be characterized by some degree of negative feedback, in order to withstand the stresses imposed by the environment and the individual members. Disturbed families are particularly refractory to change and often demonstrate remarkable ability to maintain the status quo by predominantly negative feedback. . . .
>
> However, there is also learning and growth in the family, and it is exactly here that a pure homeostasis model errs most, for these effects are closer to *positive* feedback.*[8]

*Conrad Waddington, a leading systems theorist, developed the conception of homeorhesis to describe the purposeful development of both the individual and the species. Whereas homeostasis

The process of deviance-amplifying feedback in interpersonal relations was recognized as an isolated concept before it was integrated into a general theory of the way systems function. Karen Horney's description of the "vicious cycle" in the neurotic's thinking process and the concept of the self-fulfilling prophecy are examples of positive feedback. For instance, if a person believes that no one likes him and thus acts in a defensive, distrustful, and aggressive manner, others will respond to his unfriendly behavior with the dislike he expected, whereupon he will become more defensive and aggressive, causing others to dislike him even more, and so on. Such a person develops ever increasing fear and paranoia. Deviance-amplifying feedback need not result in a catastrophic or undesirable consequence; instead it can lead to an intensely positive outcome. For instance, if one begins with the premise "I am loved," he is likely to trust others and to behave affectionately toward them, thereby encouraging them to respond warmly to him. These responses will in turn compound his loving feelings and openness, further enhancing the love of others for him, and so on. Such a person creates unlimited possibilities for experiencing the essence of love.

Systems in Evolution

Positive or deviance-amplifying feedback increases change from the original standard or norm in a system. If there were only negative feedback in systems, they would always remain static; there would be no change. There is a preponderance of negative feedback in systems that do not evolve, whereas in those that are modifying themselves, positive feedback plays a more significant role. If negative feedback in a system is slight, deviance-amplifying feedback may lead to a significant alteration in the system. The shift may be a "quantum jump" through which the system suddenly reorganizes itself in a new and more comprehensive way.

Until the functioning of positive feedback was identified, the scientific view of the universe—including physical, biological, psychical,

---

refers to regulation around a static point, homeorhesis refers to regulation around a developmental path. In regulation through homeorhesis, if one part of development occurs at a relatively accelerated rate, it will eventually slow down in order for another part to catch up. Piaget has incorporated the conception of homeorhesis into his theory of development. Positive feedback cycles do not lead to systematic growth but simply to change, unless they are regulated by homeorhesis.

and interpersonal functioning—emphasized the tendency of systems to maintain a steady state. But with increasing understanding of the process of positive feedback, science is turning toward a conception of systems as evolving. Those in the forefront of systems theory have focused on the way in which the universe is evolving, self-generating, and self-organizing as a result of deviance-amplifying feedback.

This conception of systems evolving themselves as a result of deviance-amplifying feedback has even been applied to systems that up to now have been considered nonliving or inorganic. As a result, the distinction usually made between living and nonliving forms may be called into question. Some theorists now believe that physical as well as biological and psychological systems undergo an evolutionary process in which they grow toward self-transcendence and ever-increasing comprehensiveness.[9] Research by Illya Prigogine, who has won the Nobel Prize in chemistry, indicates that even chemical structures undergo such an evolutionary process. As a result, "life no longer appears as a thin superstructure over a lifeless physical reality, but as an inherent principle of the dynamics of the universe."[10] Those in the forefront of this thinking conceive of the universe as "an evolutionary process or organismic whole aiming toward higher orders of creative synthesis. As such it has the properties of a living being rather than those of an inanimate mechanism."[11]

From this perspective, there is a hierarchy of systems in the universe. An example is an atom within a cell, within the pancreas, within the digestive system, within the person. Each system has its own organization within a more comprehensive system: "Every entity is simultaneously a 'whole' within itself and a 'part' within a larger matrix."[12] The universe consists of a hierarchy of systems within systems within systems. Each system may be thought of as a limited field of consciousness that is ever evolving to increase its own comprehensiveness. As a system becomes more all-embracing, awareness of and mastery over systems lower down on the hierarchy is achieved. "In this perspective, life becomes a much broader concept than just survival, adaptation and homeostasis: it constitutes the creative joy of reaching out, of risking and winning, of differentiating and forming new relations at many levels, of recognizing and expressing wholeness in every living system. Creativity becomes self-realization in a systemic context."[13]

Here we have a conception far removed from the theory of mechanical systems in classical physics. Perhaps through this paradigm science will actually lead humanity to a spiritual conception of existence quite different from the spiritual conceptions held in the past by Western man. Newton conceived of a God who stood outside of a mechanical universe he had created. Later, positing a Creator was thought to be unnecessary and God was done away with, but interest remained in studying the mechanical universe. Newton and those religionists who preceded him began with God, or the universal consciousness, and then described that which was created. Systems theory and other teleological theories understand the universe from the other direction: the perspective is from the unevolved system reaching upward to experience ever more comprehensiveness. What had been called God before the abandonment of metaphysics is here thought of as a potentially evolved, extremely encompassing or all-embracing system that includes all less inclusive systems within itself. From this point of view, the all-embracing consciousness cannot stand apart from the manifest world, in the manner that God has traditionally been envisioned in Western religion: "In a world which is creating itself, the idea of a divinity does not remain outside, but is embedded in the totality of self-organization dynamics at all levels and in all dimensions. . . . God, then, is not the creator, but the mind of the universe."[14]

A further implication of the models generated from general systems theory is that each entity, including the human being, is evolving toward universal consciousness. General systems theory is helping us to envision human beings, and the universe as a whole, as continually evolving to an ever more comprehensive organization and understanding, an ever more comprehensive recognition of the unity that underlies all diversity.

Comparison of General Systems Theory with Other Psychological Models

A similar conception to that which has arisen out of general systems theory has been presented by Teilhard de Chardin in a more overtly spiritual context. This multifaceted man was a Jesuit theologian and a paleontologist who lived in the first half of this century. He spent most of his adult years in China, where he participated in the discovery of the

Peking Man. Teilhard was prevented by his superiors within the church hierarchy from expressing his ideas and from having his manuscripts on theology printed. In the past, other spiritual thinkers whose conceptions transcended antithetical dualism experienced similar censorship.

Drawing upon his paleontological studies, Teilhard conceived of the universe as being a process in which consciousness evolves toward greater complexity and inclusiveness. Teilhard posited a law of complexity,

> a tendency for all things to become more and more complex. . . . Every step higher on the scale of evolutionary appearances is accompanied by a higher degree of complexity. . . .
>   . . . the degree of consciousness which is exhibited corresponds to the degree of complexity. . . . Teilhard suggests that there is some degree of consciousness at every level of reality, even including the primordial stuff of the universe.[15]

According to Teilhard, as the forms of the universe evolve, consciousness purposefully evolves through definite stages until it reaches proximity to a supreme or universal consciousness, called the omega point. He stated: "Evolution is an ascent towards consciousness. . . . Therefore it should culminate forwards in some sort of supreme consciousness."[16] He described this omega point as "a *distinct Centre radiating at the core of a system of centres.*"[17]

Some theorists who describe the process of evolution have maintained a reductionist position, concluding that the more comprehensive consciousness is an outcome of the evolutionary process rather than its origin. For example, J. C. Smuts in his book *Holism and Evolution* asserted that "Idealism is wrong where it fails to recognise that the Spirit or Psyche, although now a real factor, did not exist either explicitly or implicitly at the beginning, and has arisen creatively in the course of organic Evolution."[18] By contrast, Teilhard maintained that the omega point is pre-existent.

Teilhard's theology, general systems theory, and Jung's psychology are similar in that they each reestablish the conception of transcendent consciousness in a form more acceptable to modern man. In these models, one does not even use the traditional concept of God but is able to conceive of a universal or unitary consciousness in terms that are more compatible with twentieth century knowledge and experience. They establish teleological psychologies.

Jung's psychology and the psychology that has evolved out of general systems theory are closer to yoga psychology than to the reductionist psychologies of the West, for yoga psychology also conceives of the individual as evolving in consciousness toward ever more comprehensiveness, reaching toward universal consciousness. Sankhya philosophy and the teachings of the Upanishads presented conceptions of the evolution of the universe ages before the concept of evolution became known in the West. "According to the Upanishads . . . all creation evolves, inanimate as well as animate."[19] In this, yoga psychology agrees with those in the forefront of systems theory.

General systems theory and the work of Jung exemplify the movement away from materialistic psychology and toward the re-introduction of a spiritual perspective for modern man. But general systems theory and Jungian psychology stop short of the monistic view of Vedanta. These psychologies actually stand midway between the reductionist model of Freud and behaviorism and the monistic psychology of the East. Neither Jung nor systems theorists conceive of that which may exist beyond the world of form and multiplicity. Systems theory, by its very assumptions, must remain forever dualistic. For systems to exist there must be at least some bifurcation, some duality; there must be two or more elements interacting to form a system. Furthermore a system has boundaries: there is an inside and an outside; there is an external environment, outside the system. Full unification, a system that encompasses all, is contrary to the assumptions of this model. From the point of view of systems theory, no matter how comprehensive a system becomes, there is still further to go. Here again, systems theory shares a common perspective with Jungian psychology.

Is it possible that there is a consciousness that is beyond manifestation and thus beyond systems of any sort? Advaita philosophy and psychology asserts that there is. It is based on the principle that ultimately there is no duality. It conceives of a unification in which all systems are dissolved as though they existed only in a dream. Dualistic psychologies, including general systems theory, differ from Vedanta in that they do not conceive of an end point to the evolutionary process. They assume that the phenomenal universe is ever evolving into more and more comprehensive systems in an open-ended expansion. But what is the basis for such an assumption? Might there be a limit, or a point at which contraction occurs? Such questions need further study.

All models within the dualistic paradigm, although they are prospective and understand present events as leading the person toward ever more unified consciousness, nonetheless posit limitations to the growth process. According to this view, one can never fully experience a unified state of consciousness. Jung himself asserted that

> just as a lapis Philosophorum, with its miraculous powers, was never produced, so psychic wholeness will never be attained empirically, as consciousness is too narrow and too one-sided to comprehend the full inventory of the psyche.[20]

> Complete redemption from the sufferings of this world is and must remain an illusion. . . . The goal is important only as an idea; the essential thing is the *opus*. . . .[21]

For those who follow the dualistic paradigm, the journey becomes an end in itself. To be sure, the transformation and enrichment of life that takes place as a result of becoming aware of archetypal functioning or more comprehensive systems is not to be underestimated. Life gains a new majesty, indeed becomes spiritualized, through awakening to the dualistic mode of experience. Yet the prospect of such a grand journey left unfinished seems far from satisfying. On this issue, the dualistic position differs dramatically from the monistic perspective. Yoga psychology has as its goal the complete elimination of suffering, not merely its reduction, and asserts that this goal is not an illusion, that it can indeed be attained.

General systems theory and Jungian psychology take the perspective of consciousness growing to become ever more inclusive. The journey is everything and the goal—psychic wholeness—is forever unattainable. Monistic psychology, on the other hand, takes the perspective of one who has attained the goal and, from this purview, looks down upon the world of form. It describes unitary consciousness from firsthand experience, and the various means by which such consciousness can be experienced. Monistic psychology does not remain fascinated with the sights and experiences along the way and does not attribute the same sense of reality to these experiences as do Western psychologies. Nor does it give nearly so much attention as Western psychologies to describing the details of the cul-de-sacs or pathological states that one may stumble into on his journey. Such interests preoccupy modern dynamic psychology, but yoga psychology has devoted itself to marking out the successful paths, to providing directional markers along those paths, and to distinguishing the final attainment of unitary consciousness from imitations that might be found along the way. Modern psychology takes up base camps along the trail. From these it goes off on exploratory missions to map out the general locale, and in its preoccupation forgets that the path goes onward. Yoga psychology, however, encourages the seeker ever onward, warning him of such distractions. Many psychologists have become diverted quite early in the journey. A very few, such as Jung, have attained a considerable height before the rarefied atmosphere, the majestic sights, and the experience of the ideal forms have distracted them from the realization of wholeness.

In Jung's dualistic psychology there is a division between consciousness and the objects that are perceived by consciousness. Even the archetypes are regarded as objects of cognition; not sensory objects, but objects of a more subtle nature. One experiences the archetypes or ideal forms as the objects of consciousness and finds greater beauty, depth of meaning, and majesty than when regarding any material object, for material objects are only adumbrations, imperfect copies, of the archetypal forms. But monistic psychology posits another way of knowing that is not based on the distinction between subject and object.[22] According to nondual psychology, subject-object consciousness is the mode of experience that is common to the majority of human beings who have evolved beyond the primitive level of awareness, but it is not the only, nor the most evolved, mode of consciousness.

Psychologies that are created out of the subject-object mode of consciousness are limited in their perspective and provide a distorted conception of the true nature of psychic life. This may be compared to the distortions introduced into one's understanding of the external world when Newtonian physics is used as the basis for understanding the nature of the entire physical universe. Monistic psychology begins with the most comprehensive perspective—that of a unified consciousness. Nothing is outside the boundaries of unified consciousness, for there are no boundaries. If one takes this all-encompassing perspective, dualistic and materialistic psychologies are seen as special cases that apply within a limited range of psychic development, just as Newtonian physics remains applicable within a limited range of phenomena in the external world, even though Einstein's view is more comprehensively correct.

Newtonian physics is clearly inapplicable when dealing with the vast distances in which astronomical phenomena take place, the minuscule occurrences within the atom, and events that involve movement approaching the speed of light. However, it is pragmatically correct as a special case of relativity physics dealing with a limited intermediate range of space and comparatively slow movements. Similarly, the dualistic frame of reference may be understood as useful for describing a limited range of phenomena within the monistic perspective, and the materialistic perspective as likewise useful for dealing with a limited range of phenomena within the dualistic understanding. This may be compared to a movement from three dimensions to two dimensions to one dimension. The two-dimensional plane and the line exist within three-dimensional space, but they are progressively more circumscribed.

As noted earlier, the reductionist, dualistic, and monistic paradigms are not incompatible in the sense that one view is correct and the others wrong; rather, they are progressively more comprehensive frames of reference.* If someone functioning from a limited perspective were to claim comprehensiveness or attempt to overextend his view to apply to phenomena beyond its range of understanding, the result would necessarily be a distorted view of those phenomena. From the point of view of Vedanta philosophy, dualistic psychology is understood as a subsystem that explains a certain range of phenomena, and materialistic psychology as a subsystem within the dualistic framework that explains a still narrower range of phenomena. At the most evolved state of consciousness, one experiences a unity that is beyond all phenomena and beyond all laws and principles governing phenomenal existence. Within this unity, at a less comprehensive perspective, the archetypes, laws, and principles of the phenomenal world arise, and within these exist the subclass of laws and principles governing mechanistic phenomena. Since

---

*The humanistic paradigm is not included in this discussion since it is not a more comprehensive frame of reference that includes reductionism. Rather it is a reaction to reductionism that attempts to prove the reductive perspective incorrect.

the monistic perspective includes within it the other two, it appreciates their value but also understands their limitations and the tendency for these less comprehensive systems to be overextended into domains inappropriate for them. It is erroneous for a less comprehensive model to claim applicability to more complex domains. Unfortunately, this is just what has happened in much of contemporary thought, where everything is understood in terms of the concrete and primitive.

Since the monistic paradigm comprehends and includes the dualistic and mechanistic models as more limited perspectives within its scope, the therapist functioning from the monistic paradigm may use interventions that have been developed by a therapist working within a less comprehensive framework. In doing so, he temporarily imposes that model on himself and works within the limited perspective of that model, but he does not accept that model as giving a comprehensive understanding of reality. In a similar way, a contemporary physicist may recognize that relativity physics is a more accurate and comprehensive model for describing the physical universe, but he may continue to use Newtonian mechanics to solve particular engineering problems. The physicist does not assume that the Newtonian model applies to all aspects of the physical realm, and neither should the reductionist or dualistic psychologist assume that his model applies to all aspects of the psychological realm or to all modes of consciousness.

Those who are confined within the reductionist-mechanistic paradigm do not comprehend the dualistic perspective, and the dualists are unable to comprehend the monistic point of view. It is for this reason that when mystics such as Meister Eckhart and Jacob Boehme described their experiences of unitary consciousness, they were branded as heretics and ousted by the authorities of the dualistic religion in which they had previously gained recognition. Reductive psychologists are not able to understand the irrational and sometimes paradoxical theories and techniques of the dualists, and dualists believe that the monists have abandoned consciousness in favor of unconsciousness or insanity. In each instance, the more encompassing perspective recognizes both the uses and the limitations of the more restricted perspective, while the more limited point of view is adamantly intolerant of a viewpoint that is beyond its range of understanding.

Beyond Piaget: Further Stages of Cognitive Development

Dualistic and monistic psychologies are based on advanced stages of cognitive understanding not usually found in the general population. Jean Piaget, one of the leading theorists in modern psychology, carefully studied the process of cognitive development. He found a specific sequence of stages in the developmental process, culminating at adolescence in the attainment of what he called the stage of formal operations. At this stage, which Piaget considered to be the ultimate stage of cognitive development in the human being, one becomes able to reason abstractly, to understand the meaning of logical propositions, to manipulate conceptual hypotheses about the world, and to think not only about what is but about what could be. Piaget recognized that cognitive development involves a progressively more refined awareness that the experienced world is a construction rather than a given, and that in conjunction with this growth in awareness there is a gradually increasing separation of the individual from his identification with the object that is being perceived. A dramatic shift in awareness occurs at the developmental stage Piaget labeled formal operations. The individual who has arrived at this stage no longer depends on the immediate perception of the object in order to reason; he can now reason hypothetically.

Might there be still more evolved stages of cognitive development in which one observes formal operations thinking from another perspective rather than identifying with that mode of thinking? Piaget believed that the developmental process ends with formal operations, but further stages in the separation of the knower from the objects of perception have been described in Eastern psychology. Western theorists and researchers have also begun questioning whether mental development necessarily stops with the stage of formal operations, and some investigators have described further stages in the thinking process that until now have been attained by only a small minority of people. The fact that such attainment is the exception rather than the rule may explain why Piaget, who was studying typical development, did not distinguish and describe these more evolved stages of mental development.

Klaus Riegel has described a stage beyond formal operations that he calls dialectic operations.[23] Riegel notes that formal operations involves noncontradictory thinking. He also equates formal operations thinking with mechanistic thought: "The theory of mechanics was built upon the traditional logic, the most important property of which is that observations, definitions, or postulates should be noncontradictory. . . . It was inconceivable, for example, that light could be a wave and a particle at the same time. Only one of these alternatives could be true."[24] Riegel contrasts this type of thought with the thinking of those who are creative and gifted. He posits a more evolved stage of cognitive development in which contradiction is valued and one achieves a greater comprehension or overview through taking into account the interaction of contradictory or opposing qualities.

Recently, a symposium was held at Harvard University in which some of the leading developmental theorists presented evidence of further stages of mental development. One researcher, Herb Koplowitz, described two such stages beyond formal operations. Those more evolved stages correspond to the dualistic and monistic modes of cognition described in this book. Koplowitz has theorized that formal operations thought, the mode of thinking of most adults, has inherent limitations that are transcended in dualistic and monistic thinking. At the stage of formal operations, one's concept of causality is linear or one-directional. One asks, "'Who started it?' 'Whose fault is it?' 'How did it begin?' These questions imply a causal chain which has a beginning."[25] One also conceives of variables as operating independently and as having closed boundaries. Furthermore, the nature and existence of objects are considered to be independent of the knower. The model of the world generated at this stage of mental development is that of a mechanistic universe. This way of thinking about the world has led to certain benefits: it has, for example, made possible the development of classical physics and mechanistic science. But there are also limitations and restrictions created by this type of thinking.

Koplowitz goes on to show that general systems theory introduces a new mode of thinking. Here the concept of causality is cyclical.* For example, a man may feel that he drinks because his wife yells at him, while his wife believes that she yells at him because of his drinking. The husband

---

*While Koplowitz confines his analysis of dualistic thinking to general systems theory, it is interesting to note that Jung's dualistic psychology also transcends the linear model of causality. His concept of synchronicity in fact transcends the principle of causality.

and wife each have linear concepts of causality that are in disagreement. The family therapist, however, operating from the perspective of systems theory, will see the way in which these two antagonists are actually supporting one another. The husband's behavior evokes the wife's, which further evokes his, and so on. Systems theory views and approaches problems from the perspective of "open boundaries." From this viewpoint, a problem is not located within a particular person or even a particular relationship.

> With a concept of boundaries as closed, one locates a problem as being inside of an individual and, more particularly, as being inside of the area where the problem is most clearly manifested. Thus, a man's drinking problem would be located inside the man himself and would be treated as though the problem were simply his drinking. An appropriate treatment, therefore, would be the administration of a drug such as antabuse which would prevent him from drinking.
>
> With a concept of boundaries as being open, neither the "problem area" nor the appropriate area for intervention has clear limits. The problem may be solved by changing the man's recreational style, helping him straighten out his finances, helping him set clearer goals for his life, etc. Or, the problem may be attacked not by intervening directly with the man but by making an intervention elsewhere in a system of which he is a part. His employer may be convinced to tell him to sober up or look for employment elsewhere. His wife may be shown how to stop taking responsibility for his problems, etc. If the problem area is seen as having an open boundary around it, a wider range of interventions are seen as opportunities to reverse the problem.[26]

The cyclical view of causality leads to a new understanding of responsibility in a relationship. Couples who are experiencing conflicts typically begin psychotherapy by blaming one another for their predicament. The wife who blames the husband's drinking for her unhappiness and the husband who says her nagging and unpleasant demeanor lead him to drink in order to escape are a case in point.

It is not unusual for beginning clients to employ such expressions as "He made me do it" or "She forced me into it," but the cyclical understanding of causality makes such blaming nonsensical and impossible. If the therapist can upgrade the client's thinking process so that the client uses systems thinking, the client will come to realize that no matter what the other person does in this mutual feedback process, he can break the cyclical chain of interaction at any time. A systems theorist may ask the complaining husband how he gets his wife to nag him into drinking, and help him to see that he can interrupt the vicious cycle. A change in his behavior will inevitably lead to a change in hers. Through this type of psychotherapy, couples begin to realize the role each plays in the vicious cycle. They may even offer to put aside some of their blaming and each accept fifty percent of the responsibility for what is wrong in the relationship. The therapist's response to this would be an attempt to get each of them to accept one hundred percent responsibility, since either party can unilaterally interrupt their fixed pattern of interaction and take it in a new direction. Sometimes, however, reasoning will not suffice, or the client may not be ready to embrace a dualistic perspective. In such cases the therapist may resort to more irrational methods.

The dualistic perspective transcends the constraints of classical logic and seeks to understand and make use of paradox in communication. Dualistic thought is an intermediate phase between reductive and monistic thought in regard to polarities. One who adopts the dualistic mode of thought tends to become fascinated with paradox because it directly challenges polarization and exposes the illusory basis upon which the two ends of a polarity are distinguished. A logical paradox embraces two contradictory propositions and may thereby lead one to a sense that something is amiss in the rigid distinctions and polarizations that one creates in the subject-object mode of consciousness. For instance, the statement "I am lying" leads one to an untenable position in distinguishing between lying and truthfulness. For if the statement "I am lying" is itself a lie, then the person who made it is not lying. And if he is not lying in stating that he is lying, he is telling the truth. As a result of reflecting on this paradoxical statement, the polarity lying/not lying dissolves into a muddle, and one's usually coherent formal operations reasoning breaks down.

Bertrand Russell's theory of logical types resolves paradoxes that involve logical contradictions. However, another type of paradox, known as the pragmatic paradox, continues to powerfully affect interpersonal relations. A pragmatic paradox (such as the command, "Be spontaneous!") offers one no rational way to respond to a communication.

"Thus if the message is an injunction, it must be disobeyed to be obeyed; if it is a definition of self or other, the person thereby defined is this kind of person only if he is not, and is not if he is."[27] Such paradoxes result in a breakdown of logical communication. This can either develop pathology or lead one to freedom from rigidly held nonproductive distinctions. A therapist working from the perspective of general systems theory is likely to believe that a great many psychological disturbances, including schizophrenia, are caused by paradoxical communications in families. These communications lead to a variety of symptoms and cannot be effectively countered from the reductive-mechanistic perspective.

The systems theorist recognizes that "if you try to change something in the direct, 'obvious' way, the system is going to treat your efforts like any other outside influence and do its best to neutralize them. The more energy you waste fighting the system head on, the more energy it will waste fighting back, and any gains you make will be only temporary at best."[28] Thus what appears to be an obvious solution to a problem from the perspective of reductive reasoning is often counterproductive.

> For example, if you want to cool off an overheated house on a winter day the "obvious" solution is to open a window. But as soon as the temperature drops a few degrees below the thermostat setting, the furnace comes on full-blast, and all you do is waste a lot of energy. If it is cold enough outside, you might actually succeed in cooling the house this way—if you don't mind having the furnace on all the time—but it would be much more sensible to just change the setting on the thermostat.
>
> However, suppose that for some reason you *can't* change the thermostat setting. You might decide instead to put a small heater—like a light bulb—right underneath the thermostat. The extra heat from this heater would "fool" the thermostat into thinking that the house is hotter than it really is, which would cause it to turn the furnace off, letting the house cool down. In other words, adding heat to the system (at the right point) can actually make it cooler! Sounds crazy, doesn't it? . . .
>
> . . . by this point you should be getting an idea of *why* a systems approach to problems is so important. Without it, people who try to solve problems or improve things, frequently pick a "solution" that doesn't work or that backfires by making the situation worse. Since their solution looks reasonable, and they can't understand *why* it won't work, they usually respond by trying even harder. . . .

System thinkers, on the other hand, realize from the beginning that all stable systems have, by definition, ways of resisting change. Instead of stubbornly fighting against the system, they study it carefully to find out where the negative feedback loops are, how they work, and where they are vulnerable. A *system* solution may be quite indirect and difficult for other people to understand, but it is more likely to work, and that is much more satisfying.[29]

The interventions made by a psychotherapist functioning out of a systems theory perspective will often seem outlandish and irrational to one functioning from a mechanistic model. For example, instead of encouraging the drinker to abstain, the therapist may actually prescribe the symptom or take other actions that in terms of formal operations seem to encourage the problem. However, by paradoxical intervention the therapist is able to modify the cyclical causality in the larger system.

From a formal operational point of view, an action is reversed by means of an action in the opposite direction. Thus, the wife yells at the husband because she believes that punishment will get him to stop his irresponsible behavior; the husband drinks alcohol, a pain killer, in order to reduce the pain of his life situation. These attempts to restore order fail, however, as the wife's yelling eventually increases the husband's drinking and his drinking increases the problems in his life which cause him pain. A therapist, on the other hand, may attempt to stop the husband from drinking by instructing him to get drunk every day, that is, by applying a force in the same direction away from the desired norm. . . .[30]

As another example, consider the case of a father who responds to his son's repeated misbehavior with added punishment. The more the father punishes his son and demands compliance, the more his son misbehaves. Despite the father's attempt to bring about change in his son, the pattern of interaction in the system remains the same and the obvious solution merely leads to an intensification of the behavior of each party. Therefore a therapist trained in general systems theory might respond to this conflict in a way that appears illogical and unexpected to one whose thinking is reductive. Using a paradoxical intervention, he may direct the son to misbehave whenever the father acts in a specified manner. This prescription from the therapist changes the way in which the components of the system interact and thereby changes the nature of the outcome.

Here is another example of how paradoxical intervention can be effectively employed by a therapist:

> A client who was anxious and worried chronically was told to set aside one hour a day to worry. She was told . . . that she would have to become a competent worrier if she could ever hope to resolve her anxieties. Effective worrying meant she had to think the worst possible thoughts and keep a list of everything that might worry her for her "worry time." Moreover, she was told to worry the full hour even if she felt like stopping early.

> Most clients for whom this method is used will find the first couple of days to be painful. They will worry the fully prescribed time. In just a few days clients typically want to stop short and resent the task. They report that they are no longer worried and think that "all that worrying" was absurd.[31]

There is a stage in mental development even more evolved than systems thinking, which is termed by Koplowitz "unitary thought." This mode of thinking is characteristic of psychology based on the monistic perspective. It is also found to a certain extent in modern physics. In unitary thought, space, time, and causation are understood as creations of the perceiver rather than as inherent in the phenomena being perceived: "Time and space are both seen as constructs, artifacts of the knower's attempt to make sense of his/her experience rather than intrinsic aspects of reality."[32] At this level one experiences the unitary interconnectedness of the universe: "One is led to a new notion of *unbroken wholeness* which denies the classical idea of analyzability of the world into separately and independently existing parts."[33]

This perspective has important implications for problem solving. Koplowitz notes that "in pre-unitary thought, a problem is something wrong, something which needs to be reversed in an individual (according to formal operational thought) or in a system (according to General Systems Theory),"[34] whereas from the more inclusive perspective of unitary thought, problems are illusory. According to monistic psychology, all human suffering occurs when one ignores the unitary perspective and takes one's constructs to be real. One thus becomes immersed in self-created melodramas. Therefore the monistic therapeutic process consists of leading the client toward unitary thought and experience, for there suffering does not exist.

In unitary thought, boundaries do not exist except as artificial constructions of the knower. The creation of boundaries (that is, defining oneself in a limited way) may serve a useful function, but if these boundaries are taken seriously and one becomes locked into them, they inevitably create suffering. In unitary thinking one learns to create, dissolve, and redraw boundaries in a lighthearted way rather than taking them to be external givens within which one remains stuck. One does not regard any boundaries as though they objectively exist. Thus, if boundaries drawn in a particular way create suffering, one is free to redraw the boundaries in a manner that eliminates suffering.

From the unitary perspective, material objects are also understood as constructions of the experiencer rather than as givens. Modern physics is in at least partial agreement; it has taken a 180° turn from the former mechanistic position, and the consensus among physicists now is that quantum fields "alone are real. They are the substance of the universe and not 'matter.'"[35] Yoga philosophy goes a step further than this and points out that even quantum fields are a manifestation of a still more primary undifferentiated existence, a unitary consciousness. As one becomes more aware of and in tune with unitary consciousness, he learns to take material manifestations with less absolute seriousness.

It is important to distinguish between unitary thought and unitary or nondual consciousness. The experience of nondual consciousness is beyond the realm of conceptual thought. It is the direct experience of nonduality. Conceptual thought, however, necessarily involves the creation of form and multiplicity. Unitary thought as described by Koplowitz is the mode of conceptual thought that results from the assumption that the nondual mode of consciousness is the ultimate reality. Unitary thought does not necessarily signify that the thinker has attained the direct experience of nondual consciousness. But the conceptualization of the existence of unitary consciousness as the source of all other states of being in the world of form can lead one to conceptually view the world from the perspective of unitary thought.

According to the monistic paradigm, unitary consciousness is the only substantial existence. The world of form and multiplicity is the playful expression of that unitary consciousness. It has no real substantiality, though it arises, is maintained, and dissolves in a lawful and orderly way. One who has achieved unitary consciousness may also maintain a link with the illusory world of multiplicity, but he does not take the forms to be real and serious. He becomes the master of the phenomenal world rather than being swept up in the forms, boundaries, and melodramas and remaining their slave. Just as a scientist gains mastery over material form by finding order in its organization, so the yogi gains mastery over various aspects of the world of form by uncovering its order in the realms of matter, energy, and consciousness.

Koplowitz concludes that an understanding of the more evolved stages of cognitive development helps one gain a new perspective on the spiritual traditions: "When the thought in spiritual traditions is considered characteristic of unitary thought, those traditions become less mysterious, more understandable, and less in conflict with scientific thought. Mysticism, a discipline of unitary thought, becomes not a rejection of science (which is a discipline of formal operational thought), but rather a transcendence of it. Science is not a rejection of mysticism but rather its foundation."[36]

The monistic perspective reconciles all dualities both within and without: it reconciles conflicts that exist within the individual between unreconciled parts of himself. These splits within one's psyche have been given various labels in different psychological theories, such as top dog/underdog; id, ego, and superego; subpersonalities; parent, adult, child; persona and shadow; and so on. Conflicts that result from dualities between oneself and others are also transcended when one takes the perspective of unitary consciousness, for one becomes aware that distinctions and boundaries are one's own arbitrary creations rather than givens. One learns to take responsibility for those creations, to understand their function or purpose, and to realize that they can be altered or dissolved.

Yoga therapy helps one to expand his cognitive development beyond formal operations, to embrace the dualistic perspective, and finally to apply unitary thought to his life, thereby transcending the problems and conflicts he has experienced. Finally, yoga leads one beyond even unitary thought to the direct experience of unitary consciousness. This experience is called self-realization, for here one realizes his true nature as the underlying center that comprehends and yet transcends all limited systems, the Self that is the substratum for all that exists.

Chapter Six

From Ego to Self

The Origin and Limitations of Ego-Consciousness

The newborn baby has little or no sense of identity and self-definition as a distinct being separate from his surroundings. The baby is born into a society that functions by way of the distinctions it makes. In the view of the adults who look after the infant, there are those who are good and those who are bad, there are insiders and outsiders, parents and children, and so on ad infinitum. The infant adopts the distinctions of those who are taking care of him, and he makes other distinctions, such as pleasure and pain, as a result of his contact with the physical environment. One of the most fundamental polar distinctions made by the growing child is *I*/*not-I*. The child begins to draw a boundary around what he defines as himself and thereby considers what is outside that boundary as not himself, as separate, different, or alien. That aspect of the mind concerned with drawing the boundary between *I* and *not-I* has been termed the ego by modern psychology.

The ego enables consciousness to reflect upon itself and to give definition to itself. It also establishes self-responsibility in the individual. The child in the pre-ego state cannot manage himself in his environment because he has no clear sense of being a distinct entity. But the child gradually establishes and elaborates the duality *I*/*not-I* and thereby creates an artificial distinction between a subject who experiences and the objects that are experienced. This construction enables the child to circumscribe a limited territory (*I*) that he is able to manage. Those who do not establish a relatively clear distinction between *I* and *not-I* (subject and object) do not become responsible members of society. They are stigmatized with such labels as schizophrenic, retarded, brain-damaged, psychopathic personality, or character disorder, according to the manner in which they fall short of being able to accept responsibility. And they may be kept in institutions where others manage for them.[1]

127

Modern approaches to psychotherapy primarily focus on helping clients cultivate the incompletely developed ego in order to establish themselves more firmly in ego-consciousness. The need for such therapy is obvious, but there is a tendency in modern psychology and in modern society (which has developed this mode of consciousness to a high degree) to rigidify the distinction the ego makes between *I* and *not-I* and to believe that this distinction is real rather than an artificial creation of the mind.

Anything manifest in the world of form comes about at the expense of the manifestation of its complement. Thus, in the case of the mastery gained through ego-consciousness, the very power and control that is acquired by drawing a boundary around oneself is gained through the creation of its complement: an overwhelming sense of helplessness and weakness. By defining itself in a very circumscribed and narrow way, the ego gains the leverage to master that small sphere called *I*. But at the same time the other side of the polarity manifests: one becomes very small and relatively weak and helpless before the vast world that exists outside of those narrow boundaries, outside of oneself as one thinks himself to be.

From the vantage point of monistic psychology, the ego actually has no ground on which to stand. This psychology views the ego as having created itself out of thin air, so to speak, through the imposition of a fictitious polarity upon nondual existence; the ego is imaginary and exists only because its complement (*not-I*) seems to exist. This polarity is an artificial superimposition upon the holistic substratum of existence. Because the ego has no ground on which to stand except what it spuriously creates through its definitions of itself, the ego is extremely vulnerable and is threatened with annihilation on all fronts. This *I* of the ego, though capitalized in English script to exaggerate its importance, actually finds itself to be small and relatively helpless in the vast and largely unpredictable world. As long as the person remains identified with a circumscribed *I*, anxiety is inevitable.

If the ego fails to maintain the polar distinctions that enable it to sustain itself, the individual may lapse back into a pre-ego consciousness that is not self-conscious. If the boundary is not clearly delineated or is weak or has gaps, one may be overwhelmed by the alien forces that the ego has placed outside its perimeter. For the ego is like a country surrounded by foreign powers: it may be overrun by any quality that it has defined as being outside of its boundary. As a consequence of its extremely insecure ground, the ego devotes a great deal of energy to bolstering its position. The ego acts like a very insecure person who puffs himself up with self-importance and boasts of his accomplishments and possessions. The ego is self-centered; it believes the world revolves around it. Experiencing from the perspective of the ego is analogous to regarding the physical universe from the geocentric perspective of pre-Copernican astronomy, which taught that the sun and all the stars revolved about the earth and which thereby necessitated the factitious creation of complex epicycles to account for the movements of the heavenly bodies around this (false) center.

The bolstering of the ego is also carried out on a collective basis through the rituals of social institutions, including those psychologies that take an egocentric perspective and attest to the supremacy of ego-consciousness. Modern ego psychology, which has developed out of psychoanalytic theory, has created cumbersome epicyclic concepts like the "conflict-free sphere" and "regression in the service of the ego" in order to keep the ego at the center, to subsume various functions under the aegis of the ego, and to make phenomena that actually transcend the ego appear to be in the service of the ego.

There is a common belief in modern psychology that ego-consciousness represents the most advanced stage in the unfoldment of consciousness and is therefore the most accurate and objective perspective possible for experiencing oneself and the world. Modern psychology, in this respect, is expressing the self-glorifying position of ego-consciousness. From this position, every other form of consciousness is regarded as inferior; for when ego-consciousness comes into power, like certain totalitarian governments it tries to maintain its dominant position by creating a closed one-party system that suppresses the recognition of alternative means of governing the human being.

Psychoanalytic psychology regards the ego as the center of consciousness; it has established the ego as the monarch of the psyche. According to psychoanalytic theory, all other structures and processes in the mature person, including the id, superego, regression, and primary process functioning, are subservient to the regulation of the ego. In the reductive model, there is no conception of a center of integration that is more comprehensive than the ego and to which the ego may itself be subservient.

In contrast to this, those who take the dualistic or monistic perspective recognize inherent limitations in ego-consciousness. Jung wrote: "All ego-consciousness is isolated; because it separates and discriminates, it knows only particulars. . . . Its essence is limitation."[2] One who identifies with a limited *I*, with its artificial boundaries and distinctions, will inevitably experience a sense of isolation, of loneliness, and a longing for all that has been defined as outside. The ego seeks to complete itself. This *I* seeks out and becomes dependent on, or addicted to, those "external" objects and conditions it has artificially separated from itself, but completion and unity cannot be attained in this way because by definition the ego remains distinct from the object. Furthermore, however many objects the ego acquires, these are few in comparison to all that continue to remain outside its grasp. Though the ego seeks to extend itself, it remains a limited system within the individual, with a limited perspective. It is inevitably constricted by preoccupations, fears, and biases created by identifying with certain qualities and excluding others. It is inherently limited because it can experience only through the subject-object mode of consciousness.

The developed ego operates through formal operations thinking and through what psychoanalysts have called "secondary process." According to psychoanalytic theory, there is a more primitive, primary mode of functioning that disregards space and time constrictions and ordinary logic. But secondary process functioning, the functioning by which the ego operates, is bound by the constrictions of space, time, classical logic, and linear causality. This mode of functioning allows the ego to achieve a great deal, but also imposes severe restrictions on one's experiences. Formal operations functioning represents the culmination of egoistic reasoning; if consciousness is to comprehend paradox, synchronicity, and monistic conceptions, formal operations must be transcended. There must come into the foreground new modes of awareness that are not bound by the limitations of secondary process reasoning and yet are not a regression to a more primitive mode of experience. Psychoanalysis has not envisioned the possibility of a more evolved mode of cognition but has insisted on interpreting all nonsecondary process functioning as primary process functioning, a more primitive level of being.

Ego-consciousness is not able to reach the dualistic mode of awareness precisely because its experience is *I*-centered, or egocentric. It does not give equal weight to both sides of a polarity, including the fundamental polarity *I/not-I* on which it is established. And it cannot reach the monistic mode of awareness because it cannot transcend polarized thinking. Its perspective, though certainly more objective than primitive thinking, is nevertheless considerably biased. In egoistic thinking, there is a greater degree of detachment and objectivity than in primitive thinking, but one remains invested in the *I* who is perceiving, with all the inevitable attendant biases and insecurities. The ego is never as objective as it purports to be. Although ego-consciousness is a necessary and very important step in the evolution of consciousness—for it establishes self-consciousness and prepares the way for another more evolved mode of consciousness—the potential aroused through ego-consciousness is not fulfilled until the egoistic stage is transcended.

Humanistic psychology helps one make the transition from the egoistic mode of consciousness to consciousness based on a larger and more integrative center. Although in humanistic psychology, for the most part, there is no conception of another, more comprehensive center of consciousness than the ego (as there is in dualistic and monistic psychologies), nevertheless humanistic therapies do foster the development of capacities that transcend the egocentric perspective. For example, Erich Fromm encourages others to replace the acquisitive orientation with a willingness to give, to share, and to sacrifice: "To be an egoist . . . means: that I want everything for myself; that possessing, not sharing, gives me pleasure; that I must become greedy because if my aim is having, I *am* more the more I *have;* that I must feel antagonistic toward all others: my customers whom I want to deceive, my competitors whom I want to destroy. . . ."[3] Fromm speaks of a "new man," whose distinguishing qualities and characteristics include a joy that comes from giving and sharing, a love and respect for life, an ever-developing capacity for love, a shedding of narcissism, and a sense of oneness with all life.[4] Other humanistic psychologists have stressed the development of creativity, dichotomy-transcendence, playfulness, and various other qualities that lead to ego-transcendence.

While modern psychology believes that the ego is the center of consciousness, yoga psychology does not regard the ego as the real center of consciousness but as the subject of the subject-object mode of consciousness. According to this view, the ego is a provisional center created to achieve a particular purpose, in much the same way that a scaffolding is erected to construct a building. If one becomes enamored of the scaffolding and spends his time decorating and admiring it, he may never complete the building. Many people have such a relationship with their egos.

Modern depth psychology conceives of consciousness as an attribute of the ego. Yoga psychology, on the other hand, regards the ego as a useful instrument of consciousness. Through the creation of the subject-object mode of consciousness, with the ego as the subjective pole, a person is able to relate to the world in a way that can be useful for certain purposes. But any instrument has limitations, and when those limitations are not understood and taken into account, a distorted perspective results. An analogy may be helpful to clarify the yogic conception. The microscope is an extremely valuable instrument in helping one to become aware of minute aspects of the environment and even in uncovering fundamental processes in the natural world that could not otherwise be observed. However, try to imagine the preposterous situation of someone who has accidentally and without awareness spilled glue over the eyepiece of his microscope, so that when he uses this instrument, he becomes bonded to it. Now he can see only through the limited perspective of the microscope. What was formerly an aid to enlarge his view and understanding of the phenomenal world has become an encumbrance from which he is eager to separate himself. Now imagine a large group of such people who have shared this predicament for so long that they have forgotten their original state and who now assume that the way they are presently perceiving is the only way, that what they are seeing is the only reality that exists. According to the yogic conception, this is the situation most people are in.

The ego, like the microscope, is an instrument for knowing in a particular way. But there is a strong tendency for the consciousness of a person to become bonded to or identified with the ego, to experience the world primarily through the ego, and furthermore to forget that any bonding ever occurred. Since most people are in a similar situation, one thinks that the world he experiences through the ego is the whole of reality rather than merely a mode of experience brought into focus by his instrument. He forgets that there was ever any distinction between consciousness and the instrument called the ego, and he identifies with the ego as the subject of all modes of consciousness. Western depth psychologies, of both the reductive and dualistic schools, adhere to this egocentric view of consciousness.

Yoga psychology offers an alternative and more comprehensive perspective for understanding human development. It recognizes and values the subject-object mode of consciousness and gives the ego its due, but it does not build an entire psychology around the ego as if it were the central aspect of the human being. Through the practice of yoga, one can become aware of the limitations of ego-consciousness, learn to loosen the hold of this mode of consciousness, and come in touch with a more unifying and comprehensive center of organization within. From the limited perspective of the threatened ego, such a development may portend regression, annihilation, or, at the very least, loss of the ego's control and supremacy. Indeed, the ego eventually does come to occupy a subsidiary role; it becomes a subsystem within a larger framework.

Ego-consciousness need not be abandoned when a more comprehensive center of organization is established; both organizations may continue to exist and work together. Instead of conceptualizing the experience of the newly won state as a regression in the service of the ego, as is done in psychoanalysis, it is more accurate to conceive of the retreat to ego-consciousness as a regression in the service of unitary consciousness. Such regression enables the individual to maintain an organization for functioning in the world; however, in this case, the person remains identified with the more comprehensive center rather than with the ego. He recognizes that the boundaries established by the ego are merely useful and temporary constructions rather than the reality of "who I am" and "who and what I am not."

Although the conception of a more comprehensive level of conscious organization than the ego has not yet gained acceptance in contemporary schools of psychotherapy, precedence for such a model can be found in other areas of modern psychology. For example, it is generally believed that the evolution of the human brain took place in successive stages or layers. With the evolution of the hindbrain, the rudimentary integrative functions of the spinal cord were superseded. This new center integrated sensory-motor reflexes and stimulation from various sensory receptors and helped maintain posture, balance, and movement. This center of organization in turn was superseded by the midbrain, then by the old forebrain, and finally by the new forebrain. While the more primitive structures integrated reflexive functions, the more evolved structures regulated affective and cognitive functioning. With each development of a new and more comprehensive center of organization, the less evolved structure did not atrophy or disappear. It continued to do its job, but was now subject to the regulation of the more evolved structure.

> The ability of the brain to inhibit actions originating in the spinal cord is just one example of a more general principle that holds true at all levels of the nervous system. The successive levels form a chain of command. Each higher level is capable of achieving a more complete integration of sensory input than is available to lower levels. If, on the basis of this more complete integration, a better or longer-range plan of action arises, the higher levels can supersede the actions initiated by the lower levels. This mode of organization allows the body to react differentially after the higher levels of the nervous system have evaluated the wide and subtle array of stimulation.[5]

Consider the case of a person whose more evolved structures are not functioning properly as a result of brain damage or the use of drugs. Such a person might remain functioning at a lower level, perhaps at the reflexive level of the hindbrain or the emotional level of the old forebrain. If in such a case the cognitive functioning of the new forebrain has not superseded the functioning of the old forebrain, one would remain at the mercy of intense, labile emotions. Similarly, in a normal person, if a higher order of integration beyond the ego has not evolved, one remains under the sway of doubts, fears, addictions, anxieties, and other limitations of ego functioning.

Yoga psychology uses the metaphor of a chauffeur and his employer to clarify the hierarchical relationship between the ego as a center of integration and a more comprehensive center. A chauffeur is able to drive a limousine and to respond to traffic lights and other external conditions; he performs an important function. But imagine that the chauffeur closes the window between the front and back seat and turns off the intercom, forgetting that the owner of the car is seated in back. The chauffeur might then take the car wherever he desires rather than doing his work, which is attending to the business and needs of the owner. Sooner or later the chauffeur will run into severe difficulties. He does not have the resources to maintain the car, to refuel it, or to use it for a higher purpose than his own satisfaction. This is exactly the situation one is in when his ego tries to assert its sovereignty.

The Self in Jungian Psychology and in Vedanta

Carl Jung was greatly attracted to and influenced by the teachings of the East even in early childhood. He stated in his autobiography: "I remember a time when I could not yet read, but pestered my mother to read aloud to me out of . . . an old, richly illustrated children's book, which contained an account of exotic relations, especially that of the Hindus. There were illustrations of Brahma, Vishnu, and Shiva which I found an inexhaustible source of interest."[6] During his formative years Jung put aside his fascination with Eastern thought, yet he later seemed to incorporate more of an Eastern than a Western perspective in his own developing theories: "When I began my career as a psychiatrist and psychotherapist, I was completely ignorant of Chinese philosophy, and only later did my professional experience show me that in my technique I had been unconsciously following that secret way which for centuries had been the preoccupation of the best minds of the East."[7] During a particularly trying period of his life Jung actively practiced yoga, and he studied Eastern philosophy and psychology intently. Of the *Tibetan Book of the Dead,* he said: "For years, ever since it was first published, the *Bardo Thodol* has been my constant companion, and to it I owe not only many stimulating ideas and discoveries, but also many fundamental insights."[8]

Jung believed that yoga and other meditative traditions had evolved a psychology far more advanced than the psychologies of the West:

"What we have to show in the way of spiritual insight and psychological technique must seem, when compared with yoga . . . backward. . . ."[9] Jung also believed that those who grew up in Western cultures had not yet evolved enough to incorporate the wisdom of the East: "The philosophy of the East, although so vastly different from ours, could be an inestimable treasure for us too: but, in order to possess it, we must first earn it."[10] Jung felt that Eastern teachings were too often misunderstood; he observed his fellow Europeans adopting the trappings of Eastern spiritual traditions without truly appreciating the insights of those traditions. Some used yoga as physical and mental culture to suppress the unconscious rather than to bring it forward to be integrated; others adopted the philosophy and trappings with uncritical and untested belief; some pedantically accumulated knowledge about yoga philosophy and methods rather than applying the philosophy and methods to lead them inward toward a more unified consciousness.

Jung stood at a point halfway between the psychologies of the West and the East. He acknowledged the superiority of Eastern psychology but did not believe that Westerners could really assimilate the philosophy and practices of yoga. He felt that it was necessary for the West to develop a yoga of its own, one better suited to the extroverted mind of Western man, and he regarded his own psychology as just such a development.

Although Jung relied heavily on yoga philosophy and psychology in developing his own theories, he differed from the monistic viewpoint on one fundamental assumption, and as a result his psychology remains within the dualistic framework. Jung followed a path toward self-understanding that in many respects was parallel to yoga, but he stopped short, unable to reach the more encompassing perspective of monistic psychology. Yoga psychology goes on to a greater purview, leaving Jung behind to take in a more limited survey of the landscape below, albeit one that is far more encompassing than that of other modern psychologies.

The point at which Jung parts company with yoga is clear. It can be seen in the way in which he practiced hatha yoga exercises: "I was frequently so wrought up that I had to do certain yoga exercises in order to hold my emotions in check. But since it was my purpose to know what was going on within myself, I would do these exercises only until I had calmed myself enough to resume my work with the unconscious. As soon as I had the feeling that I was myself again, I abandoned this restraint upon the emotions and allowed the images and inner voices to speak afresh. The Indian, on the other hand, does yoga exercises in order to obliterate completely the multitude of psychic contents and images."[11] It is evident that Jung sought to travel beyond ordinary awareness to experience the world of archetypal forms. He was primarily interested in experiencing and studying the underlying forms of psychic life, much as the atomic physicist is interested in studying the underlying forms of the physical universe. In contrast to the yogi, Jung was not interested in exploring further, in going beyond these forms to arrive at a consciousness that is prior to, and underlies, the archetypes. Jung stated that "the Indian's goal is . . . the condition of *nirdvandva.* He wishes to free himself from nature; in keeping with this aim, he seeks in meditation the condition of imagelessness and emptiness. I, on the other hand, wish to persist in the state of lively contemplation of nature and of the psychic images. I want to be freed neither from human beings, nor from myself, nor from nature; for all these appear to me the greatest of miracles. Nature, the psyche, and life appear to me like divinity unfolded—and what more could I wish for?"[12]

Jung doubted that a state of unitary consciousness is attainable, and, even if it could be experienced, whether it would be of any worth. He firmly believed that the only form of consciousness is ego-consciousness, or the subject-object mode of consciousness. According to Jung, consciousness requires that one must have the experience of being a subject who experiences the objects of thought.

> To us, consciousness is inconceivable without an ego. . . . If there is no ego there is nobody to be conscious of anything. . . . The Eastern mind, however, has no difficulty in conceiving of a consciousness without an ego. Consciousness is deemed capable of transcending its ego condition; indeed, in its "higher" forms, the ego disappears altogether.[13]

> The realization of the One Mind . . . creates the at-one-ment. But we are unable to imagine how such a realization could ever be complete in any human individual. . . . One cannot know something that is not distinct from oneself.[14]

Jung believed that one could let go of the ego but that such a state inevitably consisted of falling back into unconsciousness[15] rather than, as the yogis believe, transcending the limitations of the ego to reach a superconscious state. It is precisely on this point that Jung parts company with yoga and remains within the framework of dualistic psychology.

The dualistic models bring forth the possibility of a more comprehensive center than the individual ego. In the older dualistic psychologies, this center was thought of as outside the ego and was called God. The goal of the developmental process was to bring the ego into harmony with that more comprehensive center by making it subservient to that center. In the Jungian model, there is a similar conception, except that this more comprehensive center is understood as existing within the individual.

Jung viewed the unconscious as stratified. He believed that the first layer below the level of the conscious mind comprises all the qualities that are opposed (opposite) to those qualities with which the ego identifies. Jung called this layer the shadow, one's dark side. Its contents are considered by the conscious mind to be negative and undesirable. For example, if the individual believes himself to be efficient and logical, his shadow may express itself in irrational outbursts and lead him to be at once both fascinated and repelled by irrationality in others. At a deeper layer of the psyche, one's ideal is found in the form of the anima and animus, the archetypes of soul and spirit that, upon being projected onto others, create the transference.

Jung believed that there is an even deeper level in the psyche beyond the anima and animus, a center of integration, understanding, and guidance within the individual that transcends the ego, for it embraces both the conscious and the unconscious mind. He considered this to be the archetype of wholeness or unity and called this center the self, acknowledging the similarity of this conception to the Self or Atman of Indian philosophy: "The union of the conscious mind or ego-personality with the unconscious . . . produces a new personality compounded of . . . both together. Since it transcends consciousness it can no longer be called 'ego' but must be given the name of 'self.' Reference must be made here to the Indian idea of the atman, whose personal and cosmic modes of being form an exact parallel to the psychological idea of the self. . . . The self . . . is the 'uniting symbol' which epitomizes the total union of opposites."[16] Jung also compared the process of attaining realization of the Self in yoga to the transformative process of analytic therapy: "To experience and realize this self is the ultimate aim of Indian yoga, and in considering the psychology of the self we would do well to have recourse to the treasures of Indian wisdom. In India, as with us, the experience of the self . . . is a vital happening which brings about a fundamental transformation of personality. . . ."[17]

In contrast to the psychoanalytic tradition, in which the ego is considered to be the center of integration for the personality, Jung believed that the ego is only the circumscribed center of the conscious mind and that the self is the more comprehensive center that takes into account the unconscious as well. In this respect, Jung's perspective appears similar to that of yoga psychology, for both psychologies help to make the individual aware of the distinction between the ego and the self as centers of determination and both lead the individual away from identification with the limited perspective of the ego to become increasingly guided by the Self.*

Despite these apparent similarities, there is a striking and crucial difference between Jung's conception of the self as an archetype and the yogic conception of the Self as the center of consciousness. According to yoga psychology, the ego is the center of a limited and circumscribed type of consciousness (the subject-object mode of consciousness), whereas the Self is the very center of consciousness that comprehends all modes of awareness. Jung, however, took the ego to be the center of all consciousness and the self to symbolize the integration of the conscious and the unconscious. He believed that the self, though comprehensive, lies beyond consciousness. According to Jung, one can never be fully conscious of the self because the self as a center of integration for the individual includes unconscious contents, and these unconscious contents can never be made fully conscious. Jung asserted that "a complete 'emptying' of the unconscious is out of the question. . . . Consciousness, no matter how extensive it may be, must always remain the smaller circle within the greater circle of the unconscious, an island surrounded by the

---

*It should not be assumed that the Self is a more comprehensive form of subjective consciousness. The Self is neither subject nor object. Subject/object is a distinction created by ego-consciousness and is not relevant to the Self. The Self is unified consciousness devoid of any such polarizations.

sea; and, like the sea itself, the unconscious yields an endless and self-replenishing abundance of living creatures, a wealth beyond our fathoming."[18] Jung concluded that "there is little hope of our ever being able to reach even approximate consciousness of the self, since however much we may make conscious there will always exist an indeterminate and indeterminable amount of unconscious material which belongs to the totality of the self."[19]

Thus, according to Jung, full self-realization is an ideal never to be attained. Consequently, human suffering can never be fully eliminated. Jung believed one could only become conscious of the self partially and indirectly through the symbols it produces. To the extent that these symbols can be grasped by ego-consciousness, one can make use of these treasures in achieving a more complete integration. However, to turn away from the ego and toward the self was considered by Jung to be dangerous. In fact, he went so far as to assert that "it must be reckoned a psychic catastrophe when the *ego is assimilated by the self.*"[20] In taking this position, Jung resurrected the dualistic religious dogma that the individual can never merge with the transcendent. Throughout history the Western mind has consistently viewed such a possibility as a threat of annihilation of the individual consciousness and has opted to remain identified with the subject-object mode of consciousness, seemingly keeping the transcendent consciousness at a distance, as an object.

Jung risked more than most in confronting the archetypes of the collective unconscious, but he preferred to enjoy the majestic splendor that he uncovered rather than to explore further to find if indeed there might be a more comprehensive mode of consciousness transcending the subject-object distinction. In this respect he was similar to Sri Ramakrishna, who upon encountering the Divine Mother became transfixed by his experience of the divine form. Even though he knew of the more comprehensive unitary consciousness, for a long time Ramakrishna could not let go of his attachment to this divine form in order to attain that greater height. Only the continued insistence of his mentor finally enabled Ramakrishna to make such a transition.

> "When I sat for meditation I could by no means make my mind go beyond the bounds of name and form. . . . The mind withdrew itself easily from all other things but, as soon as it did so, the intimately

familiar form of the universal Mother . . . appeared before it as living and moving and made me quite oblivious of the renunciation of names and forms of all descriptions. . . . this happened over and over again. Almost despairing of the attainment of the Nirvikalpa Samadhi, I then opened my eyes and said . . . , 'No, it cannot be done; I cannot make the mind free from functioning and force it to dive into the Self.' Scolding me severely, the naked one [Rama-krishna's mentor] said very excitedly, 'What, it can't be done!' . . . 'Collect the mind here to this point.' With a firm determination I sat for meditation again and, as soon as the holy form of the divine Mother appeared now before the mind as previously, I looked upon knowledge as a sword and cut it mentally in two with that sword of knowledge. . . . The mind . . . transcended quickly the realm of names and forms, making me merge in Samadhi."[21]

Vedanta psychology clearly disagrees with Jung's belief that the Self can never be known directly. The very aim of Vedanta is to fully experience the Self, which is the center of pure consciousness. According to Vedanta, the assimilation of the ego by the Self, rather than being a psychic catastrophe, results in a state of illumination. In striking contrast to the dualistic position of Jung, Shankara, the most respected exponent of the nondual philosophical position, unequivocally asserted: "You are pure consciousness, the witness of all experiences. . . . Cease this very moment to identify yourself with the ego, the doer. . . . Its intelligence is only apparent, a reflection of the Atman, which is pure consciousness. It robs you of peace and joy in the Atman. By identifying yourself with it, you have fallen into the snare of the world—the miseries of birth, decay and death."[22]

The difference between Shankara's nondualism and Jung's dualism is resolved when one takes into account the relative viewpoint of each position. Jung experienced the world through the waking state of ego-consciousness, and from that perspective all other modes of experience seem to be unconscious. Each night we go to sleep and pass through the cycles of dreaming and deep sleep, but most individuals do not remember much of their dream experience upon awakening, and practically no one recalls any experiences from deep sleep. So to the person who is awake, these appear to be unconscious states. In terms of the waking state, experiences from the other two states become conscious only if they can be brought over and integrated into waking consciousness.

But suppose that the dreaming state and the state of deep sleep were actually states of consciousness in which the person has experiences as real as those in the waking state but is unable to make a correlation between one mode of experience and another. Then the person would be a sort of split personality. When he entered one mode of consciousness, he would lose awareness of the others, in much the same way that a person with a split personality may become unaware of his other personalities when he is identified with one particular personality. In such a case, the individual in the waking state would experience a blanking out of consciousness when he entered the dream state or the state of deep sleep. If the individual realized that he periodically passed through the other states but in coming out of those states he partially or completely lost awareness of those modes of experience, then he would consider only the state he was in at present to be conscious, and the other states to be states of partial or complete unconsciousness.

Now suppose that the individual were able to achieve a connection between these three states so that he remained able to observe himself while in each state and while passing from one state to another. Now each of these states would appear to be a limited form of consciousness, while the most comprehensive consciousness would be that which is aware of all three states and their interrelationships.

This supposition may seem farfetched to the ordinary person who regards himself as conscious only when awake. However, according to Vedanta psychology, this is not a supposition at all but an accurate description of the nature of consciousness. Vedanta psychology regards the dreaming state and the state of deep sleep as modes of consciousness that are just as valid or invalid, real or unreal, as the waking state. In fact, according to the Mandukya Upanishad, the other two states are in certain respects superior to the waking state.[23]

The ordinary person cannot correlate these three states. When he is in one state, he is not conscious of the other two. In other words, he is exactly like a multiple personality: each part is unaware of the others. So a person in the waking state regards that state to be the state of consciousness and the other two states to be states in which one is not conscious. However, there are yogic methods for achieving a correlation between these states, and one who has attained such a correlation realizes that each is a state of consciousness and that the ability to observe all three states leads to a fourth state of consciousness that is comprehensive and is identical with the Self.[24]

It should be understood that the dream state does not refer only to those experiences one has while asleep. The dream state is actually with us all the time as a layer or mode of consciousness that in modern psychology is referred to as the unconscious. It is the world of primary process experience, the psychotic mode of experiencing; it is the realm of myth, of all symbolic expression, and of psychism. It is all that is usually meant by the term "unconscious" in modern psychology. The ordinary person in the waking state remains essentially unaware of this realm, though he is continually influenced by it. Some for whom the dream mode of consciousness intrudes may experience psychic phenomena. Others may reach this mode of consciousness through the use of psychoactive drugs. Those people who have not adequately developed their waking consciousness may walk about in a kind of somnambulistic dream. They are to a greater or lesser extent overwhelmed by the dream world and carried away by it. Such people may be labeled schizophrenic or psychotic. Their task in life is to strengthen their waking mode of consciousness; if they succeed, their dream mode may become obscured except during sleep. Only after the person has developed the potentials of waking consciousness to a high degree will he be able to open the door to dream consciousness without being swept away in it. Then he will have the potential for integrating the two realms. If he achieves this integration, his waking consciousness will then be enhanced by another dimension, and he will enter the realm of dualistic thought.

Those rare individuals who have evolved their consciousness to the degree that they can remain aware in the stage of deep sleep have described that state as devoid of all objects, a seeming void, the obverse of the waking state. In the Buddhist tradition, this state has been referred to as nirvana. When one enters this state, he cuts himself off from awareness of objects. He remains still and is completely withdrawn within. To the external observer, he may appear to be unconscious: "Objectively viewed, the individual . . . appears to enter a complete state of ecstatic trance, in which there is a suspension of vital and conscious process. . . . This is all that the physical scientist qua physical scientist can observe. And if the observer holds to the theory that the Sangsaric type of consciousness is the only possible consciousness, then he would say the trance involved the total extinction of consciousness in every sense. Some psychologists take this position, but since they are unable to trace what they cannot see, they are quite unqualified to pass judgment upon the state in question."[25]

Franklin Merrell-Wolff, a contemporary of Jung who successfully followed the Vedantic path to achieve a correlation between these states, agrees with Jung to a certain degree. He acknowledges that, for some, the experience of this state can be a kind of regression: "Some writers conceive Nirvana as being like the state of the newly born infant, wherein there is little or no self-consciousness. . . . In this view there is a part truth and a great error. Without full self-consciousness, this state may be likened to a sort of original nascent consciousness, such as must precede the development of organized consciousness. It is entirely possible for an individual who is not sufficiently developed in the capacities of organized consciousness to sink back into such a nascent stage. Therefore, Nirvana is not the immediate goal for immature men and women. In fact, the immature entering of the state is a sort of failure."[26] Dr. Wolff acknowledges that giving up the subject-object mode of consciousness may indeed be a return to unconsciousness, but he attests that this is not inevitable: "For most individuals the center of consciousness in the Spatial Void is a state like dreamless sleep, in other words, a psychical state that analytic psychology has called the 'Unconscious'. . . . It is possible, however, to transfer the principle of self-consciousness into the Spatial Void, in which case it is no longer a state like dreamless sleep."[27]

This state of nirvana may be conceived of as the opposite or complement of the waking state. One who is able to remain self-conscious in this spatial void experiences a state of ongoing ecstasy far in excess of any pleasure experienced through the waking mode of consciousness. Though this is a state of mystic bliss devoid of all the pain and suffering experienced in the waking state, it is not the highest state of consciousness. The most transcendent state of consciousness is that which transcends all polarities, including the primary polarity between nirvana and the world of names and forms. This is a state that comprehends and encompasses the waking state and the nirvanic state along with the dreaming state of consciousness. According to the Upanishads, this is the fourth state of consciousness, the nondual state, in which all limitations of form are transcended. It cannot be defined except perhaps by paradox or by negating any form that may be attributed to it.

Jung was able to make the correlation between waking consciousness and dream-consciousness—a great and rare achievement—but he was not able to correlate the state of deep sleep with the other two states of consciousness. This in a nutshell explains why and how his position differs from other psychologists and also how it differs from nondual psychology. Jung's entire life was devoted to exploring the dream state in its own right and translating his experiences into waking consciousness. This led to a great deal of struggle in certain phases of his life as he tried to maintain the correlation between the dream state and egoistic consciousness. He was more than amply rewarded for his struggle, for he explored majestic and heavenly realms whose doors remain closed to all but a few. But Jung was not able to integrate into his awareness the state of deep sleep nor to reach that state of consciousness that comprehends both the world of form and its polar opposite, the world of nirvana. He thus was not able to experience the Self directly, and as a result he posited as part of his psychology that the Self *could not* be directly known.

Ordinary human consciousness does not have the capacity to comprehend the transcendent unified state of consciousness any more than a being who lived in a two-dimensional world could imagine the experience of someone living in three dimensions. The mind can create maps and metaphors to give one clues to the nature of this transcendent state, but all these necessarily remain within the framework of the subject-object mode of experience and therefore are distorted and far from complete. Furthermore, looking at a map is far different from experiencing that which the map is designating. The seer-philosophers who have experienced this unified consciousness have attempted as best they could to describe it to those who are functioning in the subject-object mode of consciousness. In some cases they have done so by negating any conceptions or distinctions that one might apply to nondual consciousness from within the subject-object framework. The Brihadaranyaka Upanishad explains it thus:

> The Self is described as *not this, not that*. It is incomprehensible, for
> it cannot be comprehended; undecaying, for it never decays;
> unattached, for it never attaches itself; unbound, for it is never
> bound.
> . . . the changeless Reality . . . is neither gross nor fine, neither
> short nor long, neither hot nor cold, neither light nor dark, neither of
> the nature of air, nor of the nature of ether. . . . without re-
> lations . . . without measure . . . without inside or outside.[28]

Other sages have also described this state in terms of the transcendence of
all polarities. Shankara, for example, said: "The absolute Reality is
beyond good and evil, pleasure and pain, success and disaster."[29] "All
sense of duality is obliterated. There is pure, unified consciousness."[30]
Merrell-Wolff has asserted that this state is "neutral with respect to every
polarity and thus in principle gives command over all polarities."[31] He has
written: "In it are blended, at once, all dualities. . . . It is the Desire and
the desire fulfilled, at this moment and forever. . . . Here is the utter
Fullness, beyond the highest reach of the imagination."[32]

Since this undifferentiated consciousness from which the world of
appearance is projected transcends all polarities, he who experiences the
Self will likewise be free from identification with the pairs of opposites
that comprise the phenomenal world. In describing the awakened sage,
Shankara said:

> Sometimes he appears to be a fool, sometimes a wise man.
> Sometimes he seems splendid as a king, sometimes feeble-minded.
> Sometimes he is calm and silent. . . . Sometimes people honor him
> greatly, sometimes they insult him. Sometimes they ignore him. . . .
> He has no riches, yet he is always contented. He is helpless, yet of
> mighty power. He enjoys nothing, yet he is continually rejoicing. He
> has no equal, yet he sees all men as his equals.
> . . . He appears to be an individual, yet he is present in all things,
> everywhere. . . .
> If a man identifies himself with the gross and subtle coverings
> within which he dwells, he will experience pleasure and pain, good or
> evil. But nothing is either good or evil to the contemplative sage,
> because he has realized the Atman and his bonds have fallen from
> him.[33]

Chapter Seven
Turning Outside In

Involution and Evolution

We have traced the process whereby the human being becomes enmeshed in the world of names and forms. He comes into the world unaware of his true nature, so he begins to develop his own self-definition. He gradually develops ego-consciousness and becomes entangled in the world of multiplicity. Identifying with one side of various polarities, he projects the unintegrated side onto the external world. Then he becomes attached to, or repelled by, his projections. In pursuing or avoiding the projected aspects of himself, he creates the various melodramas that make up his life, mistaking them for reality. He comes under their sway and experiences the kicks and bruises and the rewards and punishments that one receives from the world, and he lives in a state of bewilderment about the meaning and purpose of his life. Through this process he creates the world he experiences, including the pleasure and suffering, the attainments and frustrations, the hopes and disappointments, that characterize the life of most human beings.

This is only the first half of the developmental process. Most modern schools of psychotherapy focus their attention on this first or projective phase, assisting in the development of ego-consciousness. Yoga psychology describes a second complementary phase in the development of consciousness that also needs to be experienced if one is to significantly reduce frustration, disappointment, and suffering in his life. Although there are notable exceptions, most of modern psychology has only dim and partial recognition of this latter or unifying phase of the developmental process.

C. G. Jung and Roberto Assagioli have recognized the need for at least two distinct types of psychotherapy related to two stages of human development.[1] Jung believed that the shift from one stage to another occurs at the midpoint of one's life: "The basic facts of the psyche undergo a very marked alteration in the course of life, so much so that we could almost speak of a psychology of life's morning and a psychology of its afternoon. As a rule, the life of a young person is characterized by a general expansion and a striving towards concrete ends; and his neurosis seems mainly to rest on his hesitation or shrinking back from this necessity. But the life of an older person is characterized by a contraction of forces. . . ."[2] Through childhood, adolescence, and early adulthood, human beings build their egos and try to prove that they are capable of functioning in the world. Once they have established ego-consciousness and competency in the world to a sufficient degree, they may go through further metamorphosis as they loosen the hold of the ego and begin to identify with a more comprehensive center of consciousness. They are then at the stage of their development in which spiritual awakening dawns. According to analytic psychology, "the individuation process . . . follows regular patterns. It falls into two main, independent parts, characterized by contrasting and complementary qualities. . . . The task of the first half is 'initiation into outward reality.' Through consolidation of the ego, . . . it aims at the adaptation of the individual to the demands of his environment. The task of the second half is a so-called 'initiation into the inner reality.'"[3]

Jung believed that an individual goes through an about-face at the midpoint in his life, turning from a preoccupation with differentiation and definition of his ego to a new focus on spiritual development: "Among all my patients in the second half of life . . . there has not been one whose problem in the last resort was not that of finding a religious outlook on life. It is safe to say that every one of them fell ill because he had lost that which the living religions of every age have given to their followers, and none of them has been really healed who did not regain his religious outlook. This of course has nothing whatever to do with a particular creed or membership of a church."[4] Jung's findings parallel a view of the phases of life that has existed in Indian culture for ages and by which the people of India have traditionally organized their lives. In this conception, the first half of life consists of two stages. In the first stage, the young person devotes himself to his studies and to self-mastery, and as he matures he involves himself with family life and with responsible functioning in the world. The second half of life also consists of two stages, but here one increasingly turns away from worldly involvement. In middle age one partially withdraws from the world and turns toward spiritual concerns, and in old age one becomes a *sannyasin,* a renunciate who withdraws completely from the outer world to devote himself exclusively to the transcendence of ego-identification and to spiritual awakening: "The last stage of the full lifetime of the individual, known as sannyasa, or monastic life, was entered into by those . . . who totally gave up the world in search of Truth and Freedom. . . . Relinquishing all longing for material happiness both here and hereafter, as well as the desire for self-gratification through progeny, wealth, or heavenly bliss after death, these monks practiced total renunciation. . . . they not only left behind material possessions but also stripped themselves of ego and desires. Material objects had no glamour for those who had realized . . . the Self within, as the source of all bliss and happiness."[5]

This way of organizing one's life is quite different from the way of the modern world, which is so oriented toward external success and mastery. Many people today remain fixated at the adolescent or some earlier stage of development and carry the preoccupations of that stage beyond its time. They continue to be caught up in bolstering their egos, in proving their self-worth, and in acquiring more and more possessions and symbols of their success in conquering the material world. And at midlife, the modern person all too often remains oriented toward external success and mastery and thus fails to make the transition to the inward life. Continuing to orient his life according to the needs and desires of adolescence or young adulthood, such a person becomes anxious or despondent when he finds that youth is abandoning him. He fails to appreciate the possibility of finding inner peace, contentment, and a deeper understanding of life's meaning and purpose. Instead, as Jung noted, "Many old people prefer to be hypochondriacs, niggards, pedants, applauders of the past or else eternal adolescents—all lamentable substitutes for the illumination of the self, but inevitable consequences of the delusion that the second half of life must be governed by the principles of the first."[6]

Yoga psychology has long recognized the two phases of life described by Jung, but it has found that many people are not yet ready to shift from one phase to another at midlife, whereas others make the shift much earlier. According to the yogic conception, the movement from one phase to another is not necessarily tied to a person's age. Just as there are those who remain in the first phase throughout their lives, there are also exceptional people who early in life move from a focus on ego development to the stage of giving up identification with the ego. Furthermore, these stages are not as exclusive as the previous description indicates: both phases may occur simultaneously at any given time. A person may be developing self-confidence and mastery of the external world in certain areas of his life while at the same time learning to give up his identification with the ego in other respects, recognizing that the ego functions as an instrument of a more comprehensive center of consciousness. The shift from one phase to another is not an absolute change but is rather a change in predominance.

In yoga psychology, the two complementary phases are referred to as involution *(shrishti)* and evolution *(laya krama)*. During infancy, childhood, and adolescence, one tends to become ever more invested in and identified with the phenomenal world: the involutionary phase predominates.* One who progresses to the subsequent phase of disillusionment with the subject-object mode of consciousness turns 180 degrees back toward whence he came, back toward his origin. He has been enriched by what he has achieved in his journey, but now begins to withdraw from involvement with the phenomenal world, and works toward freeing himself from the world of names and forms and its constraints. He is in the evolutionary phase of his journey and will eventually undo all that has been created in the world of form, methodically untying all the knots of entanglement in the phenomenal world so that the Self stands revealed. Ultimately this process leads to the

---

*There is confusion in the use of the terms *involution* and *evolution,* but not in the underlying conception, among various writers who describe these two phases of unfoldment. The author agrees with Sri Aurobindo's use of the term involution to refer to the process of becoming involved with form, and evolution to refer to the phase of dissolving one's identification with the world of names and forms in order to evolve to more comprehensive consciousness. This usage seems to be in accord with the English dictionary's primary definition of the term involution to mean "the act of involving or the state of being involved," and the term evolution to mean "a gradual process in which something changes into a . . . more complex or more sophisticated form" (definitions taken from *The American Heritage Dictionary*). However, other writers reverse the application of these terms. They use the term evolution to refer to the establishment of the world of form, and the term involution to refer to a turning inward toward the source of manifestation, the nondual consciousness.

recognition of oneself as unitary consciousness unencumbered by the limitations of names and forms.

In each aspect of a person's life, the ego must be securely established before he is ready to loosen the grip that the ego maintains on the personality and allow the ego to function in the service of a more embracing center. In each area, the phase of ego development is a necessary precursor to the phase of spiritual awakening and must be completed if one is to become capable of maintaining self-consciousness as he progresses through more evolved modes of consciousness.

The distinction between the two phases of life and the necessity for going through the phases successfully is inherently recognized by society. This is clearly seen in the way society relates to individuals at different stages of personal development. For example, children are encouraged to develop pride in their accomplishments, although spiritual teachings assert that pride stands in the way of one's development ("Pride goeth before a fall") and those who join a monastic order are encouraged to give up all sense of pride in favor of humility. These two ways of dealing with pridefulness seem to be at odds with one another, unless one views these two approaches from a developmental perspective. Imagine a child coming home from school with a drawing he had just made and his mother saying, "Don't be too proud! I'm sure other children in the class did better. You should learn to be humble. God doesn't like children who are vain!" Such a response would obviously undermine the child's sense of self-worth. Far too many children have suffered because a point of view that is valid under certain conditions is applied without considering the child's stage of development. Each way of dealing with pride is correct for a particular stage of life. The child must build ego-consciousness and along with it a sense of pride, but a renunciate has passed that stage of development and no longer needs pride. Pride now stands in his way to further evolution.

Modern psychology has generally made the mistake of carrying forward models that focus on building an ego, inappropriately applying such models to those people who are in the process of transcending identification with the ego. Psychotherapy that focuses on ego development is necessarily different from the form of therapy that is effective in the evolutionary phase of development. Either the psychotherapist must adjust his orientation and his methods so that he can assist clients in each of these phases, or he must learn to refer clients to therapists whose approaches are in accord with the client's developmental phase. Though yoga therapy is an inclusive approach applicable to both phases of development, it is uniquely effective in providing an understanding of and assistance with the evolutionary phase of development.

The involutionary phase begins with a simple thought that creates a polarization and then a projected object that appears to be external to oneself. The object then allures its creator and becomes a desired goal that motivates his behavior. He thinks of means to attain the desired object, and this creates desires for those means as well. Thus one desire leads to other desires. In this way, desires multiply. An entire universe with innumerable melodramas can arise out of one simple thought. The creator of that thought is easily swept into and taken over by his creation. He forgets that he is the creator and thinks that he is merely one of the characters in a reality imposed upon him from the outside. The myth of creation, as it appears in the ancient Sanskrit scriptures, is based on this understanding.

> The Creator, Brahma, the . . . world-producing aspect of the Godhead, sat . . . bringing forth, from the enlivened depths of his own divine and all-containing substance, the universe and its multitudes of beings. . . . suddenly the most beautiful dark woman sprang from his vision, and stood naked before everyone's gaze.
>
> She was Dawn, and she was radiant with vivid youth. . . . Her eyes, like dark lotus calyxes, had the alert, questioning glance of the frightened gazelle; and her face, round as the moon, was like a purple lotus blossom. Her swelling breasts with their two dark points were enough to infatuate a saint. Trim as the shaft of a lance stood her body. . . .
>
> [Then Brahma created a second being, whose name was Kama, or desire.]
>
> "You will go wandering about the earth," he said, "striking bewilderment into men and women with your flower-bow and shafts, and in this way bring to pass the continuous creation of the world. . . . And I myself . . . shall be given into your power. . . ."
>
> . . . They were all set wild together, and their senses thickened with lust. Indeed, the entrancement was so strong that when the Creator's pure mind apprehended his daughter through this aggravated ambient, his awakened susceptibilities and compulsions directly opened themselves. . . . And in the meanwhile, the woman

was exhibiting, for the first time in the long romance of the universe, the signals of her own agitation. Affectations of shyness were alternating provokingly in the dim dawn light of this morning of the world with overt efforts to stimulate amorous admiration. . . . Brahma, beholding her performance, broke into a steam; desire for her conquered him entirely. . . .

. . . A longing to possess the incarnation of his desire groaned in him. . . .[7]

In the evolutionary phase of unfoldment, the process that led to the creation of the universe is reversed in order to dissolve the forms that had been created. In yoga psychology, the second phase in the development of consciousness is known as the stage of dissolution, for one goes through a process of dissolving all identification with the phenomenal world that had been established in the phase of involution. The process of dissolution "implies moving against the current of life. In subjective terms it means thirsting for a higher state of consciousness, suppressing the 'lower' by ascending the ladder of multiplicity into unity, a spiritual itinerary which takes the form of a return to . . . the *a priori* state before experience begins. Such a return shifts the centre of the personality from a fragmented awareness of his ego-centric consciousness to cosmo-centric wholeness, and brings about the union of the individual and cosmic consciousness. . . . The entire discipline of . . . meditation is directed towards this single goal, a return to the Supreme Centre."[8]

The universe is created through the projection of progressively more dense forms that enwrap this "Supreme Centre" in successive coverings. In order to experience unitary consciousness, the individual must reverse this process. One must withdraw from his absorption in the forms that enwrap the Self, journeying inward and successively becoming un-involved with each wrapping until he knows the Self directly. Shankara in the *Viveka Chudamani* has explained: "All the names and forms finally return to the same Atman whence they have sprung. He who can remain absorbed in the Atman alone is indeed a sage."

The various practices of yoga are directed toward this end. One reverses the process which he went through in building up his involve-ment and entanglement in the world of names and forms. He withdraws back into himself that which he projected and gradually recognizes that all is within. As the projections of one's complementary aspects are withdrawn inward, each antithesis is reconciled with its opposite and the polarity is transcended. One comes to experience the underlying unity behind each polarization. He begins to realize that the external forms that have been projected are weak adumbrations of the inner archetypal forms and that those archetypes are themselves illusory projections of unitary consciousness. He thereby frees himself from entanglement in the world of names and forms, yet he remains free to play within the phenomenal world if he chooses. He surrenders his identification with ego-consciousness and begins to experience guidance from a more comprehensive and unifying center within. Finally, he comes to know himself as unitary consciousness.

The Withdrawal of Projections

The process of creating an ego and projecting that which is alien to it has a useful and necessary function in the unfoldment of consciousness. This process establishes a limited reflective consciousness with manageable boundaries. Projecting the unintegrated aspects of oneself onto the external world enables one to create situations in which one interacts with those projections and thereby gradually assimilates them. Projection occurs in the involutionary phase of development; in the evolutionary phase there is a reversal of the projecting process, a progressive withdrawal of all that has been projected so that consciousness can become unified. But this unified consciousness is not the same as that which existed before the process of differentiation into the world of form. It is a consciousness capable of reflecting upon itself. Through the process of assimilating one's projections, a person's understanding of himself gradually extends until reflective consciousness embraces all and becomes unitary consciousness as well. One comes to realize that indeed everything that is experienced outside has actually been projected from within, that nothing is apart from oneself.

In Jungian psychotherapy, the withdrawal of projections is central to the individuation process. "The development of consciousness," Jung wrote, "requires the withdrawal of all the projections. . . . everything of a divine or daemonic character outside of us must return to the psyche, to the inside of the unknown man, whence it apparently originated."[9] The process of reassimilating one's projections occurs with respect to all three layers of the personality that have been distinguished by Jung: the shadow, the anima, and the self. One first assimilates those unwanted and unacceptable projected qualities that constitute his dark side or shadow. Next he begins to realize that the ideals that have been projected onto others or experienced as deities outside of himself in the transference are also aspects of himself. Finally, he recognizes that the pure consciousness from which the ideal forms and their adumbrations arise does not exist outside and apart from himself, but is in truth the essence of his being.

As one withdraws the projections of his dark side, he realizes that his enemies are merely shadow figures with no substance. They are only the antithesis of his conscious identifications. As he lets go of each one-sided identification and embraces its complement, each side of the polarity loses its seriousness, substantiality, and intimidating power over him. Both sides of the polarity are seen as created and imaginary forms with which he can play, and he thus becomes the master of those forms rather than being mastered by them.

Those projections that create the transference lead to the worship of external forms. Without an adequate carrier of those ideals, one inevitably experiences an endless series of disappointments, as the carrier of each projection is eventually seen to be different from what was projected upon him/her/it. Disappointment, however, is the vehicle that induces one to travel onward rather than remaining entangled in a transference. One projects the ideal onto one carrier and becomes disappointed, so he looks for another, and then another, experiencing a series of disappointments until he realizes that he is searching for something beyond all the carriers. Eventually, he will discover himself as the originator of the projected ideal.

The projected forms constitute the external aspect of maya, the multifarious illusion that one experiences as the objective world. When the projections are withdrawn inward, one experiences the majestic and awe-inspiring world of the unconscious more directly. In ordinary experience, one is typically swept up in the projected forms and in the external melodramas that result from those projections. The withdrawal of projections, however, leads one beyond the ordinary sphere to a deeper and grander realm in which one becomes aware of the ideal forms within. Here the polarities dance and weave in their idealized forms. Having left the external melodramas, one may become absorbed in the majestic inner dramas taking place, as the gods and the mythological values that had formerly been projected onto the macrocosm are now recognized as residing within. Jung noted that "the withdrawal of projections makes the anima what she 'originally was: an archetypal image which, in its right place, functions to the advantage of the individual. Interposed between the ego and the world, she acts like an ever-changing Shakti, who weaves the veil of Maya and dances the illusion of existence. But, functioning between the ego and the unconscious, the anima becomes the matrix of all the divine and semi-divine figures, from the pagan goddess to the Virgin, from the messenger of the Holy Grail to the saint."[10]

Jung remained fascinated with this splendrous world of archetypes, and he devoted himself to its exploration. But in doing so, his journey remained unfinished, for from the nondual perspective, at this stage the withdrawal of projections is partial and incomplete. Jung withdrew the projections from the outer world into the inner sphere of the psyche whence they had come. He then discovered a heavenly grandeur within and remained enchanted by an inner world populated with divine forms. But whence came this inner drama? Could it itself be a projection of something more subtle than the world of archetypes? This territory Jung failed to explore, for he was caught by his fascination with experiencing the archetypes, much in the same way that the ordinary person may be caught up with and enchanted by his projections upon the external world. To be sure, Jung traveled much closer to the unitary source than have other modern psychologists, and the form of maya which he encountered was ever more subtle and arresting than the world experienced by the ordinary person. But from the nondual perspective, it is maya nevertheless. The jnana yoga texts warn the seeker that in order to reach Self-realization, one must pass beyond fascination with and absorption in not only the physical realm but the heavenly realm as well.

Jung correctly noted that the unfoldment of consciousness involves a withdrawal of projections, but he appreciated only the first phase of this process: their withdrawal from the external world. He did not fully comprehend that even after those projections are withdrawn inward, they still remain as projections of consciousness. Jung failed to carry through to the further step of withdrawing consciousness from involvement with the more subtle archetypal projections within the mind itself. He mistakenly thought that such a withdrawal would lead to an annihilation of consciousness rather than to a more comprehensive consciousness. Jung did recognize the dangers of identifying with any particular archetype, and sought to gain objective knowledge of the archetypes by dispassionately witnessing their functioning rather than being swept up in them. But he remained absorbed with comprehending the ideal forms and could not envision a meaningful state of consciousness beyond that. At this juncture, Jung clearly parts company with Vedanta philosophy. Jung stopped here; Vedanta does not.

Freud and his followers studied the personal unconscious in great detail but could not see beyond to further depths of the psyche. As a result, psychoanalytic theory is severely circumscribed and skewed: it gives a distorted picture of the human being. Jung explored further to the depths of the collective unconscious and unearthed a vast treasure of psychological wisdom, but failed to penetrate to an even greater treasure. Yoga psychology goes on ahead to explore the way that leads beyond the collective unconscious studied by Jung. In the same way that Jung enlarged on Freud's concepts by viewing the psyche from a more comprehensive perspective and seeing deeper and more extensive implications for those concepts, so the broader perspective of yoga psychology vastly extends Jung's conceptions.

The similarity of concepts that have been employed in modern psychology and in the ancient psychologies of the East is striking and points to an underlying order in psychic processes that has been uncovered in vastly different times and locales. However, the depth of penetration in understanding that order differs markedly from one system to another. We see time and again that Freudian psychology newly unearths an archeological find for modern man but uncovers only the topmost layer of that which lies buried. As a result, it remains ignorant of that which lies further below, and its theories about what is to be found at a greater depth are far from complete and are often based on false assumptions or misinterpretations of the bits of evidence that were initially unearthed. A few of those who came later found other clues and developed new and more comprehensive theories. Of all modern psychologists, Carl Jung has achieved the greatest penetration and the most comprehensive theory to account for the data at the level that he reached. His depth of penetration into the unconscious is truly astounding. Nevertheless, he falls far short of real comprehensiveness, and certain distortions appear when he is led to speculate about what lies beyond his level of penetration.

It is precisely here that yoga psychology takes up the way for modern man, for long ago it penetrated to the utmost depths. While at times yoga psychology employs an ancient and foreign language to describe the treasures that have been unearthed, when modern man carefully deciphers that language and follows the path of those who have gone before, he too can attain that comprehensive understanding. It may be that any conception is but an adumbration, a distorted and very limited approximation, of the underlying laws of psychological functioning. Yet there are degrees of obscurity in the way the underlying order is formulated for our understanding. There is a progressive decrease in that obscurity as one moves from reductive to dualistic to monistic psychology in explaining such processes as polarization, projection, transference, and other aspects of psychological functioning.

In the spiritual traditions of the East, attaining more evolved states of consciousness is sometimes described as "reaching the other shore." Between the secure ground on which one ordinarily stands—that is, ego-consciousness—and that other shore—that is, fully awakened consciousness—lies the vast sea of the unconscious mind. To reach the other shore, one must cross that sea. The dangers of the journey are many, and only a few succeed in the attempt. Some drown (that is, become overwhelmed by the unconscious, as happens in the psychotic state), many lose their bearings, most become diverted from the goal. The competent teacher who represents a meditative tradition serves to bear one safely across the sea of the unconscious mind.

The possible experiences and dangers in this journey have been described in the great epics, myths, and fairy tales that Jung and his followers have studied in depth. These archetypal stories have always aided mankind in the journey to expanded consciousness. They shed light on what is likely to be experienced as the unconscious unfolds itself to consciousness, and they describe landmarks and dangers along the way as well as the means of facilitating an easy voyage. In Homer's *Odyssey,* for example, Odysseus meets a series of obstacles on the "wine-dark sea" that could prevent him from reaching home. At one point he encounters the sirens who, with their singing, cast their spell on all who approach them, leading captains to cause their vessels to founder on the rocks. Homer states, "There is no homecoming for the man who draws near unaware and hears the sirens' voices." Only through divine intervention and guidance is Odysseus able to experience the sirens' alluring melodies without being destroyed. He is instructed to keep his purpose foremost and govern the ship from a detached state. Ordering his men to sail on despite all orders that he might give to the contrary, he has them plug their ears and is himself tied to the ship's mast. This myth symbolically portrays the dangers inherent in confronting the unconscious mind, the need for maintaining a more objective consciousness, and the necessity of passing beyond the allurements of the unconscious.[11]

The unconscious mind is filled with endless lures and enchantments. Each new experience tempts one to become preoccupied with what is taking place at the moment and to forget that he is on a journey to a far more profound and encompassing awareness, a journey to his true home. Seeking after or becoming infatuated with unusual experiences is thus actively discouraged in yoga psychology. The purpose of meditation is to lead one safely across and beyond the realm of the unconscious mind to the pure consciousness, a unified and abiding state of awareness from which all limited forms of consciousness spring. The traveler must systematically let go of each fascination in order to see beyond it and then let go again to see beyond that. Such is the process that occurs in the practice of meditation.

According to yoga psychology, as long as one remains identified with the creations of the mind, spiritual attainment is impossible. The mind is merely the instrument of consciousness; one must go beyond the mind to realize his true nature. The Katha Upanishad states: "Beyond the senses is the mind and beyond the mind is the spirit" (chapter 6, verse 7). "The spirit is eternal among things that pass away, the pure consciousness of conscious beings" (chapter 5, verse 13).

Pure consciousness is the final goal of meditation and contemplation, and with that goal in mind, the teacher of meditation helps the student avoid becoming entangled with the transpersonal or archetypal experiences that arise as he encounters the unconscious mind. The basic process of meditation consists of letting go of *all* limiting identifications, whether worldly or fantastic, earthly or heavenly, in order to reach pure consciousness, which is unfettered by any form whatsoever.

The Nondual Conception of Projection

Vedanta psychology goes beyond Jung and other dualistic thinkers; it asserts that the entire universe, including the inner world of archetypes, is a projection of a unified and undifferentiated consciousness:

> The projecting-power of māyā creates the entire universe . . . and all the objects dwelling therein.
>   . . . But this projection is only an appearance; it is not real. . . . Non-dualists differ with dualists . . . as the latter take the creation to be real.[12]

According to Vedanta philosophy, this world is an illusion, a mirage. The material universe seems to the senses to have substantiality, but in fact it is the denial or absence of that which is substantial. This denial does not diminish that which is. It merely creates the illusion of an apparent something which is really an absence.

This conception is difficult to comprehend because it is quite foreign to ego-consciousness and directly contradicts one's sensory experience, which tells him that the material forms are real and substantial. To better understand the universe as an absence of substantiality, imagine a formless, timeless existence that first projects itself in the form of superabundance. This superbundance is beyond comprehension through conceptual thought, but if one were to attempt to convey its qualities, he might describe a ceaseless overflowing of sheer ecstasy, bliss, radiant love, and all-encompassing wisdom. These qualities emanate from a center of unlimited abundance like molten gold and seek beings through which they can flow. There is such a surfeit that the flow cannot all be absorbed. From this center, love radiates outward and reaches out to touch, care for, and nurture each and every creature no matter how much its consciousness denies love's existence. This center is the source of a torrential river of wisdom that flows with inspired words, sentences, and books of sacred scriptures and the most profound awareness of the order, plan, and conception of the universe and that which lies beyond.

Now imagine that all of this is overflowing from a center existing within the human being, but he has sealed up the avenues through which this superabundance flows and has denied its existence. As a result of that denial, desire for the very qualities being denied is created. One desires love, acceptance, ecstasy, and knowledge and then projects or imagines a world of objects, people, and situations that he believes will fulfill those desires. He chases after those objects, people, and situations, but they turn out to be mere appearances or filmy bubbles that burst just as he takes them in his grasp. This person's way of being is actually a self-created joke, for he already is the very things he seeks; that which he seeks externally is but an insubstantial reflection of that which he really is. Poor man—who is wealthy beyond all conception and does not know it. He does not comprehend the chimerical nature of the world. If he were to open the avenues to the abundance within, he would laugh to realize that he has been taking the absence to be fullness, and the fullness to be absence.

The source of this superabundance is found in the nirvanic state of consciousness. From the perspective of the subject-object mode of consciousness, this state appears to be a void, a negation, for it is devoid of objects. But in another sense, it is a state of abundance, and the world of objects is a negation of this abundance. Turning away from one's investment in objects opens one to this superabundance, which is as substantial as the world of objects is not. From a more encompassing perspective, the subject-object state is seen as an absence of that abundance, in which one chases after empty things that have only a negative existence created out of denial.

Both the nirvanic state and the subject-object state, as well as the dream state, are themselves manifestations or projections of the nondual state of consciousness. That consciousness which projects the universe is not external to the individual, but it is the core or essence of each being. It only appears to be external in the subject-object mode of consciousness because in that state everything which is not within the sphere of the ego appears as though it were an object. The goal of yoga is to recognize that this illusory world is superimposed upon a consciousness that transcends form. Consciousness in its pure form may be realized by disentangling oneself from identification with the world of form. The ordinary human being identifies with the insubstantial world of objects and calls it reality, while the yogi is engaged in disentangling himself from his identification with that illusory world. His goal is to fully experience that which lies beyond the illusion. The difference between the common person and the yogi is clarified by Shankara in the following manner: "Compare a man who knows what a mirage is with a man who is ignorant of its nature. The former turns away from it; the latter runs toward it to satisfy his thirst. The man of realization is no longer lured by the world of appearances—that is his evident reward."[13]

According to yoga psychology, ignorance of the underlying reality is the first and fundamental cause of human suffering. In his ignorance, a person mistakes the unreal for the real. He takes the ego to be the center of consciousness and the projected objects to be real, and then he reacts to them accordingly. He becomes attracted to and fascinated with the projected objects. He experiences apparent beauty or the longed-for goal in those objects, not realizing that the beauty is merely a poor reflection of that consciousness from which it was projected. Most people are enchanted with the projected forms, remaining ignorant of the source from which they come. They look for fulfillment in the objects of experience, whether those be external forms or the archetypal forms created by the mind, never realizing that that unitary consciousness from which the forms are manifest is the real source of fulfillment.

The Transcendence of Polarities

A tightrope walker must maintain perfect balance. If he leans too far in either direction, he loses his equilibrium and falls. To enhance his ability to balance, he may use a long pole that extends far out on either side of him. He maintains awareness of the extremities of the pole while remaining at a neutral or balancing point. In a similar way, the sage walks a tightrope between the polarities that exist in the mind. If he were to lean too far in either direction, he would lose his tranquility and fall into an identification with one side of a polarity. But by remaining aware of both ends of the polarity, the sage remains centered on the neutral point about which the polarity is balanced. This neutral point is not a compromise between the two extremes but an encompassing awareness of the extremes, the continuum, and the unifying center from which the polarity emerges.

Roberto Assagioli has distinguished between compromise (finding a midpoint between the two ends of a pole) and attaining equilibrium through a more comprehensive understanding that transcends the polarity.[14] For example, sympathy and antipathy (aversion) may be considered to be two ends of a continuum, with indifference being the midpoint. Indifference is a limited perspective that does not comprehend sympathy or antipathy. However, one may rise above the continuum and arrive at a center of equilibrium—benevolent understanding—that comprehends the two endpoints and the midpoint as well.

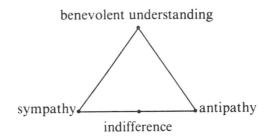

benevolent understanding

sympathy   antipathy

indifference

This is an objective consciousness of a higher order. From this vantage point one can comprehend the dramas and predicaments created when one identifies with the positions on the continuum; one can remain free from identification with the polarity and the limitations and predicaments that such an identification engenders. However, if one so chooses he may act from either pole or from any point in between. "The essential requirement," Assagioli has stated, "is to avoid identifying oneself with either of the two opposite poles, and to control, transmute, and direct their energies from a higher center of awareness."[15]

Other psychological theorists have also made a distinction between the attempted solution of problems through a change of content within a polarity and a resolution achieved by gaining a perspective on the polarity itself. Paul Watzlawick and his co-workers have named the former "first-order change" and give the example of a dreamer who makes attempts within his dream to avoid danger. By contrast, in "second-order change" the whole melodrama is transcended: "The way out of a dream involves a change from dreaming to waking . . . a change to an altogether different state."[16] Likewise Jung observed that the way his clients resolved important life problems was not by solving the problems logically but rather by achieving "a new level of consciousness" from which the problems "faded out": "What, on a lower level, had led to the wildest conflicts and to panicky outbursts of emotion, from the higher level . . . now looked like a storm in the valley seen from the mountain top."[17]

Though some of the techniques of yoga therapy are directed at first-order change (for example, the substitution of one habit for another), the focus of yoga therapy is on helping a person achieve a more comprehensive perspective, a second-order change, wherein his former problems and conflicts are no longer experienced as difficulties even if the external circumstances remain unchanged. Paradoxically, struggling against an unwanted situation may keep it from changing; arriving at a more encompassing purview, however, frees the external situation to change. For when one is caught up in a polarity, his very resistance to the unwanted pole maintains it; but when one lets go of his polarized attitude through attaining a metaperspective, the circumstances evolve into a new form. The emphasis on achieving a metaperspective or second-order change is characteristic of dualistic thinking. Dualists apply the techniques of achieving second-order change to resolve numerous problems that result from taking a polarized position. Monistic psychology extends this approach and applies it to the modes of consciousness themselves, thereby enabling one to reach a profound insight into the very nature of consciousness and its relationship to form.

The phase in which one becomes involved in worldly delusions is known in yoga as *samsarika chetana.* In this phase one experiences a seeming something, which is actually a relative absence of consciousness. The polar opposite of worldly consciousness is nirvana, or the withdrawal from worldly experience into what seems to the person who is identified with samsara to be a nothingness or void. But one who is able to maintain consciousness of the seeming void experiences utter fullness and considers worldly consciousness to be a negation of that fullness and thus a relative emptiness.

The contrast between the two phases may be exemplified by analogy with the difference between day and night. The unfoldment of a human being's consciousness may be compared to the movement of the sun from dawn to dusk. For the ordinary person, sunrise represents the phase in which one awakens to life in the world and increasingly involves himself in and identifies with worldly life. Midday represents the height or zenith of worldly activity. The withdrawal of projections and the transcendence of polarities may be compared to sunset and the ensuing darkness of night, during which one withdraws from his investment in worldly life.

For one who has reached the state of unitary consciousness, however, the analogy would be reversed. The Bhagavad Gita speaks of this reversal of perspective when it says, "In the dark night of all beings awakes to Light the tranquil man. But what is day to other beings is night for the sage who sees."[18] For such a person the phase of becoming increasingly involved in and identified with worldly life is analogous to twilight and the coming of night, for this process entails a gradual obscuration of consciousness of the Self and an apparent diminution of consciousness. The sage sees that to become absorbed in the worldly plane is to move about in a darkness only slightly illumined by the glimmers of the reflected light of the Self. Thus, for the yogi, dawn is the symbol of giving up one's identification with the world of names and forms and awakening to self-realization.

The typical human being remains caught in *samsara,* the cycle of worldly life, and in the polarities that abound within this illusory realm. But when one enters into the phase of evolution, he gradually learns to withdraw from the world of objects and eventually experiences its polar opposite, nirvana. However, there is a still more encompassing perspective that comprehends and transcends even this polarity. One who has systematically learned to regulate the focusing of his consciousness through yogic disciplines can attain a metaperspective in which he comprehends both poles in the complementary and mutually supportive relationship that exists between samsara and nirvana. He can then recognize that this polarity is a manifestation from a more unified field of consciousness.[19] The same figure that was used to illustrate the attainment of a metaperspective with regard to various polarities can also clarify the relationship between the three modes of consciousness.

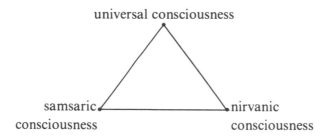

universal consciousness

samsaric
consciousness

nirvanic
consciousness

As previously stated, in the phase of evolution one reverses the process of manifestation. Resolving and transcending polarities leads to an ever greater appreciation of and unification with universal consciousness. First one comes to terms with and integrates the less encompassing polarities, and then he resolves those of progressively higher orders of comprehensiveness. He comes to understand that both sides of each polarized quality within the realm of samsara exist within himself. He transcends such distinctions as inside/outside, I/not-I, and subject/object, and realizes that there are no such distinctions except in an illusory dreamlike manifestation. Finally he experiences both samsaric consciousness and nirvana as two ends of a pole that is itself an illusory projection of unitary consciousness. He realizes that there is only one unified consciousness and nothing else.

Awakening

As one moves from reductive to dualistic to monistic psychology, the view presented seems increasingly nonsensical. It is progressively less comprehensible to the subject-object mode of consciousness. The modes' of experience upon which dualistic and monistic psychologies are based are increasingly removed from the subject-object mode of consciousness. For example, in our earlier description of the dualistic frame of reference, the view was presented that one grows upside down, from the future to the present. And monistic psychology takes the position that although the human being has the experience of being on a never-ending journey toward ever more comprehensive consciousness, the journey is actually an illusion: there is no place to go. One is already there but does not realize it.

Monistic psychology does not negate the usefulness of the dualistic model and its methods nor even the usefulness of the reductive mode. Rather it adds another layer of understanding that incorporates those perspectives and methods, while also comprehending their limitations. From the monistic perspective, it becomes clear where those models have overextended themselves to claim completeness as though they could account for all psychological phenomena and have thereby created a distorted conception of the human being.

The dualistic psychologies that explain the nature and progression of the individual's journey toward an ever more comprehensive consciousness are extremely valuable in helping the individual evolve. For the journey, though ultimately illusory, is not experienced as such. It has a certain order to it, and dualistic psychologies have helped to illumine the path and remove some of the obstacles that impede progress. Specific archetypal themes characteristically appear repeatedly, and one tends to become entrapped in the dramas that unfold out of them. The methods that have evolved out of the reductive and dualistic models are useful for dealing with certain obstructions and have long been incorporated into yoga therapy. But those models create obstacles of their own in much the same way that a medicine may alleviate the presenting symptoms yet create new problems. Final and complete extrication from the melodramas of life and the conflict and suffering they engender can come only by realizing the illusory nature of the journey itself. For that task only the nondual paradigm is adequate.

The following allegory is told in the monistic tradition to help one understand that the evolutionary journey described by the dualists is illusory, that there is really no place to go. The story states that there were once two children who had been separated from their father for a long period of time. They repeatedly pleaded with their mother to take them to see their father. Finally she agreed but warned them that the journey would be long and arduous. They would have to travel by foot, crossing numerous rivers and traversing several mountain ranges. During part of the journey they would have to pass through blizzards and biting cold weather, and at other times they would feel overwhelmed by the intense heat of the sun. But the children were so eager to see their father that nothing could dissuade them from undertaking the journey. So after long and careful preparations, they all set off.

The journey proved even more difficult than the children had been warned it would be. Sometimes along the way they encountered robbers and thieves; at times they went hungry; and they often became lost. As the journey progressed, they developed courage, patience, and concern for one another. After years of traveling, they came to a meadow. The mother pointed to a house in the distance and said, "That is your father's house. Finally we have arrived." Overjoyed, the children hurried to the door and knocked loudly. Their father came out and recognized them immediately. He bent down and picked them up in his arms and embraced them. The day was filled with love and joy. After the sun set, the children became tired. Their father opened a door to show them to their sleeping room and when the children went through the door, they were astonished. For beyond the door they found their own room, in their own house, just as they had left it at the start of their journey.

This story illustrates the way in which the dualistic and monistic perspectives complement one another in describing the attainment of unitary consciousness. From the dualistic perspective, one seems to be on a journey. But according to monistic psychology, one has the illusion of being on a journey, while in fact all that he has ever envisioned as a goal has been one with him all along.

The ultimate purpose of monistic therapy is to help one to awaken to the realization of his true nature as unitary consciousness. The ordinary individual is living in a kind of dream world or hypnotic state in which he believes that he is less than he really is. He further believes that he must acquire something outside of himself to be fulfilled and complete.

A noted English psychiatrist, R. D. Laing, has asserted that most individuals are hypnotized in childhood by their parents into accepting limiting attributions for themselves.

> I consider many adults (including myself) are or have been, more or less, in a hypnotic trance, induced in early infancy: we remain in this state until—when we dead awaken . . . we shall find that we never lived.
>
> Attempts to wake before our time are often punished, especially by those who love us most. Because they, bless them, are asleep. They think anyone who wakes up, or who, still asleep, realizes that what is taken to be real is a "dream" is going crazy.

It is my impression that we receive most of our earliest and most lasting instructions in the form of attributions. . . . One is, say, told one *is* a good or a bad boy or girl. . . . In the family situation, . . . the hypnotists (the parents) are already hypnotized (by their parents). . . .

. . . I think many children begin life *in* a state like this.

We indicate to them how it is: they take up their positions in the space we define. They may then choose to become a fragment of that fragment of their possibilities we indicate they are. . . .

What we indicate they are, is, in effect, an instruction for a drama: a scenario.

For example, a naughty child is a role in a particular family drama. . . .

. . . he learns that he *is* naughty, and *how* to be naughty in his particular family.[20]

Laing points out that one who begins to wake up from the dream world may be induced back to sleep or driven crazy by those professional therapists who are themselves asleep. "Anyone in this transitional state is likely to be confused. To indicate that this confusion is a sign of illness, is a quick way to create psychosis. . . . A psychiatrist who professes to be a healer of souls, but who keeps people asleep, treats them for waking up, and drugs them asleep again . . . helps to drive them crazy."[21]

In nondual psychology, the entire world of names and forms—with its polarities and melodramas, archetypes, and illusory evolutionary journey of consciousness—has been likened to a dream. If one frees the mind from its involvement and fascination with those forms, he awakens to a new mode of consciousness, just as one awakens from dream consciousness into the so-called waking state or subject-object mode of consciousness. While dreaming, the dreamer becomes involved in the drama being enacted: he thinks that it is real. In the dream, he may try to attain something or believe that he has attained it, but when he awakens from the dream, he realizes that the dream had no substantial existence. Similarly, when one awakens from the hypnotic enchantment within the subject-object mode of consciousness, he realizes that all that had been experienced and taken to be real is as insubstantial as a mirage. The dream world he called reality is no longer able to entrap him. He now knows that all of the limited attributes he thought were his and the limited attributes he projected onto others are merely superimposed upon his true nature, and he ceases to identify with them. The iron fetters that had seemed to bind him are found to be as weak as flimsy strips of paper and are broken in an instant.

Vedanta philosophy and psychology repeatedly asserts that the world of names and forms is an intricate illusion from which one must awaken. Shankara forthrightly declared: "You may dream of place, time, objects, individuals, and so forth. But they are unreal. In your waking state, you experience this world, but that experience arises from your ignorance. It is a prolonged dream, and therefore unreal."[22] The *Yoga Vasishtha,* a revered Vedantic text, uses allegory to make this perspective clear. It tells the story of a young man who is passing the day with his close friend. As the day wears on, his friend falls asleep. Now this young man has some yogic powers: he is able to make his mind one-pointed and direct it to experience the thoughts of another person. So, not having anything better to do, he decides to find out whether his friend is dreaming, and if so, what is occurring in the dream. He concentrates on the thoughts of his friend and finds that indeed a dream is taking place. In order to experience what is going on more fully, he decides to enter into the dream. He finds that his friend had been dreaming about a young man growing up in a foreign land. He enters into the thoughts and experiences of the young man in his friend's dream and becomes the young man in order to experience his world. He finds that as the young man, he lives in a small village. He is in love with the daughter of a merchant.

As the dream continues, he marries "the girl of his dreams." He starts a business of his own and begins to raise a family. As the years go by he prospers, but he continues to have a gnawing feeling that has been with him as far back as he can remember: he feels that he does not really belong to the place where he is living and that he is not like everyone else who seems to fit in so well and to take this life so seriously. Instead, he is a misfit, always wondering, Who am I really? What is my purpose in being here?

After years of such doubts and questions, he decides to consult a man who is reputed to be very wise, a man who is called "Swami." The swami says, "I know very well why you have those doubts. It's because you don't really belong here. You are not of this world, but you have become absorbed in this life and have forgotten your true identity. You have entered into a dream world, and you will never be satisfied until you come back out of this dream world to experience your true self." The man asks the swami, "How can I awaken from this dream?" The swami replies, "You will have to learn to let go of your attachment to the forms of this dream. You will have to make your mind one-pointed through meditation and withdraw your mind from its involvement here. Then you will be able to disengage from this dream world and return home."

So the man practices meditation and other yogic methods of self-mastery for several years until he is able to make his mind one-pointed on the object of meditation and to let go of his identification with the dream images. One day while deeply absorbed in this practice, he finds himself leaving the dream world behind. He comes out of the dream and discovers that he is sitting by his friend who is still asleep and still dreaming. Only a few minutes have passed.

According to Vedantic philosophy, the world we call reality is exactly like the dream in this story. We have all become absorbed in such a dream and forgotten our true identity. Only by withdrawing from our identification with these material forms can we awaken and realize our true nature.

As previously stated, yoga therapy helps one to awaken from the illusory world of names and forms with which he has become entranced. Yoga psychology does not encourage one to enter a trance state. Instead, it encourages him to awaken from the trance state of the subject-object mode of consciousness. This trance is experienced when one identifies with the thoughts in the mind. Those thoughts may be acquired as a result of the attributions of others, as Laing points out, or from other experiences. One thinks: I am weak, I am incompetent, I am afraid. A person ordinarily gives embodiment to his thoughts; he fills them out and gives them a seeming mass and weight by believing he is those thoughts and then acting on that belief. Awakening from the hypnotic or dream state requires a reversal of this process; one must let go of identification with his thoughts.

The most systematic presentation of yoga psychology, the Yoga Sutras of Patanjali, compiled in the second century B.C., clearly states the basic principles of yoga psychology in its opening aphorisms:

Yoga is control over the mind and its modifications (thought patterns, emotions, and desires) and the direction of mental energy toward attaining the purpose of life.

When the mind and its modifications are controlled, the experiencer abides in his true nature.

When they are not controlled, consciousness becomes falsely identified with the modifications.

In Western models of psychology, development is understood as a process of acquiring something new, adding to that which one is or that which one knows or understands. Nondual psychology emphasizes the other side of the process, pointing out that change involves giving up that which one has thought himself to be. While Western psychology and psychotherapy emphasize acquiring knowledge and skills, Eastern psychology emphasizes that the growth process consists of letting go of the limiting false ideas with which one has identified. Waking up is described as recognition and as recollection. By letting go of, rather than identifying with, one's thoughts and desires, one becomes aware of a treasure that has been there all along but that has been forgotten. It is pure consciousness, the source of all names and forms, which is itself beyond the limitations of form. It is the source of all knowledge, being, and bliss. Change does not occur in yoga therapy by acquiring more ideas but by disengaging from the innumerable limiting ideas with which one has identified. The process may be compared to that which a sculptor goes through as he removes that which is superfluous to reveal the beauty that had been hidden in a block of material.

Another simile may help to make the process more understandable. Speaking of the *atman,* one's true self, Shankara has said:

The Atman remains hidden, as the water of a pond is hidden by the veil of scum.
    When the scum is removed, the pure water is clearly seen. It takes away a man's thirst, cools him immediately and makes him happy.[23]

The unitary consciousness already exists as the true nature of each being. When that which is obscuring it is removed, one's true nature stands revealed. Let us examine this analogy in more detail.

Imagine that a person has been imprisoned all his life and is suddenly freed. He has never seen his reflection and would like to know how he looks. There are no mirrors available but there is a lake nearby. He is told that if he looks into the lake, he will be able to see an accurate reflection of himself. So he goes to the lake's edge and peers down, but he does not see his reflection, for the lake is very polluted. Not only are algae and weeds growing in the water, but scum and garbage are floating along the lake's edge, and there are even a few dead fish, suffocated by the pollution, floating belly-up on the surface. Since this person is unusually naive, he looks down into the mess and thinks, So that's what I look like.

That this simpleton could mistake the pollution for his image may seem a little far-fetched, but that is exactly what happens when one asks the questions, Who am I? What am I? and looks into his own mind for answers. When one tries to catch a glimpse of his real nature by examining his mind, instead of seeing what he really is he experiences the thoughts floating in the mind and mistakes them for a reflection of his true self.

In order to see one's true reflection in the lake, it would be necessary to remove the pollution from the lake, to prevent new pollutants from entering, and to eliminate any turbulence in the water. Then the lake would become a clear mirror. In order to look inward to see one's true reflection, one must do exactly the same. Nondual psychology helps one clean up the lake of the mind and eliminate mental and emotional turbulence so that one's true nature can be recognized. The process is not conceived of as acquiring something new but as eliminating that which is superfluous. The pure water is already there in the lake, but other things have been mixed in with it. If one were unfamiliar with unpolluted lakes, he might never realize that it is possible to remove the impurities and be left with pure water. Likewise, those unfamiliar with pure or nondual consciousness find it hard to imagine that by eliminating the thought waves in the mind, unitary consciousness can be revealed and experienced.

Letting Go of Identifications

The concept that growth consists of letting go of one's limited perspective is not unique to yoga psychology; it is a view common to many schools of psychotherapy. Therapists recognize that their clients are suffering because they are caught up in and identifying with a part, role, response pattern, limited self-concept, or expectation. Various approaches to psychotherapy help the client to let go of his identifications and to transcend his limited perspective, but schools of therapy differ in how far along the path of dissolving identifications they are prepared to lead the client. Some schools of therapy are content simply to help one let go of behavior or thought patterns that are directly linked to the presenting symptoms, while other therapies deal with underlying complexes. Psychoanalysis leads the patient to let go of parental introjects and expectations that have been created as a result of past experience. Jung goes further, helping one to give up his identification with archetypal themes. In discussing the anima and animus, Jung wrote: "Although the two figures are always tempting the ego to identify itself with them, a real understanding even on the personal level is possible only if the identification is refused. Non-identification demands considerable moral effort."[24]

In order to extricate himself from identification with the illusory world of names and forms, the yogi cultivates an attitude of nonattachment. This term is often misunderstood by those in the modern world, who take it to imply a withdrawal from relationships. Actually nonattachment can lead to more fulfilling relationships rather than leading away from relationships. Nonattachment in yoga psychology means nonaddiction or nondependency. One can tell when he is attached or addicted to something by imagining what it would be like to let go of it or by actually giving it up. To the extent that he then experiences withdrawal symptoms (physical or psychological suffering), he is addicted to, dependent on, or attached to an illusory form and is obscuring his true nature—the pure consciousness from which all forms arise. The goal of yoga is to become independent of the world of illusory forms, but not necessarily to become unrelated to the world of forms. Independence allows relationships; addictions constrict relationships.

Nonattachment means love. When one lets go of expectations and demands, he frees himself to really experience another and to respond to the other person's needs. But if one is addictively dependent on a relationship, object, or experience, he constricts himself, focusing on what he feels he must have instead of remaining open to the possibilities inherent in that relationship. He narrowly concentrates his energies on attaining or maintaining that to which he is attached rather than experiencing the fullness of the moment. In this regard Jung wrote: "In general, emotional ties are very important to human beings. But they still contain projections, and it is essential to withdraw these projections in order to attain to oneself and to objectivity. Emotional relationships are relationships of desire, tainted by coercion and constraint; something is expected from the other person, and that makes him and ourselves unfree. Objective cognition lies hidden behind the attraction of the emotional relationship; it seems to be the central secret. Only through objective cognition is the real *coniunctio* possible."[25]

Clearly, Jung recognized the importance of developing nonattachment. He observed that "whenever we are still attached, we are still possessed; and when we are possessed, there is one stronger than us who possesses us."[26] But Jung, like most modern therapists, believed that only limited nonattachment and nonidentification are possible or desirable: "Like the alchemical end-product, which always betrays its essential duality, the united personality will never quite lose the painful sense of innate discord. Complete redemption from the sufferings of this world is and must remain an illusion."[27] Modern psychotherapy, in agreement with this view, does not attempt to really eliminate human suffering. It attempts to cultivate nonattachment and nonidentification only in certain limited areas and only to a certain degree.

On this point, the approach of modern psychology differs markedly from that of yoga psychology, which seeks to eliminate all human suffering through the cultivation of complete nonattachment, the transcendence of all addictions and dependencies. The yogi learns to be responsive to the experiences that come his way rather than creating demands or expectations for particular objects or experiences. The Bhagavad Gita, one of the three major sources of Vedanta philosophy and psychology, emphasizes this principle:

> The man who moves among the objects . . . free from either attachment or repulsion finds peace. In this peace the burden of all his previous sorrows and miseries falls from him.
>
> (2:64-65)

Let the yogi unceasingly exercise control over his mind, hoping for nothing, desiring nothing.

(6:10)

This attitude, though misunderstood by the masses, has been recognized in different cultures and historical periods as characteristic of the most evolved state of consciousness. Thus John of Ruysbroeck, a fourteenth century Flemish mystic, stated that "man must be free and without ideas, released from all attachments and empty. . . . He must be untouched by joy and sorrow, profit and loss, rising and falling, concern for others, pleasure and fear, and not be attached to any creature. . . . It is in this that the 'unity' of his being consists."[28] Franklin Merrell-Wolff has termed this awareness the "High Indifference," and Meister Eckhart spoke of it as disinterest, saying that "a mind unmoved by any contingent affection or sorrow, or honor, or slander, or vice, is really disinterested— like a broad mountain that is not shaken by a gentle wind. Unmovable disinterest brings man into his closest resemblance to God. . . . It is an achievement of the grace that allures man away from temporal things and purges him of the transitory. Keep this in mind: to be full of things is to be empty of God, while to be empty of things is to be full of God."[29] And Jung has testified that "the art of letting things happen, action through non-action, letting go of oneself as taught by Meister Eckhart, became for me the key that opens the door to the way. . . . this is an art of which most people know nothing. Consciousness is forever interfering. . . . It would be simple enough, if only simplicity were not the most difficult of all things."[30]

For one who has not yet attained consciousness of unity in diversity, nonattachment is the end and also the means: to the extent that one practices nonattachment, he experiences unitary consciousness. Though this teaching is found in the writings of many great mystics, it is contrary to almost all that is taught in our modern civilization, in which the desire to attain and succeed in the outer world reigns supreme. As a result, the mystic is not understood and may even be seen as a threat by the masses as well as by those in authority. That is as it must be. For modern society is concerned with helping people establish themselves in the process of involution, whereas such self-realized beings are guiding those for whom the complementary phase of evolution predominates.

When the aspirant finally experiences the transcendent fullness and completeness found in the state of nonattachment, the things to which he had previously been addicted completey lose their alluring and enchanting qualities. For, as Shankara has said, "How could a wise man reject the experience of supreme bliss and take delight in mere outward forms? When the moon shines in its exceeding beauty, who would care to look at a painted moon?"[31]

In order to reach that state, one must surrender all identification with limited forms and limited conceptions of himself. In yoga psychology, the surrender of artificial distinctions created by the ego and the surrender of all desires for those objects that one has defined as external to himself play an important part in leading to the transcendence of ego-identification and the awakening to unitary consciousness: "When one renounces all desire and his spirit is content in itself, then he has indeed found peace" (Bhagavad Gita, 2:55). Through surrender, one ultimately arrives at a state in which he experiences the transcendence of all polarities, including such fundamental polarities as I/not-I, good/bad, internal/external, and subject/object. There are then no distinctions; nothing is separate from oneself as pure Being. The Sanskrit term for that state of consciousness is *sat-chit-ananda:* existence, consciousness, bliss. In that state there are no goals because there is no future in which to attain a goal, there is only the here and the now. Nor is there anything to be attained, for nothing is distinct from oneself as unitary consciousness: one is conscious of being the all in all, the ever-existent Reality.

Part II

APPLICATIONS OF YOGA THERAPY

Introduction to Part II

The Ecology of Consciousness

Monistic psychology posits that consciousness alone is self-existent and that all else only apparently seems to exist. All distress comes from ignoring the underlying reality and identifying with the world of names and forms. Yoga science studies and explains the way in which a person's consciousness has become absorbed in the world of names and forms and provides the means to lead him out of this ensnarement. Yoga is an ecological science: it attempts to comprehend, in all of its aspects, the environment in which a person is involved, and then to free him from his entanglements.

Modern psychology identifies the human being with his personality and thoughts and considers his environment to be his external surroundings, including the air he breathes and his home and work space. But yoga psychology considers consciousness to be the essence of a person, and all else to be the environment in which consciousness is embedded. In addition to one's external environment, which exists outside of his skin, one has an internal environment, which includes his body, emotions, thoughts, desires, and appetites. In much the same way that a worldly environmentalist would be concerned with restoring a polluted lake to its natural state of purity and equilibrium, the yoga therapist is interested in leading a person from the experience of disturbance to the consciousness of equilibrium and tranquility.

The monistic model is based on two underlying principles; the wide variety of interventions used in yoga therapy is a consequence of the application of those principles. When the principles are clearly understood, the underlying unity behind the apparent diversity of focuses in yoga therapy becomes discernible. The first principle is that self-realization is a process of purification; one has only to remove the impurities and encumbrances that obscure one's true nature as pure consciousness in order to be free of all distress and suffering. The principle of purification runs throughout all the techniques of yoga science and is applied in working with each facet of the human being. Since one is already pure unlimited consciousness, the process of growth consists of discarding all other beliefs and assumptions and recognizing what one is and always has been. Those unreal qualities that one has superimposed upon himself may be regarded as pollutants in much the same way that one regards smoke to be a pollutant of the air. Just as the removal of smoke leaves air pure and uncontaminated, so the removal of limiting self-concepts allows pure consciousness to become unveiled. Yoga therapy in all its phases consists of nothing but the removal of the various pollutants that obscure pure consciousness, which is one's true essence.

Those pollutants are found in various forms and in all aspects of our being. In the ordinary person, each instrument of pure consciousness is encumbered by pollutants. The first phase of yoga science consists of freeing those instruments from the pollutants, enabling them to serve as fit vehicles for the expression of the Self in the manifest world. The body is polluted by toxins it cannot assimilate, and in a similar way the mind is polluted by thoughts that do not reflect the underlying reality. The person identifies with those thoughts, and his awareness of the Self is therefore obscured. But when those pollutants are removed through the practice of meditation, one experiences his true nature.

The second principle of yoga therapy is holism. Yoga science applies the process of purification to each aspect of the human being. The ecological situation in which consciousness finds itself includes a person's living environment, his body and all of its functions, the air he breathes and the food he eats, his relationships and his manner of relating, his emotional and ego states, and his habits, desires, and thoughts. Yoga psychology takes into account all the variables in the world of form, however gross or subtle, that may affect the ability of a human being to be aware of his true nature, and step by step seeks to unravel the complex knots that bind the person to those forms. The entire ecological situation must be considered, including the interconnections between the various aspects of the environment, if one is to become free of the hold that one's internal and external environment apparently has over consciousness. Yoga psychology does not concentrate on one aspect or a few aspects of the human being, but helps consciousness disentangle itself from every facet of its environment. Thus, yoga is truly a holistic science.

The Holistic Model

Although analytic, atomistic, and reductive theories and methods have predominated in modern psychology and psychotherapy, there have been significant schools of psychology that have stressed the holistic and purposive functioning of the organism. Those schools have come predominantly from the German philosophical tradition. Two such schools that emerged in the first half of this century are gestalt psychology and organismic psychology. Recently the holistic perspective has begun to establish a foothold in modern medicine and psychotherapy. Theorists in this emerging field have attempted to define the basic principles upon which holistic therapy is based.

In the more orthodox Western therapies, mind, body, and spirit are separated into three distinct areas, with specialists to deal with each facet of the human being independently, and with little interaction among the specialists. As a result, it is not unusual for the different specialists treating a person in each of these areas to be working at cross-purposes. However, in the yogic model, medical, psychological, and spiritual needs are dealt with synergistically. The yoga therapist relates to the human being as a whole and seeks to understand how the various aspects of a person function together. A fundamental tenet of yoga therapy is that there is body-mind-spirit integration. Physical functioning, mental functioning, and one's relation to ultimate values and purposes are all of a piece, reflecting one another. The yoga therapist is aware of this inter-relationship and leads his client to become aware of it as well. He uses techniques that are effective on each level.

In the medical model followed by the vast majority of physicians in our society today, a specialist treats the organ system in the body through which symptoms are expressed. He may give the patient suppressive drugs which clear up the symptoms in that organ system, but since the underlying disturbance remains untreated, it will continue to develop and sooner or later will express itself through another channel. Furthermore, the pharmaceutical agents that are ingested typically create imbalances in the organism, causing reactions as the organism attempts to adjust or throw off the foreign substance. As a result, additional imbalances are likely to appear in other systems within the organism. These mental, emotional, or physical disturbances are usually considered to be merely annoying and unimportant side effects, but all too often they turn out to be more disturbing to the organism than were the original symptoms. Thus suppressive treatment may result in serious symptoms in other organ systems that neither physician nor patient recognize as being an outcome of the earlier treatment. So the patient goes to another specialist who deals with the organ system now affected and receives another pharmaceutical agent that suppresses the new symptom. This chases the disturbance to still another area, and actually has the effect of imbedding the original imbalance more deeply within.

For example, eczema may be treated with symptom-suppressive ointments that seem to be quite effective on the surface: the treatment appears to be successful, and the skin rash clears up. But after some time the patient may develop an asthmatic condition and consult a specialist in respiratory diseases. The patient has no idea that his present respiratory distress is related to his previous skin condition—and unfortunately his physician is probably also unaware of the possibility of there being a connection between the two conditions. A careful study of the two conditions, however, reveals that when either asthma or eczema is treated with suppressive drugs, the other condition often appears. The effect of the suppressive treatment of eczema is to drive the disease deeper within the organism, resulting in an asthmatic condition. An even worse situation is created if treatment of the asthma drives the disease still deeper to a more subtle level of functioning, resulting in mental disturbance. If the asthmatic condition is treated with symptom-suppressive steroids, as it usually is, the natural adaptive functions of the body deteriorate further and result in the atrophy of the adrenal glands, and out of that condition a psychiatric disturbance may emerge. The situation may be even more complex than already described. Strange though it may seem, those who have worked extensively with families have found that the treatment of one family member may lead to the emergence of related symptoms in another member of the same family. It is therefore necessary for a truly holistic model to consider the family as an organism and to be aware of the effects that symptoms and their suppressions have on other family members.

The yoga therapist trains himself to become acutely aware of the interconnection between various facets of human functioning, and he helps his client to become sensitive to himself in the same way. The practice of yoga science leads one to become more attuned to all aspects of functioning and to gradually gain mastery over every aspect of his ecology. The process is akin to learning biofeedback in each area of one's functioning. However, instead of relying on machines to amplify and give him feedback about changes in his internal ecology, the student of yoga learns how to become sensitive to his internal processes without the aid of machines, so that inner changes register more clearly in his awareness. For instance, in the process of learning hatha yoga, one becomes increasingly sensitive to physical tension and discomfort in the body and learns processes of self-regulation to reduce or eliminate those symptoms. He also becomes aware of how his breathing pattern, diet, thinking patterns, habits, and way of relating to others contribute to the physical tension or relaxation he experiences and how his physical state affects those other aspects of his experience.

The yoga therapist may work together with other professionals who complement his own expertise to jointly provide training for his client. Training in self-awareness and self-regulation of the body, diet, breath, habit patterns, emotions, states of mind, values, will, unconscious processes, desires, and relation to archetypal processes and to transcendent being—which are treated in isolation in various therapies— must be integrated in a truly synthetic approach to optimal functioning. If any area is left out, the therapy is incomplete. Furthermore, for treatment to be effective, there must be awareness of the way in which intervention at one level of functioning affects the other facets, for example, how a change in diet alters the breathing pattern and the mental state. At best, the techniques used at different levels not only complement one another but work synergistically as a unit.

The yoga therapist is not limited to a single modality of therapy, or even to a few: he has a wide array from which to choose. He may meet with a client individually, or he may meet with a couple or with a family. If he has the resources, he may provide a therapeutic environment in which the client can work on various aspects of his functioning—physical, emotional, interpersonal, and spiritual. The ashram or residential environment is a form of milieu therapy in which students can work jointly on expanding self-awareness. This type of environment provides the opportunity for regular practice in each aspect of yoga therapy, including diet, hatha yoga postures, breathing, meditation, solitude, self-study, and ego transcendence. There is also a chance to deal with projections and transference in interpersonal relations. In such an environment, there is frequent consultation with the teacher to help the student deal with the conflicts and difficulties that inevitably occur.

Materialistically oriented practitioners treat primarily the physical organism and behavior, and if internal psychological processes are considered to be significant, they are dealt with along mechanistic lines. Some therapists and physicians are currently enlarging their scope, however, and are paying attention to areas of functioning that had previously been ignored. But no modern approach to treatment works with the various facets of a human being in an integrated way; most so-called holistic therapies focus on just a few facets. Only the monistic model offers the possibility for a truly comprehensive approach to the elimination of human suffering.

In most medical and psychological treatments, the spiritual dimension of life is discounted. And many therapists who consider themselves to be holistically oriented, in the sense that they are aware of the body-mind interaction and of the extent to which physical disorders are actually psychosomatic, do not understand the place of the spiritual dimension of life in holistic treatment. Actually, if we trace the etymology of the word "holistic," we find that it has first and foremost a spiritual meaning and is derived from the same root as the word "holy": "The word 'holistic' is derived from the Greek word *holos*. . . . Holos means the entirety or completeness of a thing and is found throughout the New Testament. The state of wholeness and of health was often equated with salvation; a person who was made whole or who was healed was saved."[1] The holistic conception is found in the words of Paul: "'May the God of peace Himself sanctify you wholly; and may he preserve you whole and entire:' (literally, 'the whole of you') 'in spirit, and in soul, and in body, without blemish.'"[2]

The dualistic paradigm, in contrast to the reductionist and humanistic paradigms, recognizes the importance of the spiritual dimension of human life, as well as acknowledging the part played by the body and mind in contributing to a state of well-being. But it too falls short of being holistic, for according to dualistic models, becoming whole is an ideal that can never be achieved. In this view, the completely unified functioning of all facets of a human being is unattainable: the human being must always remain incomplete; there is always something more that is yet to be integrated. Such a conception is inevitable in the dualistic perspective. In fact, it is its very basis. For if complete integration could be achieved, the conception would not be dualistic, but monistic. The very word "dualism" implies a basic split and therefore an orientation that is not truly holistic.

The monistic model, however, is based on the assumption that unity alone exists. All functioning and all facets of the human being are guided and integrated by that unity. In the monistic paradigm, unity already exists within the person and needs only to be uncovered and recognized, whereas in all other paradigms unity does not and cannot exist. In the other paradigms, the therapist can only approximate a holistic attitude by understanding the way in which certain diverse aspects of a person are functioning in some interrelated way. Only the nondual paradigm is truly holistic.

Dimensions of Yoga Therapy

Yoga is a vast science. Its therapeutic applications cannot be fully encompassed in this volume. To describe each facet of yoga therapy in depth would be, at the least, an encyclopedic undertaking. What follows in this book is merely a small sampling of some of the main aspects of yoga therapy. The way in which the various facets of a human being are dealt with in yoga therapy will be described, beginning with the more material aspect of human existence and progressing toward the more spiritual. When appropriate, illustrations from actual therapy sessions are given.

The content of each psychotherapy session originates primarily from the client: the therapist is responsive to the client's immediate needs and issues. The therapist does not usually respond with didactic teaching, although he may do so occasionally at the request of the client. As is appropriate to the symptoms or issues raised by the client, the therapist at times focuses on body work, breathing techniques, diet, biofeedback, or meditation, but training and practice in such areas is usually not the primary focus of the psychotherapy. Often, but not always, a client working with a yoga therapist has been learning hatha yoga, correct breathing, meditation, and other yogic techniques in classes and is practicing each day outside of the therapy session. The yoga therapist may occasionally help the client to overcome obstacles or refine his practices in those areas. He often works together with holistically oriented physicians, yoga instructors, and other professionals. The psychotherapy itself usually focuses on the psychological and spiritual concerns of the client. The emphasis may be on developing ego strength, dealing effectively with concerns related to sex, work, and eating, changing habit patterns, improving interpersonal relations, resolving inner conflicts, developing self-acceptance, transcending limited identifications, understanding one's purpose in life, or cultivating an awareness of the transcendent.

Chapter Eight

Body and Behavioral Techniques

Diet

At some point in the process of yoga therapy, clients may begin to change their dietary habits. Diet is being discussed first in this section, not because it occupies the central place in psychotherapy based on the yogic model, but because it most clearly illustrates the approach to purification, which is the basis of yoga therapy in working with each aspect of human functioning.

If the client is to experience physical, emotional, and mental ease and comfort, his body needs to be free of contaminants and intoxicants. When one has a cold or influenza, he becomes acutely aware of the effects that toxins in his body can have on all aspects of his functioning. He feels restless and ill at ease; he has difficulty concentrating and experiences other mental and emotional disturbances. In a similar but more subtle way, if one absorbs chemical additives in his food or ingests stimulants or intoxicating drugs that upset his internal chemical balance, his mental and emotional equilibrium will be disturbed. The effects of stimulants and additives can be seen most readily in hyperactive children, many of whom begin to behave normally when put on a pure and natural diet.

Yoga science divides food into three categories: those which create restlessness and disturbance (*rajasic* foods), those which create lethargy and dullness (*tamasic* foods), and those which lead to a peaceful, joyful, relaxed yet energetic state (*sattvic* foods). The client may be encouraged to slowly eliminate foods that leave toxins in his system and that create disturbances and to eat a more pure and natural diet. He may be further encouraged to work with other professionals who are more knowledgeable about the effects of diet and nutrition or who can assess deficiencies in his biochemical makeup and

189

guide him in correcting them. Work in this area can have a profound effect on personality, mood, and cognitive functioning.

The following comments by a young man in yoga therapy illustrate the way that diet can affect one's emotional state and the way he relates to others. This excerpt also points out that discussing and making changes in one's diet can be a meaningful component in psychotherapy.

Yesterday I fixed myself a heavy breakfast. About an hour afterward, I became sluggish and depressed and I was totally despondent for the rest of the day. The energy wasn't in my work. After work when I was driving home, I was screaming, "What's wrong with me?" I felt like my system was messed up in some way, and I was crying. Today I've had only juice. That helped quite a bit; my work went fantastic and I was very friendly with the people that I work with.

I feel I've messed up a lot of relationships. I was talking with a girl yesterday and I was weak and irritable. I want to be consistent; I don't want to be snappy with anyone. Today I felt like going over to where she works. I felt I could be very friendly and energetic and have a real good time. If I could feel generally like I do today, I think my personal relationships will work better. I won't be dwelling on myself; I'll start thinking about the other person.

I'm going to test myself with different foods. Tomorrow I think I'll make a light soup and see how I feel. I stayed off wheat for a long time and then ate it to see how it would affect me because I heard that wheat can cause allergies. I need to do that more—go by my own experiments, not by what Joe Blow says with his latest diet. In the past, I would watch my diet for a week, and then I would pig out and feel miserable. This time I'm going to stick to it and watch what happens. After we talked about my liver last week, I also began paying more attention to that part of my body. I noticed that sometimes I get a sharp pain down there after I eat certain things.

All too often therapists ignore dietary imbalances that may be drastically affecting a client's emotions and behavior. The yoga therapist helps his client become more aware of the way that specific foods affect his physical functioning, his personality, energy level, thinking process, and relationships.[1]

Body-Mind Interactions

Working with the body is an important part of yoga. Body language has been thoroughly studied by yoga psychology, which analyzes all the postures, gestures, and movements found in both animals and human beings. The yoga therapist observes these characteristics in his clients as clues to their inner states. Many people mistakenly associate the word "yoga" with body work alone. Conversely, an equally large group of people think of yoga as a means of reaching a state of consciousness that transcends awareness of the body. But yoga leads neither to pre-occupation with nor disregard for the physical level of being. Rather it seeks to optimize functioning at this level in order to free one from identification with the physical being and to bring the physical into harmony with more subtle levels of existence. The yoga therapist helps one to transform his physical being and behavior through such means as proper diet and postural and behavioral techniques, but yoga does not create an entire philosophy and world view based on the physical level of existence alone: it uses physical and behavioral methods in a way that is integrated with and respectful of more subtle levels of functioning.

Tension carried in the body is intimately related to emotional and mental tension. When one learns to stretch and relax muscles that have been chronically tensed, he experiences a state of relief and ease that he may not have experienced since youth. Each person develops his own characteristic defensive patterns that are expressed in posture, movement, and chronic tension in specific parts of the body. One person may have hunched shoulders, another a rigid chest, a third may pull in his abdomen, and so on. Wilhelm Reich, who studied this subject in depth, used the term "character armor" to refer to the way we chronically tense particular parts of the body in an attempt to protect ourselves: "Reich asserted a functional identity between the individual's character structure and his muscular armoring—that is, the armoring *is* the character structure in its physical form. Therefore if one can break down the armoring, one will to the same degree change the neurotic character structure. But since the rigidity of the character is locked into the body, in the armoring, it is more effective to loosen the armoring than to try to change neurotic character traits by forms of talking-out therapy like psychoanalysis."[2]

The practice of hatha yoga leads to effects similar to those attained through such diverse psychophysical disciplines as bioenergetics, chiropractic, rolfing, and massage. The character armor is gradually broken down through the sustained practice of hatha yoga postures (asanas), and the emotional blocks that accompany characterological muscle tension also give way. As one stretches and relaxes muscles usually held tense, he experiences relief from tension in all aspects of his being. He learns to let go and to trust, becoming aware of a new sense of comfort within. One becomes more in touch with himself at all levels through the practice of hatha yoga. As he learns to pay more attention to his experience of his body while he maintains a posture, he becomes increasingly sensitive to the body's tensions and its dis-ease. He experiences physical relaxation and the emotional and mental states that accompany this relaxation.

The following excerpt taken from a therapy session with a woman in her midthirties illustrates the awareness of body-mind integration that can occur as a result of practicing yoga asanas and discussing one's experiences in the context of yoga therapy.

I have felt very stiff in the last few months, but yesterday I went to a yoga class and I was really amazed at what I was doing. I realized that I have been holding myself back. At times I have the feeling that my hamstrings have been very tense; there is some sort of blockage in the back of the knees, in the hamstrings. I'm very conscious of what I show in front, but the whole back area from my thighs down past my knees is an unconscious part of me. I'm not conscious of it and I imagine that no one else is conscious of it. I have bad circulation in that area, too.

I wonder if the tension there is related to my wanting to kick? Lately I have been feeling a sense of pent-up rage inside of me. Soccer is the only sport I like to play. When I was younger, I kicked a lot when I fought. My sister would hold me down, but I used to pull hair and kick.

Another woman reported:

> When I was in my teens, my shoulders and hips were in proportion; later I became very narrow in the shoulders and wider in the hips. My shoulders became very tight, as though I became ashamed of my breasts, my femininity. In yoga I've opened my shoulders more. Since I've been working with you and doing yoga, my body has gone through some changes. I have a different type of body, more womanly.

The greatly enhanced sensitivity to inner processes and the experience of serenity that come with the practice of hatha yoga encourage one to make changes in other facets of his life, bringing about a greater sense of well-being. For instance, one may become keenly aware of the aftereffects of eating rich foods on his physical, cognitive, and emotional states, and as a result begin to change his diet. Or he may more readily tune in to the physical and emotional discomfort that results from a conflictual transaction with another person. This awareness can be the first step toward making changes in that relationship so he can maintain the feeling of well-being he has learned to cultivate through yoga.

According to yoga science, posture is an expression of a psychological state. Modern psychologists know that a person's posture can tell a great deal about his inner feelings and his attitudes about himself and others. But psychologists are not generally aware that by purposefully assuming a certain posture, one can induce a particular psychological state. Each of the postures practiced in yoga brings about a particular mental-emotional state in the person who is maintaining the posture. While one posture promotes receptiveness, another may lead to an attitude of superiority. Other postures can help one develop various qualities such as fortitude, steadiness, vigor, equilibrium, humility, balance, and courage.

If one seriously practices asanas and studies their origin and symbolism, he also discovers that yoga postures are actually enactments of archetypal modes of being. In maintaining a prescribed posture, the student brings forth the expression of a particular archetype. Hatha yoga teaches the posture of attainment, the posture of prosperity, the posture of the teacher, the hero's posture, and many more. Assuming one of these postures brings about the corresponding attitude and mode of experience in the yoga student. One's repeated practice of a posture leads to greater awareness and integration of that mode of expression in different aspects of his being.

Along with physical postures, yoga therapy employs relaxation exercises that involve concentration on specific muscles and parts of the body as one consciously relaxes those body parts. There is a series of exercises leading to progressively more subtle and complete states of relaxation. Many of the more elementary techniques of yoga relaxation have been adopted by behaviorally oriented schools of modern therapy, but the techniques that lead to the deeper levels of relaxation are unknown to modern psychology.

Yoga relaxation exercises are effective in the modern world in reducing anxiety and psychosomatic complaints and in releasing repressed emotionality. Such techniques enhance a parasympathetic nervous system response to acute and chronic anxiety. With the use of these relaxation techniques, one can acquire the ability to remain calm and alert despite his external surroundings or internal thoughts. Emotional arousal requires nervous system response, and if the nervous system is trained to remain balanced, disruptive emotional states will not occur. Thus the individual can learn to be less reactive and to more quickly recover a state of equilibrium following an emotional reaction.

Biofeedback training, which has sometimes been called Western yoga, is a helpful adjunct to relaxation training. Some psychologists say that it may simply constitute an elaborate method for teaching relaxation. Biofeedback involves the use of electronic instrumentation to amplify the subject's internal autonomic functioning, thereby making him immediately aware of it. With this kind of training, also known as visceral learning, one eventually learns to recognize tension and relaxation in the body and to use "passive volition" to attain a state of relaxation. In yoga one learns to become increasingly sensitive to internal states so that he can regulate them without the aid of amplifying devices. When one is relatively insensitive to inner processes, electronic instrumentation may be helpful, but as one gradually becomes more keenly aware of inner processes through the continued practice of various aspects of yoga, he goes beyond what can be differentiated or measured by such instruments.

Regardless of the relaxation intervention employed, the same basic breathing pattern eventually emerges. This relaxed breath pattern is slower, deeper, smoother, and more abdominal than breathing in other states. Thus the breath can be viewed as an organic mobile biofeedback device, a readily available indicator of autonomic nervous system activity. From time immemorial yogis have known how to use their breathing to monitor and regulate such activity (and numerous other systems as well).

Relaxation may be learned by the client in separate classes or individual training sessions, but it is sometimes also useful in the therapeutic session itself. A short period of sitting quietly to practice the relaxed breathing pattern, or relaxation in a supine position, may help the client to become centered within himself and more aware of issues and emotions lurking just beneath the surface. It is sometimes helpful for the therapist to guide a client through a relaxation technique and to help him discover areas of tension in the body that are related to emotional issues. One young woman, for example, who always spoke with a soft high voice, complaining that others did not accept her, was led through a relaxation practice by a yoga therapist. There was considerable tension apparent in the throat area, and more time was accordingly spent in relaxing this area. When the tension was released, the young woman experienced a surge of tears and subsequently discussed the lack of self-worth that she feels and how she creates situations that prevent others from nurturing her. Thus the relaxation exercise helped her to experience her emotions more clearly and facilitated her ability to realize and openly deal with her own responsibility in creating her experience of not being accepted.

Breath

Breathing is one of the most neglected aspects of human functioning in modern therapy. There are, of course, inhalation therapists who attempt to treat severe disorders in breathing, such as chronic emphysema. But respiratory therapy by itself is incomplete; indeed, it does not even attempt to deal with more than its own very select area of concern. Some psychotherapists teach the rudiments of breath awareness in relaxation training, and those trained in bioenergetics, rebirthing, and rolfing teach their clients to become aware of and alter their breathing patterns. But there is almost no focus on breathing in most approaches to psychotherapy; there is little awareness that the way one breathes affects all aspects of his life. Breath is the vehicle that links all facets of one's functioning; breathing, posture, and thinking are interrelated, and they influence one another. In yoga psychology, the breath is a tool for regulating all of one's emotional and mental states, and even the way in which one behaves.

Most people take the process of breathing for granted; they assume that breathing is a natural process that need not be given any special attention. But this is not so. Very young children breathe with little inhibition or disturbance of natural breathing rhythms. But as one grows up, he experiences traumas, imitates others, follows erroneous advice, and thereby develops incorrect breathing habits. These lead to chronic distortions in the breathing pattern and consequently to disequilibrium in other functions. Most adults breathe irregularly or they chronically tense some of the muscles involved in the breathing process. A child may develop the habit of raising his shoulders and collapsing his chest in response to frightening situations. If he is often frightened, this may become a chronic posture accompanied by a distortion of his breathing process. A soldier may be taught to stick out his chest and pull in his stomach in order to look more manly. A teenage girl may likewise learn to keep her stomach pulled in to appear more attractive. In each case, a habit is superimposed on the natural breathing process and this alters the process and in turn affects one on many levels, including his physical health and personality.

Swami Vivekananda has said: "The breath is like the fly-wheel of this machine, the body. In a big machine you find the fly-wheel moving first, and that motion is conveyed to finer and finer parts until the most delicate and finest mechanism in the machine is in motion. The breath is that fly-wheel, supplying and regulating the motive power to everything in this body."[3] If the motion of the fly-wheel is not regulated, the motion of the entire machine is disturbed. The breath affects more than the body, for the rhythms of the body in turn affect one's emotional and mental life. In yoga science, the breath is considered to be the main link between body and mind.

It has long been accepted that emotions affect the breathing process; indeed, people commonly ascertain the emotional states of others by observing such breathing patterns as gasping, sighing, sobbing, laughing, and yawning. It is becoming equally clear that breathing patterns affect emotionality, and an increasing number of studies have been carried out to investigate this understanding, which has always been integral to yoga science. Scientists have verified that the slightest change in respiration induces changes in the rest of the autonomic nervous system, and that physiological reaction is an essential component in emotionality.

Respiration affects the right vagus nerve, which in turn controls the autonomic nervous system, and this system regulates the secretion of adrenaline, thyroxin, and other hormones of the body. The secretion of these hormones plays a major role in creating one's emotional states. By learning to effect changes in the autonomic nervous system through conscious alteration of the breathing pattern, one can modify autonomic arousal and modulate subsequent levels of emotionality. A few schools of modern psychology and physiotherapy utilize this concept. For instance, Alexander Lowen, who helped to establish bioenergetic therapy, has stated, "Breathing creates feelings, and people are afraid to feel. . . . Inadequate respiration produces anxiety, irritability and tension. . . . The inability to breathe normally [is] the main obstacle to the recovery of emotional health."[4] A respected physiotherapist, Magda Proskauer, has declared that "the breath forms a bridge between the conscious and unconscious. Our breathing pattern expresses our inner situation."[5]

When one begins to pay close attention to the breath, the link between breath and emotions becomes obvious. One can readily observe that whenever he or another person becomes emotional, the breath becomes erratic. Emotions such as anger, depression, and fear all have their characteristic patterns of irregular breathing. When one is angry, he tends to hold the breath after inhaling, while depression is often characterized by deep sighs and long pauses after exhalations. Through yoga, one learns to consciously alter his breathing and thus his emotional state.

There are many yogic breathing exercises, each of which achieves specific, well-defined results. Breathing techniques have been developed with a wide range of effects, such as increasing the amount of oxygen in the blood, raising or lowering blood pressure, or promoting relaxation. There are also breathing techniques that induce altered states of consciousness. Yoga therapists have experimented with the effects of breath regulation and have found that striking improvements in one's emotional state can be produced by regulating the breath. For instance, one can attain a calm and alert state through smooth and even diaphragmatic breathing. A client who finds himself becoming emotional in his day-to-day activities may be taught to breathe slowly, deeply, and evenly. He is likely to be surprised at how simple it is to gain control over even intense emotions through this means. Clients often report that when they practice slow, even breathing at a time when they are angry or upset, they find themselves becoming quite calm within only a minute or two. This technique does not lead to the repression of one's emotions but to the ability to witness the emotional part of oneself and regulate it, rather than remaining identified with the emotional state.

Many yogic breathing techniques lead one toward deep relaxation. One of the first methods taught to a beginning student of yoga is diaphragmatic breathing. This is a key factor in teaching a person to relax physically and mentally and in helping one to become cognizant of feelings that have been held outside of awareness. Here is an excerpt from a therapy session that focuses on this issue:

C: I had a rough time this week. You suggested that I pay attention to the way I breathe, and it was very difficult. I've been crying a lot. It's related to my mother, I think. I've often had the fantasy that when I was a fetus, her intestines were like a rope which became entangled around my neck and choked me. She didn't want the pregnancy. Later, as I was growing up, I had a tightness in my throat and my breathing was very irregular. I'm breathing better now, but every now and then I feel like I'm suffocating, like I'm choking; I can't get the air in. At other times, I feel a catch in my breath.

T: Have you tried to change the way you are breathing?

C: I don't have any system. I don't know how to change it yet.

At this point the therapist taught the client a breathing exercise to be practiced at home. The exercise includes relaxation of the abdominal muscles and diaphragmatic breathing. After practicing this exercise for a few minutes in the therapy session, the client reported:

C: I'm afraid to be relaxed. I remember often being complimented as a girl because I used to have a very flat stomach and a very thin waist. I was holding everything inside.

T: Was your stomach tense?

C: It must have been. My stomach was very hard. There was always a fear of being relaxed. I was always anxious. Even now I'm wanting to please. I become anxious trying to please.

T: What would it be like if you weren't trying to please?

C: I'd be more relaxed. I'd just let go and be able to be myself instead of looking for approval all the time; I'd lose a certain anxious self-consciousness. I've had an image in my mind that for a woman to be attractive, she has to have a flat stomach, but I'm beginning to learn that it's okay to be relaxed and to have the stomach sticking out. When the stomach is relaxed, is it naturally sticking out? I'm so used to it being the other way that relaxing doesn't feel natural.

T: Have you ever watched children when they breathe? Do their stomachs stick out?

C: It is loose. That is the way it is naturally, I assume. They have a pulsation there with their stomach.

T: It might be useful for you to observe yourself breathing in front of a mirror. My sense is that when you hold your stomach in, it also holds in and inhibits feelings.

C: I realize that when I relax my abdomen, I feel more sensuous. It's like the difference between the ballerina and the belly dancer. Certainly the belly dancer is more sensuous looking, more human looking.

T: In ballet you were taught to hold in the stomach?

C: Very much so. If you stick out, the teacher comes and pushes it in. I was really very good at it. My stomach was the flattest.

Later in this session, the therapist and client went on to explore the client's relationship with her mother and the intense anger that was being kept inside through tensing her diaphragm and inhibiting her breathing.

Alexander Lowen, in describing irregularities in breathing that are related to emotional disorders, has commented that "most people are poor breathers. Their breathing is shallow, and they have a tendency to hold their breath in any situation of stress. Even in such simple stress situations as driving a car, typing a letter, or waiting for an interview, people tend to limit their breathing. The result is to increase their tension."[6] In order to breathe more fully, one must learn to properly empty the lungs with each exhalation. Most people, and particularly neurotic individuals, fail to exhale fully. Lowen has pointed out that "the neurotic person finds it difficult to breathe out fully. He holds onto his reserve air as a security measure. Breathing out is a passive procedure; it is the equivalent of 'letting go.' Full expiration is a giving in, a surrender."[7]

Yoga employs an exercise called the complete breath to teach one how to correct for shallow breathing, to inhale and exhale fully, and to increase his breathing capacity. In practicing this exercise, one learns to become aware of each of the muscles used in the process of breathing. After exhaling completely, there is a slow, deliberate inhalation, beginning with the lowering of the diaphragm and continuing as one gradually expands his chest and finally raises the shoulders to completely fill the lungs with air. The process is then reversed with a step-by-step deliberate and complete exhalation. This slow complete breathing may be repeated for some minutes as needed or desired throughout the day.

As mentioned, particular breathing irregularities are associated with specific emotional and psychosomatic disorders. For instance, those experiencing depression or asthma are found to be breathing primarily through their left nostril, and a person who is anxious or restless tends to have a right nostril predominance. Usually simple postures or breathing exercises can easily correct such imbalances. Clinical research has led to the conclusion that six to ten percent of the people seen in medical outpatient clinics are actually suffering from chronic hyperventilation that usually goes undetected.[8] The symptoms described by these patients include dizziness, headaches, chest pains, anxiety, panic attacks, exhaustion, and a variety of physical and emotional complaints. Typically, the physician can find no physical cause for the complaints because the basis is an imbalance in the oxygen/carbon dioxide ratio in the blood, and the physician does not test for this imbalance. Such patients often go from one doctor to another without receiving medical treatment and acquire a reputation as hypochondriacs. They may eventually be referred to a psychiatrist for what is considered to be a hypochondriacal or hysterical disorder. But the symptoms can easily and quickly be erased simply by learning diaphragmatic breathing and an altered ratio of inhalation and exhalation. In a few training sessions, a chronic malady can be easily corrected.[9]

There are many subtle variations in the way human beings breathe. Some people characteristically breathe in slowly and deeply and breathe out in a quick spurt; others breathe in quickly and exhale deliberately. Some inhale or exhale through the mouth, while other individuals hold the breath momentarily at certain points in the breath cycle. One's pattern of breathing is as unique as one's handwriting. The breath may vary along several dimensions from one individual to another or from one time to another in the same individual. These dimensions include: (1) the ratio of inhalation to exhalation, (2) the evenness or unevenness of the air flow, (3) the degree of pause at the end of exhalation or inhalation, (4) the muscles that are used to expand and contract the lungs, (5) the nostril through which the air predominantly moves, (6) the depth of the breath, (7) the frequency of breaths, (8) the force of the exhalation, and (9) the pattern of air flow through the nostrils. As part of the systematic self-observation carried on in yoga science throughout the centuries, the subtle variations in breathing and their effects on all aspects of one's being have been studied in great depth.

In therapy sessions, when a client becomes emotional, his breath may become shallow, with frequent pauses. Such a change is not likely to be observed by a therapist who is not trained in the science of breath, but would be apparent to a yoga therapist. As with diet and body work, breathing techniques may be learned outside of the psychotherapy sessions. However, there are occasions when the breath may become the focus of a therapeutic session. The yoga therapist notices if a client's breathing becomes shallow, if he is tensing the diaphragm and breathing with his chest, if he is holding his breath momentarily. When the therapist becomes aware of irregularities in the client's breathing, he may call attention to those irregularities in order to make the client aware of them. The therapist and client can then explore the relationship between the client's breathing and his emotional or mental states. The therapist may then instruct him in a particular breathing exercise that can help correct the irregularity.[10]

Habits

Behavior change is an important component of the process of self-transformation through yoga therapy. Yoga psychology has long recognized that habits play a major role in maintaining one's characteristic behaviors. The human personality is composed of habit patterns, and without changing those patterns the personality cannot be transformed. Most strong and deep-rooted habits are in the unconscious. Since one's habit patterns are outside of one's awareness, it is difficult to break them. Helping a client to change habit patterns constitutes a significant part of yoga therapy.

Most people try to change habits through the use of will power. They attempt to deny the habit expression, and thereby create a battle within themselves. For instance, if one wants to give up drinking coffee, he will deny himself, and a struggle will ensue between the part of the person that desires to repeat the previous behavior that brought satisfaction and the part of the person that does not want to continue a behavior that he believes is harmful. Typically, there is a tug-of-war, with one side or the other gaining an uncertain advantage. Lasting change does not usually result when one attempts to alter habits in this way.

A theory of the way in which habits become established and how they can be permanently modified has been offered by Patanjali in the Yoga Sutras. In the yogic approach to self-transformation, one does not concentrate on the undesirable habit that creates obstacles in his unfoldment. Instead, he turns his attention to establishing a more desirable habit in its place: he repeatedly engages in a new behavior that is incompatible with and antithetical to the undesirable habit. Practicing a new antithetical habit does not allow one to continue the old incompatible habit pattern. This understanding is the key to eliminating undesirable habits.

In the first stages of establishing a new practice, one may have intense desires to engage in the unwanted behavior that he previously found rewarding in certain respects. However, as he continues to practice and find satisfaction in the new habit, his memory of the pleasure gained through the old routine fades, and with it, the attachment of the old habit pattern. For example, if one has been in the habit of drinking each evening but now begins to meditate at night, he will initially experience conflict in giving up his accustomed pleasure and establishing a new routine. While meditating, he may have intermittent intense desires to carry on his usual habit of drinking. But if he perseveres and continues to faithfully meditate, this practice may bring new satisfactions, and the attachment to drinking as a means of finding pleasure will diminish or be eliminated. The yoga sutras are explicit in describing the necessary conditions for practice to firmly establish a new habit pattern. The sutras say that one should be fully committed to the new practice and should practice consistently for a considerable period of time.

To be successful in this approach, it is important to find a new practice that provides considerable satisfaction. That makes it easier for one to eliminate the old behavior. For instance, each time one wants a cup of coffee, he might substitute another hot drink, and if he finds a new drink that is genuinely satisfying, the desire for coffee will diminish and eventually all but disappear. As a result of consistent practice, the new and more favorable habit becomes established, and the undesirable habit is extinguished.

This ancient procedure, which underlies the concept of practice in all aspects of yoga, has its modern counterpart in the reciprocal inhibition techniques used by behavior therapists. In modern behavior therapy, the client may be placed in anxiety-provoking situations and taught to practice relaxation. Since the new response—relaxation—is incompatible with the experience of tension, the person ceases to react to the stressful situation with anxiety. In this regard the approaches in yoga therapy and in modern behavioral therapy are similar; however, yoga psychology extends the application of this principle to a much broader range of habits. Yoga psychology uses this approach to change behavior of all sorts but also goes beyond a focus on behavior to modify habits of thought as well. In the past few years, behavioral psychologists have also expanded their approach to work with changes in cognitive habits.

Any unwanted habitual behavior, attitude, emotion, or thought pattern that the client has may be altered by cultivating a new habit incompatible with the first. Thus the yoga therapist may offer specific practices to replace the client's undesirable habits. It is not unusual for the yoga therapist to give his client "homework" or "prescriptions" for behavior to be practiced between therapy sessions. The prescriptions given by a yoga therapist are usually specific to a particular behavior that the client wishes to change. The therapist may ask the client to keep a journal and thus monitor the extent to which he is practicing the new behavior and the results that come from his practice. The client and therapist can then review what occurred and modify the practice to deal with any difficulties.

While one facet of yoga therapy focuses on helping a person to change habit patterns, another aspect teaches a person to transcend the conditioning process. Modern psychology has amply demonstrated that reward and punishment play a major role in the development and maintenance of habits. A person ordinarily follows those routines that bring him reward and avoid punishment. The practice of meditation helps one to more fully experience the present moment and to let go of anticipations of reward and punishment, and in yoga therapy sessions one also learns to give up addictions and aversions and thereby become free of the effects of punishment and reward. One begins to act in the moment rather than being preoccupied with the consequences of his action. The Bhagavad Gita advises: "Set thy heart upon thy work, but never on its reward. Work not for a reward. . . . How poor those who work for a reward!"[11] The student of yoga psychology learns to attend to the action itself, to act with awareness, care, and attention. As a result, his acts become more successful. Instead of viewing the current situation as a means to a future end, he uses each circumstance to become more aware, more conscious. He learns to transcend the polarity of success and failure. Here is an example of a client who is cultivating this way of being:

> In the past, I've felt that happiness or sadness is based on what happens, good or bad. Today I was working on a different attitude, allowing what happens externally to be okay, no matter what it is. I'm just maintaining a good feeling and it's not affected by failure or success. Today there was no fear of failure at all, and consequently I just said all kinds of things that I've never been able to say. I did my best at work and I had my boss's best interest in mind, but I wasn't afraid of what he was going to say to me. I was more aware of what we had in common rather than being aware of him being a vice-president and judging me.

Transcending Polarities

Many theorists agree that the basis of suffering is one's experience of being split into conflicting factions. Jung declared that neurotic suffering is the result of inner polarization. "Neurosis," he asserted, "is an inner cleavage—the state of being at war with oneself. Everything that accentuates this cleavage makes the patient worse, and everything that mitigates it tends to heal him. What drives people to war with themselves is the suspicion or the knowledge that they consist of two persons in opposition to one another. The conflict may be between the sensual and the spiritual man, or between the ego and the shadow. It is what Faust means when he says: 'Two souls, alas, are housed within my breast.'"[10] Theories differ in the way they conceptualize the fundamental or typical splits within the person. Psychoanalysis focuses on the conflict between the id and superego, while gestalt therapy is concerned with the conflict between top dog and underdog. Transactional analysis deals with parent, adult, and child ego states, while psychosynthesis helps one to resolve conflicts between subpersonalities. Still other theorists have concerned themselves with the split between a person's verbal and nonverbal communication.

Psychotherapy based on yoga psychology is also concerned with healing the divisiveness that can occur within a person, as well as the divisiveness between oneself and others. Only psychotherapy based on the monistic paradigm can heal all the splits that occur within and without. All other therapies assume a fundamental unhealable division as a result of the assumptions on which the theories are based, but the monistic model leads to a truly unified consciousness. Each of the various means used in yoga therapy is directed toward this end.

The two initial steps in the system known as raja yoga or ashtanga yoga consist of ten principles. The first five, which constitute the first step, deal with interpersonal relations. These are: noninjury, nonlying, non-stealing, nonsensuality, and nongreed. Next come five principles of internal purification: purity, contentment, austerity, self-study, and devotion.[13] If one makes a commitment to follow any one of these ten principles, he will sooner or later realize that it leads away from dualistic consciousness and toward a consciousness based on the recognition of unity. While many aspects of yoga therapy lead one first to understanding and subsequently to a change in behavior, working with these ten principles brings about a change in the other direction: one first modifies his behavior, and that leads to a change in his understanding. Old behavior patterns that lead one to experience duality and conflict (lying, stealing, and so on) are systematically replaced with new behaviors that manifest harmony and unity. Learning and working with these principles can be a significant part of the process of yoga therapy.

In order to better understand how this process works, let us consider the practice of nonlying. This principle has many parallels in modern psychotherapy. Leading theorists have noted that being dishonest with oneself and with others is at the root of both neurotic and schizophrenic functioning. For instance, Helmuth Kaiser has advanced the theory that duplicity is "necessary and sufficient for the existence of neurotic disturbance."[14] More recently, Virginia Satir has asserted that "the troubled families I have known all have handled their communication through double-level messages."[15] Both Kaiser and Satir have shown that in disturbed communication there is a discrepancy between verbal (conscious) and nonverbal (unconscious) expression, whereas in healthy communication verbal and nonverbal expression are unified and one is fully behind what is being expressed. Healthy communication is characterized by what Satir calls "leveling."

> The message is single and straight.
>   . . . it represents a truth of the person at a moment in time.
>   . . . The position is one of wholeness and free movement. This response is the only one that makes it possible to live in an alive way, rather than a dead way.[16]

In their book *The Structure of Magic,*[17] Richard Bandler and John Grinder point out that disturbed functioning involves deletions and distortions both in one's communications and in the way that one represents the world to himself. After analyzing the therapy of Satir, Perls, and others, Bandler and Grinder concluded that the therapist functions to correct those deletions and distortions in the patient's communications and thereby changes his inner world of experience as well. In most forms of modern therapy, the development of self-honesty and honesty in communication is at the core of the therapeutic process. It is also central to the process of self-transformation in yoga.

In working with the principle of nonlying, the yoga student is encouraged to become aware of distortions, deceptions, and dishonesty in his thoughts and in his communications throughout each day. To better develop self-observation skills, he may also be asked to keep a diary and to note each day's experiences of being dishonest with himself or others. He may also be encouraged to anticipate the coming day's interactions in order to consider how he might put the principle of nonlying into practice. In following this practice, one first becomes aware of his more obvious deceptions. As he becomes more sensitive to the issue, gradually more and more subtle distortions in his thoughts and communications begin to surface and are corrected.

The practice of truthfulness is not intended to lead toward confrontative or aggressive behavior, for it is balanced by another principle: noninjury. Nonlying helps one to become aware of self-deception and of the way that one deceives others to gain an advantage. The practice of nonlying may also lead one to confront an underlying insecurity and an inner feeling of nonacceptance that motivates him to practice deception. He can then begin to face and deal with those feelings more directly rather than attempting to cover them up. The practice of nonlying also helps one to realize how he forms conflictual polarities through his deceptions, creating opposition between different aspects of himself and also between himself and others. With continued practice, the person experiences an ever-increasing sense of integration; his felt sense of opposition and conflict gradually dissipates. In this way nonlying (and each of the other nine principles) leads one from a feeling of divisiveness to a recognition of the underlying unity of being.

The following excerpts provide an example of a client in yoga therapy working with the principle of nonlying over the course of three therapy sessions.

First session:

C: My friend and I met for lunch just before he was about to go on a trip. I didn't tell him what was on my mind. I was playing a role and I didn't realize it, although I was very aware that it was a real shallow get-together. I was denying the fact that I depended on him. I told myself that it didn't matter that he was going away for a while, totally denying the fact that I would miss him. I also told myself that I shouldn't feel sad. I think denial is what leads me to eat so much. I cover over my feelings and it leaves me with an uncomfortable sensation in my stomach. I use food to deal with that.

T: What could you have done instead?

C: Told him how I was feeling, that I was going to miss him, admitting, "I don't know how I'll deal with this loneliness while you're gone." But my attitude was real cocky: "Don't worry, I'll take care of myself." I was pretending it wasn't happening; I made myself numb. Overeating helps numb everything, helps suppress that feeling in my stomach. And once I start denying feelings, I create an unreal world. I made sure that I wouldn't miss him and get lonely. It even affected me when he came back. How could I have any good feelings on his return if I'd been denying all the time he was gone that I missed him? There were all these feelings that I was denying and being dishonest about.

Second session:

C: Over the weekend, I decided to do some writing about honesty. I became aware that if I had something to eat between meals, I wouldn't tell my friend. If I had two apples, I would lie and say that I had only one. If I had three colas, I would tell him I had two. I found that I want to control the situation by saying something that the other person wants to hear. I also found that being totally honest frees me up from trying to control anything except me. It makes me responsible for my own feelings. When I give excuses rather than the real reason for something, I start playing with how people are going to react to what I say, and it just snowballs. I saw how dishonesty was creeping into other areas of my life, and it didn't feel good. I saw that I had been wanting to make myself appear a little better than I was, not totally admitting where I was.

T: Did your behavior change after you wrote about this?

C: I'm more aware when I say something dishonest. I've stopped being dishonest about food and find I'm able to deal with my food intake. If I had a heavier breakfast or lunch this week, I was able to deal with exactly what I had and figure out what I was to have for dinner and still feel good about it.

I was surprised at how dishonesty was creeping into different parts of my life; for example, in not giving the real reason why I was late for an appointment. This morning was a perfect example. I was late for an appointment. I had trouble getting my car started, but even if my car had started right away, I still had gotten a late start. When I had trouble with my car, the first thing that went through my head was: I can tell him this is why I'm late.

It was really funny because I immediately recognized that that is the kind of behavior I want to change. It didn't make me feel good. So when I got there, I said, "I wasn't very motivated this morning. I was slow and that's why I'm late." I became aware that I was still reacting slowly, and we ended up laughing about it. That was an isolated situation, but a lot of little isolated incidents make me end up feeling not so good about myself, and those are the things that I found myself writing about. By committing myself to writing down my experiences, I set aside some time to myself. Even when I didn't write, I thought about what I was going to write.

T: Would it be useful to take ten minutes every night and review the events of the day to become more aware of how honest or deceitful you were?

C: Sure, it would be good to commit myself to writing ten minutes every night. That might keep me from avoiding some issues.

Third session:

C: I'm more aware of how uncomfortable I feel when I'm not honest with someone. I had something to deliver. It was supposed to come from the supplier by midmorning, so I made arrangements to deliver it at noon. But the supplier didn't show up until five o'clock in the afternoon, and when the guy finally came, he brought the wrong thing. I really wanted to run away. It is so hard for me to call my client and be upfront and just say, "We have a problem, and this is it." In the past, I would have made up some excuse. Instead, this time I simply told my client what had happened. Many little incidents like this have happened in the past few weeks. In the past, I avoided them or made excuses for them without even realizing it. Every time these incidents come up now, I feel: Here is another chance for you to practice being level with a person.

I have been thinking a lot about energy. It is as though I have a jar full of energy for the day. I can spend it negatively or positively. Every time I do something, I let a little bit of it out and by the end of the day, I want to see if it went toward productive things rather than worrying or making up excuses.

The practice of nonlying does not give one the right to act aggressively toward another. As the following client is beginning to realize, nonlying and noninjury actually work hand in glove:

I've been trying to be more honest. Before, being honest meant trying to tell other people how I feel, but how I feel is usually based on my emotional reaction. A lot of times that hurts other people and it hurts me because my emotional reaction is not necessarily what is true about the situation. I've been real near-sighted in that sense. For example, my husband did something that made me angry. In the past, I would get totally wrapped up in expressing what I felt at the moment and I'd forget that two hours before, he'd done something really considerate. My whole attitude about what's honest is turning upside-down right now. I'm trying to be a little more far-sighted and objective when I'm in a tense mood.

To further understand the way the ten basic principles or commitments of yoga work to transform one's behavior and understanding of himself, let us consider an example from the second group of five qualities, those that deal with inner attitudes. One of those qualities is *santosha,* or contentment. As is true with all the principles, contentment helps to heal the fundamental split within oneself and between oneself and the external world. Contentment is the highest of all wealth. If a person has a million dollars and is not content, he is poor; if he has little means and yet is content, he is wealthy. In the modern world, many people live in a chronic state of discontent, experiencing a gap between where they are and where they would like to be. Most of their time and effort is spent in trying to change their circumstances, in striving to be someplace else. Yoga psychology encourages a contrasting or complementary attitude that relieves the chronic sense of dissatisfaction and engenders harmony both within and without. The following interchange illustrates the application of the principle of contentment to a person who had been expressing chronic dissatisfaction with herself. It also illustrates how yoga therapy can help one gain insight into the paradoxical nature of the phenomenal universe.

C: I overlook the ninety percent good I do and dwell on the ten percent that I consider bad. I always think that if I would have done something a little differently, it would have turned out better.

T: One of the yogic principles, you know, is contentment. Have you ever worked with that principle?

C: No, contentment is one of those things I can't grasp. It is hard for me to imagine. I feel that I make mistakes in my decisions a lot.

T: Is it possible for you to feel that nothing you do is a mistake?

C: I don't understand. Do you mean is it possible for me to believe that whatever I do, I do for a reason?

T: It has a purpose.

C: But there still is such a thing as a mistake, isn't there? Are you trying to tell me that there's no such thing?

T: I'm wondering if there is such a thing. In *your* psychology there is the idea that there is such a thing as a mistake, but in reality I don't know.

C: That's an interesting thought. When you say that, I see a little light: viewing things as mistakes is being judgmental. I just don't want all this tension about having to change. If I put a concentrated effort into changing, I can't seem to do it.

T: There *is* nothing to achieve; that is what contentment means. If you are trying to make something be different, you are not content.

C: So if you are content, things in yourself don't need to be changed? You just accept yourself as you are? It's like giving up all criticism. And I suppose, I shouldn't put contentment out there as a goal either, and criticize myself when I'm not content.

T: I don't know if you *should*. You can put it out there as a goal, but it's not contentment if you do. You can't get to it as a goal, because contentment is already where you are.

C: If contentment is already where you are, why is it so hard?

T: Because you keep setting up those false goals, those ideals: "This is the way it must be done."

Contentment, like many other qualities characteristic of unitary consciousness, cannot be reached by striving toward a goal, but can be realized only by letting go and experiencing where one is at the moment. Contentment does not lead to complacency, however, as many people imagine. The principle of contentment creates an inner sense of calm and peace, but it does not prevent one from working outwardly to bring about change. In working with the principle of contentment, one becomes increasingly aware that there is an ongoing growth process which makes change inevitable. He learns to be in harmony with the current situation even while he is bringing about change; he becomes increasingly peaceful and undisturbed by so-called failure or success. This dual attitude of being content and yet being in harmony with the process of change replaces the chronic restlessness, dissatisfaction, and stagnation so characteristic of many people's lives. The cultivation of contentment leads one from emotionality and from a preoccupation with narrow and petty concerns, which do not allow one to envision the many paths leading to his goal, to a sense of greater calm and openness. Paradoxically, the more one is content, the more he is open to change.

When one is content, it frequently has nothing to do with his objective circumstances. Discontent is an inner attitude that often would remain even if the person were to change his situation. The discontented person is not necessarily seeking change. He may be assuming a posture that actually makes change difficult. Yoga therapy helps such a person to relax his posture, to begin to accept his situation and open himself to possibilities of growth that he had not considered when he assumed his posture of dissatisfaction. Yoga therapy leads one to playfully explore alternative ways of acting and reacting in the world.

Many modern psychologists believe that if a person is content, his motivation dies. They believe that one must be restless and ill at ease to be creative and productive. But yoga psychology sharply distinguishes between contentment and satisfaction. Contentment refers to one's expectations. If one is not content with the fruits of his actions, he will be miserable. But one may be content with the results of his actions without remaining satisfied. Nonsatisfaction helps one to make efforts, without in any way preventing him from being content with the results of those efforts.

Instead of avoiding difficult situations, the student of yoga comes to view all situations as learning experiences, turning problems into opportunities for growth. A good example is provided by the woman quoted previously who felt she often made mistakes in her decisions. As she progressed in therapy, she found her attitude toward her job undergoing a change:

C: All these little exercises that you have given me really help me enjoy my job a lot more. The other day, I had a choice of where to work in the restaurant, and I picked the place where I would have the most confrontation. My girlfriend asked, "What's wrong with you?" Everybody avoids that area because for some reason that is where anyone that would give you a hard time ends up sitting. I said, "Well, I figure it's an opportunity." She said, "I don't know what is going on with you." Afterward I thought about how much time I spend worrying that I might have to work there and trying to avoid it. There must have been some kind of change of attitude for me to pick that section to work in. And as it turned out, that section was really easy and it was waitresses in other sections who ended up complaining about problem customers.

T: Are you saying that it's your attitude which creates the situations you face?

C: I see that a lot. The waitresses who are looking for a hard time always get it. I have seen it work so fast. I don't know what it is about a waitress's body language or the look on her face, but somebody will give her the hardest time about something. Sometimes I tell her that I'll go talk to him, and he's really nice to me. You can see how people create their own environment. And when I got over my fear of certain situations, I stopped creating those situations to deal with.

Chapter Nine

The Relationship Between Therapist and Client

Responsibility

It is important to reevaluate where the responsibility lies for making a person well. In modern medicine, the physician is considered to be the expert in fixing the body when it breaks down. His role is analogous to that of a mechanic fixing an engine, although of course the human body is far more intricate than any engine. There is little the patient can do but rely on the doctor's expertise and passively receive the treatment administered. The patient is expected to surrender his judgment to the expertise of the physician. This attitude toward treatment has carried over into the treatment of mental and emotional symptoms in what has come to be known as the medical model in psychiatry. It is not uncommon for the patient to enter therapy with the attitude that the therapist is an expert who will administer a treatment that will cure him while the patient himself remains relatively passive. Of course, this model of therapy fits in with some of the patient's needs and fantasies. The patient may prefer to avoid facing certain conflicts and weaknesses in himself and thus escape the considerable effort involved in changing. The appropriateness of generalizing from the medical model and applying it to problems of living has been called into serious question,[1] and certainly there are many psychotherapists who are not in agreement with it. However, the medical model continues to be prevalent in much of modern psychiatry.

In addition to standard medical treatments, there are other physical treatments that encourage a relatively passive attitude on the part of the client and emphasize the expert's responsibility in bringing about a cure. These approaches may have a marked temporary effect, but if the client does not learn to take continuing responsibility for his functioning and to change previous habits, the symptoms that led him to seek treatment are likely to reappear. Such passive treatments occur in the psychological sphere as well.

215

Hypnosis is perhaps the most obvious example. It can produce marked changes in symptoms, but there has been a long-standing controversy over whether such changes are lasting, whether symptom substitution occurs, and whether a person who undergoes hypnosis is giving up responsibility for himself.

The movement from treating symptoms in isolation to dealing with the whole person leads to a change from the medical model, in which the expert takes responsibility for the patient, to the conception that the main work of the physician or psychotherapist is to teach the person how to take increasing responsibility for his own life. By concentrating on the suppression of isolated symptoms, the physician or psychotherapist can frequently create the illusion that in his bag of tricks he has the means to make the patient well. But when one recognizes the role of symptoms as signals of underlying disunity, the focus moves to the underlying discord itself. From this perspective, the work of the physician or therapist is to help clear the way for the client to alter his way of living and being in order to become unified within himself. The physician or therapist can assume the role of coach or teacher, but he cannot "fix" the patient, as is assumed in the medical model. He in fact encourages the client to take increasing responsibility for the various facets of his life.

Yoga is a holistic training program rather than a method of treatment.[2] The yoga therapist does not treat patients; instead he may teach, coach, guide, or otherwise assist fellow players in the game of life. His method of teaching is not didactic, but consists of an ongoing dialogue with the client. He may provide guidance, but it is up to the client to practice the techniques of self-transformation. The client gradually learns to take responsibility in each aspect of his life—physical, interpersonal, mental, emotional, and spiritual.

The issue of responsibility is vitally important. Therapists have noted that the neurotic person does not take responsibility for his words and actions.

> The rifts in the neurotic's personality do not permit him to be "present" to the same degree in his actions and words as are healthier personalities. . . . A comparatively healthy person will . . . retain the feeling that he made a decision. . . . A severely neurotic person . . . will be inclined . . . *to feel:* I have no choice.

> . . . neurotics feel, "I did it, but I did not want to do it." Or, "I wanted to do it, but at the same time I did not want to do it." . . .
>
> . . . such a patient does not feel at one with his own words and actions. . . . It is the analyst's task to make the patient feel responsible for his own words and his own actions. . . .
>
> . . . *making the patient feel responsible for his own words* is equal to *curing the patient.*[3]

Typically, the client entering psychotherapy feels at the mercy of outside forces; he does not feel that he is freely choosing his way of being. This is reflected by the words he uses. The client denies responsibility in using such expressions as "I have to" or "he made me." The client will say, "He made me angry" or "He hurt my feelings." The yoga therapist may respond to such a statement by asking whether the client could have chosen any other response than anger or hurt. Gradually, the client learns that he chooses to respond in a particular way.

"Shoulds" and "have tos" also play a large part in the lives of many clients. One client reported:

> When I was growing up, my mother would give me the feeling that to take any option other than the one she wanted me to take would be bad. Her attitude was, "This *should* be done right now in *this* way." If I did it any other way I'd be doing it the wrong way. Now I have a sense of guilt if I don't do things I feel are expected.

When a client says "I should" or "I have to," he is expressing his unwillingness to stand behind his actions and accept full responsibility for them. To the yoga therapist, such expressions are jarring and make no sense, because they imply an inherent disunity within the personality. The therapist may challenge the perspective on which they are based and offer another in its place. The interchange between client and yoga therapist may go something like this:

C: Doesn't everyone live with shoulds?
T: I'm not sure. I wonder what it would be like to live without them for a day.
C: But then I wouldn't have any controls over myself. I might do anything.

T: Gee, that sounds exciting! I wonder if you'd be willing to try and live
     without shoulds and have tos for a few hours one day this week.

One client was told she *should* never do what someone tells her she *should*
do. This paradoxical injunction helped to free her from the "tyranny of
shoulds" which is experienced by so many neurotic patients.

As therapy progresses, the client begins to replace "I have to" with "I
choose to." He learns to take responsibility, to become integrated or
whole rather than split by conflict between "what I want" and "what I am
supposed to do." He also comes to understand that it is counterproductive to impose shoulds on others, for it often leads to a response
which is the antithesis of what is sought. A client who had been in therapy
for some time and had been working on this issue described the following
interchange with her daughter:

C: This morning I told my daughter that she should wear her boots
     today. "Should" just automatically came out. She said, "I don't want
     to wear my boots today." I told her that there was snow on the
     ground. She said, "I don't like boots." Then I thought about how
     we've talked here in therapy about the feeling that we "should" do
     something. So I said, "Actually, I guess you really don't have to, but if
     you don't, your feet will get wet." She said, "I like my feet to get wet." I
     told her, "I don't like my feet to be wet. I like to wear my boots, but if
     you don't mind your feet being wet, then I guess you don't need to
     wear your boots." She said, "Okay." She started out the door without
     them and then she came back in, saying she had decided to wear her
     boots, and she put them on.
          We are just so inundated with these shoulds, like, "Your room
     should be neat." It took me a long time to give up that one. Right now
     at this point in my life, I feel that there is nothing more important than
     allowing my children to know what their own feelings are rather than
     telling them that they should or should not behave in a certain way. I
     can point out possible consequences of what they do, but I also
     acknowledge that they may not care about those consequences in the
     same way that I do. If they are not burdened with a should, they can
     do something and learn from it. Then they won't have this big hangup

that they did the wrong thing. If my daughter catches a cold from going without her boots, it doesn't seem like a big thing.

T: Do your children respond differently since you've adopted this way of relating to them?

C: Yes, I think so. One day my daughter said "That is just your opinion" to a friend of hers. It gives them a certain amount of freedom, and they can tell me what they think or feel. It works out good in my family to say, "It's just your opinion," and it's not the almighty word that is being passed along. They can disagree with it. I might make them do it my way anyway, but at least they are free to know they don't always have to do it my way or think the way I do.

The emphasis on self-responsibility in yoga therapy extends to the therapist as well. While a physician who follows the medical model assumes responsibility for curing the patient, he may take little responsibility for his own physical, psychological, or spiritual well-being. In the same way that a mechanic's ulcers or obesity have little effect on his ability to fix an engine, in the medical model the physician's well-being or lack of it is considered to be irrelevant to his ability to operate on his patients or to prescribe for them. He need simply apply the techniques he has learned. He may give "sound medical advice" about diet, smoking, exercise, and so on, whether he himself follows the advice or not. This contrasts with yoga therapy, where the principle "Physician, heal thyself" is of primary importance. Jung was in agreement with this perspective. He unequivocally asserted that

> analytical psychology requires the counter-application to the doctor himself of whatever system is believed in—and moreover with the same relentlessness, consistency, and perseverance with which the doctor applies it to the patient.
>
> . . . The demand . . . that the doctor must change himself if he is to become capable of changing his patient, is . . . a rather unpopular one. . . . because it is sometimes exceedingly painful to live up to everything one expects of one's patient.[4]

The Role of Modeling

While imitation as a means of learning is given little importance in modern psychology, in other cultures modeling has been regarded as an extremely important mode of learning. For example, the Ramayana, an ancient epic of India, gives little in the way of direct instruction. Rather it teaches through the examples of the characters in the epic. In describing Rama, the hero of the epic, the Ramayana tells us: "Whatever he did he ennobled by the way he did it." Rama and his wife, Sita, were exemplars for the entire society to emulate. The Bhagavad Gita directly states that a good role model is essential. Krishna, the enlightened teacher who is free from all desire and the need to act on his own behalf, tells Arjuna, his disciple:

> In the actions of the best men others find their rule of action. The path that a great man follows becomes a guide to the world.
>
> I have no work to do in all the worlds. . . . I have nothing to obtain, because I have all. And yet I work.
>
> If I was not bound to action, . . . men . . . would follow my path of inaction.
>
> If ever my work had an end, . . . confusion would reign. . . .[5]

In yoga therapy, the relationship between the teacher and the student takes precedence over the teaching of mechanical procedures, abstract content, and behavioral prescriptions. When content is taught, it is within the context of a relationship, and what is conveyed by the relationship is considered to be more important than the content. Likewise in yoga therapy, the presence and way of being of the therapist plays a greater role in influencing the client than the content of what the therapist says.

Some of the most enlightening examples of the way in which teaching occurs through imitation and of the power that ensues when verbal instructions are congruent with the expression of one's entire being are found in the life of Mahatma Gandhi. Gandhi did not advocate anything that he did not practice himself; he always experimented on himself and found what the results would be before he taught anything to another person. The story is told that one day a mother brought her child to Gandhi and informed him that the child was eating a great deal of sugar. She said to Gandhi, "Please tell my child that sugar is harmful and that he should stop eating it. He won't listen to anyone else, but he respects you so much that he will listen to you." Gandhi thought for a moment and said, "Bring your child back in two weeks and I will talk to him." The mother and child lived far away and the mother was annoyed that they would have to make the long trip a second time. But she wanted the child to stop eating sugar, so she agreed. When they returned two weeks later, Gandhi simply told the child that sugar is bad for one's health and that he should not eat it. The mother was grateful, but her annoyance grew. She asked, "Why did you have us come all this way again?" Gandhi replied, "Two weeks ago, I was still eating sugar."

Self-Acceptance

The approach of the yoga therapist in working with behavior change may be straightforward. The therapist may recommend that the client undertake specific practices that lead to more functional behavior. But many clients do not respond to this direct approach. Although they may say they are highly motivated to change, they fail to practice new routines on a regular basis, if at all.

A client's thwarting of the goals of therapy, his reluctance, unwillingness, or inability to follow the therapist's guidelines or pre-scriptions, is labeled "resistance" by many psychotherapists. In physics, the term resistance refers to a force that tends to oppose or retard motion. Freud adopted this concept and applied it to what he believed is the ego's opposition to the recall of unpleasant experiences. Subsequently, the use of this term broadened. The term is now used to indicate that the client is resisting the process of change: "Resistance may vary from rejection of counseling and overt antagonism, on the one hand, to subtle forms, such as hesitation and inattention, on the other. Clients may say: 'I know what I want to say, but I can't say it'; 'I'll have to leave early today since I want to study for a test'; 'I don't think that applies in my case'; 'I'm sorry I'm late, but I almost forgot about our interviews'; 'I thought you were supposed to be the expert.'"[6] The use of the term "resistance" reflects the egocentric perspective of the therapist who has, singly or with the client, defined a goal and views the client as not carrying out his part in attaining that goal. The client's behavior is considered to be defensive.

From a less egocentric perspective, however, one might say that it is the therapist who is resisting the client, for the therapist is neglecting to consider that the client may not actually be failing to progress toward the client's real goal. The client's goal may simply be different from what was stated verbally, agreed upon, or expected by the therapist. The therapist is not taking into full account all that lies behind the client's agreement to carry out a task and his subsequent unwillingness or seeming inability or failure to do so. From this perspective, resistance is a two-person game that the therapist helps to create. The payoff is that the therapist can blame the client for not changing, while the client concludes that the therapist must be incompetent, since the therapist is not bringing about an alleviation of his symptoms. If the client's goal is to defeat the therapist, he may be quite successful.

Seen in a more positive way, it may be important to the client to establish his independence and autonomy by failing to carry out prescribed behavior. If the therapist looks behind the verbal contract to the unspoken interchange, he is likely to discover that these are initially quite at odds with one another, and that they merge only when the therapeutic process has succeeded. If the therapist tunes into, deciphers, and responds to the unspoken dialogue and to the client's frame of reference, he may view the client's behavior not as resistance to growth, but an expression of his attempt to grow.

From this perspective, the client is never resisting; he is always in the process of growth. If the therapist helps the client become aware of the way in which his attitude or behavior is part of the growth process, he can avoid the stalemates that often occur by labeling behavior as resistance. The client enters therapy complaining of symptoms or qualities within himself that he would like to eliminate. The yoga therapist, however, may help the client to experience their positive value. For attempting to eliminate a quality perpetuates it, whereas recognizing its value helps one to become less preoccupied with or fixed upon that quality and allows him to move on.

What is labeled resistance is actually the externalization of an inner conflict that the client experiences between two aspects of himself. One part of the client makes a demand, and another part asserts itself against the demand. It is important that the therapist not become aligned with either side, that he maintain a neutral position with regard to all polarizations within the client. If the therapist feels that the client is resisting him, it is because the therapist has aligned himself with one side of a polarity. Resistance is an illusion. Demands necessarily create resistance. Resistance dissolves to the extent that demands are given up.

As long as the client focuses on what he defines as unacceptable feelings, thoughts, and actions, and attempts to eradicate them, he creates a tug-of-war within himself between the "good" or judgmental part of himself that demands change and the part that is resisting being eliminated. The energy on each side of the polarity is equally matched, so neither side can ultimately win. One side may temporarily overcome the other, as when an obese client refrains from eating sweets for a week. But the temporarily subdued side will sooner or later gain its revenge; the contrary part will eventually reassert itself and become dominant: the client will one day call his therapist to tell him that he has just eaten four chocolate bars and a large piece of cake. A therapist who identifies with one side of the client's internal battle will inevitably be disappointed. The therapist may become dejected as a result of his imagined failure, or he may take out his frustration on the client.

Paradoxical interventions can be extremely valuable in helping the client and therapist out of these deadlocks. While such interventions, which involve the encouragement of symptomatic behavior, have found increasing use in modern psychotherapy, they are not a new discovery. They have long been used in spiritual traditions to lead students out of the stalemates they create for themselves. The following anecdote from the life of Rabbi Wolfe of Zbaraj from the Hasidic tradition exemplifies "the acceptance of symptomatic behavior, with a view toward the creation of a context where change is possible."[7]

> People came to him to denounce some Jews who were playing cards late into the night.
> "And you want me to condemn them?" he cried out. "Why me? And in the name of what? And for what crime? They stay up late? It's a good thing to resist sleep! They concentrate on the game. That is good too! Sooner or later they will give up card-playing—what will remain is a discipline of body and mind. And this time they will place it in the service of God! Why then should I condemn them?"[8]

This story illustrates the way in which "the therapeutic paradox accepts the symptomatic behavior, but creates a context within which it can be put to more productive ends. It draws on the client's . . . strengths, so that when the problem-supporting context is transcended, these strengths remain to be utilized in the service of growth."[9]

In Zen Buddhism, paradox is used in a different way. In the Zen tradition the spiritual guide may use a koan to encourage the student to exaggerate symptomatic behavior—in this case, his rationalistic reasoning process—until the student becomes so frustrated that he experiences a breakdown in that framework, and a new mode of consciousness emerges. The koan is "a mental exercise whose absurdity or paradoxical nature blocks the faculty of rational comprehension and thereby makes it fail. What then enters into consciousness is an awareness of one's world image precisely as *an image* of reality and not reality *itself.* Indeed, there is reason to assume that the so-called mystical experience occurs when . . . we manage to leave . . . our world image and for a fleeting moment succeed in seeing it 'from the outside' and thus in its relativity."[10]

Akido and other Eastern martial arts use a similar principle. In these arts, instead of opposing the force of an attack with a counterforce, one uses the energy and momentum of one's opponent, turning the opponent's own force against him. One may accentuate the thrust of the opponent's attack and thereby help it to complete itself in a way that defeats its antagonistic purpose. One continues to turn the aggressor's thrusts back against the aggressor until the attacker surrenders, defeated by his own efforts.

In psychology, if the therapist creates expectations or opposes the client's "resistance," the client and therapist may become locked into a tug-of-war. But if instead the therapist aligns himself with the antagonistic or "resistive" client, the client's position as antagonist becomes untenable. If the client wishes to continue as an opponent to the therapist who is encouraging "resistance," he must adopt a new position—one that is identified with growth. Or the client may give up the game and arrive at a more spontaneous way of relating and being, which is not based on one-upmanship. In either case, the client must change.

The therapist, for instance, may find that the client will not carry out behavioral prescriptions. Instead, the client attempts to set up a power struggle in which the therapist is supposed to get the client to change or improve, while the client's role is to maintain his symptoms or get worse. In such a situation the yoga therapist may direct the client to increase his symptomatic behavior. In one case, an anorexic client was given weekly prescriptions for behavior change, but they were not directly related to eating. This was done in order to determine how she would respond to directions. The client would return each week and report that she had been unable to follow through on the instructions. The therapist then told her that she was too heavy, and agreed with her that food is repulsive and that she should not force herself to eat. He suggested that she go on a fast and lose a minimum of one pound in each successive week. He continued to express his disappointment as the client returned each week to report a slight increase in weight.

The yoga therapist may join in the client's perspective and up the ante. At a superficial level it may seem that he is not taking the client seriously, that he is discounting or mocking the client, but actually it is the client's ploy or the limiting role with which the client identifies that the therapist does not take seriously. The therapist's unwillingness to be involved in the transaction that the client is attempting to set up may lead to more intimate and genuine sharing between client and therapist.

One client who consistently did not follow his therapist's prescriptions enjoyed giving lengthy and detailed descriptions of his inability to overcome his problems. The therapist then made a show of beginning to record their sessions, telling the client that he was writing a book on failures in psychotherapy and that the client was an excellent case upon which to base his book. Furthermore, whenever the client began complaining about his lack of success, the therapist would indicate for the tape recorder that this was a section of the therapy session to be transcribed for his book. As the client's complaints diminished and he instead began to describe positive changes in his life, the therapist began to complain that all the time and effort he had spent in collecting material for his book had been wasted. After a time, the client improved considerably and began giving credit for his improvement to all of the people who he said had helped him. The therapist then complained that he expected to receive all the credit and that furthermore he expected the client to go around telling everyone else how much he had been helped by the therapist. The client soon began asserting that he himself was responsible for his own behavior, and not others.

The yoga therapist may express the client's negativity or doubt in an accentuated or exaggerated way, or he may encourage the client to exaggerate or advertise his plight to others. One client reported that he felt burdened with obligations, as though he were always carrying a heavy weight on his shoulders. He expected the therapist to make suggestions about how he might be relieved of his burden, but instead the therapist encouraged him to accept and pay greater attention to his experience, even to make it worse. The following interchange took place:

C: I let the load build unconsciously without feeling it at all for a while, and then gradually I just begin to feel worse and worse without realizing why. Finally, I feel so miserable that I say, "All right, what's the matter?" or I'll be rude or feel like I want to withdraw.

T: I had a crazy notion of you getting some canned food and taking the labels off and then relabeling them with your burdens, like "taking care of the dog," "getting my papers done for school," and so on. Then you can put the tin cans into a sack and carry them on your back. Your sense of being burdened and the burdens themselves would be more obvious to you. You could really feel the weight of those burdens.

C: Everyone would know then.

T: Not necessarily. The cans would be inside the sack, so people would just know you're carrying something.

C: I could set them out in front of me and just stare at them, or I could measure the weight; I'd know if they were growing.

T: Yes, you could actually add or subtract weight as your burdens change.

C: It would drive home the point. I guess I could keep in the back seat of my car a box of canned, prepackaged, unspecified burdens of various sizes—one-pound, two-pound, three-pound cans—and I could label them as needed. Well, that would sure bring it home to me. It's such a senseless pattern. It's like carrying around a bag that I don't have to carry around simply because I got out of the awareness of carrying it. I forget I'm carrying it around.

The yoga therapist may lead the client to side with the unwanted part of himself, and he may also encourage the client to side with another

person who is antagonistic to the client. Clients often describe problematic relationships with parents or with others who they find demeaning and disrespectful. Some clients have sought love and acceptance
from a parent for years on end, but each contact brings simply another
rebuke, to which the client responds by feeling dejected, inadequate, or
angry. This pattern is repeated again and again. The client envisions no
alternatives except to try once more to win his parent's love. In such
situations the yoga therapist may help the client to respond to the parent
much in the same way that an akido master deals with someone who is
trying to be an adversary. If a woman is criticized by her mother each time
they speak on the phone, the therapist may suggest that she anticipate her
mother's criticism and side with her. The daughter may be instructed to
begin the conversation by criticizing herself. In this way she steals the
mother's thunder. She takes control of her mother's anticipated thrust
and completes it in a way that is not painful to herself. Furthermore, since
the daughter is now occupying her mother's position, her mother has little
choice but to give her daughter the support that she had been seeking all
along.

　　In dealing with inner conflicts, the therapist may encourage the
client to accept and appreciate both sides rather than identifying with one
and rejecting the other. One client who had been so encouraged reviewed
her recent therapy sessions in the following words:

> A month ago, we talked about my ambivalence about money.
> You suggested that I approach it by setting aside one or two days a
> week for dealing extensively with money—paying my bills, studying
> about investments, and so on—and another day or two a week for
> avoiding money completely. I realized that my tendency was to try to
> force myself to choose between two opposite inclinations rather than
> making room for both. I had a flash of intuition: I perceived that
> behind your suggestion was the idea of respect—respect for all the
> different sides of myself.
>
> 　　I tried to imagine what it might be like to exercise this kind of
> respect in my life, and the first thing that popped into my mind was:
> sweets. My craving for sweets has always been one of the things I
> really dislike in myself, not only because it contributes to my being

overweight, but also because it conflicts with my interest in good nutrition. And yet it always seemed that the more I resisted it, the more it tried to take me over. I wondered if it would be possible to respect the sweets craving and allow it expression rather than being at war with it. So I determined to try it out.

For about two weeks, I ate good meals for breakfast and lunch. Then for dinner, I ate only sweets—as much as I wanted. It became a great game to find the most gooey, delicious, high-calorie extravaganzas available. Chocolate nut brownies with thick frosting became my favorite, so the game became finding the best brownie in the city. Eventually, I began to crave good food with my sweets dinner. So I started eating protein and vegetables at dinner, and sweets didn't fight back. I began eating fewer sweets overall, but always made sure to set aside at least one time during the day that was sweets time. Right now, I am satisfied with a dish of ice cream after lunch, along with an occasional goodie at other times when the idea of sweets jumps up and demands attention. I don't spend nearly as much time and energy as I did before either thinking about what sweets to get or trying to resist the urge.

In order to allow the client this sort of freedom and acceptance, the therapist must remain a neutral witness, free from attachments to either side of the polarity with which the client is struggling at the moment. He may attempt to clarify the struggle that the client is putting himself through, but he remains a model of one who has disengaged from identification with polarities and their ensuing dramas.

If a client assumes that he has failed at something and then generalizes and labels himself a failure, he creates and will remain caught in a vicious cycle. Since he already sees himself as a failure, he will lack the self-confidence and enthusiasm to succeed, and so is bound to fail at any new venture. If the therapist encourages him to be a success, he will fail at that as well, and the therapist will inevitably experience disappointment. But the yoga therapist is likely to respond to such a client by defining him as successful no matter what he does. The yoga therapist helps the client to adopt this new perspective and thereby replace the negative cycle with a positive one. Ultimately he will lead the client beyond the polarity of success and failure.* From the monistic perspective, polarities are all considered to be illusory. Resistance/compliance, success/failure, and so on are illusory conceptions that make no sense from the monistic point of view. How can one fail when every experience is part of the process of awakening to one's full nature? With this view, the yoga therapist may confront his client's illusions. Here is an example of such a confrontation:

C: I'm afraid of failure.

T: What do you mean by failure?

C: I failed at my marriage.

T: I don't understand the word failure; that word doesn't make any sense to me. Haven't you learned anything from that relationship? Haven't you grown from it?

C: Well, I got a divorce.

T: Okay, but why do you call divorce a failure? You have a preconceived notion of the way it's supposed to be and when it doesn't turn out that way, you call it failure. Then you spend your time blaming yourself, feeling guilty, and programming yourself to feel incapable rather than productive. What if you didn't create that gap, but accepted yourself as you are? In my mind, there is no such thing as a failure.

The way I see it, you grew to the extent that you were able to in that experience; you learned what you were ready to learn. It's true you didn't come close to an ideal relationship, but then you weren't ready for an ideal relationship. Rather than accepting where you were, your limitations and their consequences, you deny the reality. You have an ideal which you project onto yourself and the relationship, and then when you don't measure up to the ideal, you call yourself a failure. What an interesting plot! It would seem to me that you and your ex-wife are still each learning what you are capable of learning from each other, whether you are divorced or living together.

From the perspective of unitary thought, what was viewed as problematic turns out not to be a problem at all, that is, the situation is viewed in a positive way.

---

*If a client were identified with being successful, the yoga therapist would also challenge this limited identification, pointing out the ways in which this self-definition does not apply. His aim would be to lead the client beyond identification with either end of the polarity.

As with a Chinese finger lock, the more one struggles, the more he becomes entrapped. Paradoxically, when one accepts himself, he becomes more fluid, and begins to change. The way out of this client's conflict is not to struggle to become a success, but to accept all aspects of himself. The ultimate goal in this case is to transcend the polarized conception of success and failure.

Many people mistakenly think that the attainment of some goal will lead to self-acceptance and acceptance from others, but acceptance based on attainments is superficial and ultimately disappointing. One really wants to be accepted and loved unconditionally for what he is underneath the masks he wears. The search for acceptance underlies everything that one seeks in life. All the melodramas in which a person becomes entangled—such as those based on identification with success and failure, and good and bad—involve a lack of acceptance by oneself and others.

To the extent that the therapist truly accepts himself, he is able to model self-acceptance and to accept his client. All psychotherapeutic methods are insignificant in comparison with the expression of unconditional acceptance. In fact, all interventions are primarily the means for the therapist to express or deny acceptance. To the extent that the therapist can express and the client can experience unconditional acceptance, growth and healing take place; to the extent that acceptance by the therapist is lacking, growth and healing are restricted.

The client comes to therapy disowning the parts of himself that he considers unacceptable. He believes that those unacceptable aspects of himself create his suffering, but it is actually his nonacceptance and disowning of aspects of himself that create all the melodramas and unhappiness in his life. When one accepts the unwanted parts of himself, they cease to dominate him. The yoga therapist, therefore, encourages the client to acknowledge all aspects of himself. The following client is beginning to see how helpful self-acceptance is:

C: I'm trembling, and it's embarrassing.
T: I wonder what it would be like if you accepted the trembling as part of yourself, instead of trying to fight it.
C: You said that to me once before, about accepting emotions, when I feel intensely angry toward my daughter. At first when you said it, I

thought, "Accept *that*? I can't accept that. That is a really despicable part of me." I've thought about it a whole lot since then and what a hard time I do have accepting aspects of myself that I don't like. I know that is what meditation is all about, letting go completely and not trying to be anything. It is so utterly simple and then at the same time it's so fantastic, so profound.

Leading one to accept all parts of himself does not mean encouraging him to act them all out—in fact, acceptance has quite the opposite effect. When portions of oneself are not accepted, a melodrama ensues in which the unwanted part is given a leading role. The unconscious acts out the unwanted part, or one projects it onto others while the conscious mind plays the complementary role. But when one befriends the unwanted aspect, both sides give up the charge which is created between them and sustained by their artificial separation and polarization. The energy that had been tied up in maintaining the polarity is then freed, and the person experiences increased vitality, inner joy, and unity. Here is an example:

C: All I've wanted to do all my life was to live up to my mother's expectations. I've always tried to be what she wanted me to be. But when I accomplished something my mother wanted, I didn't feel any different. For instance, I didn't feel any more worthy for being on the football team, and so I had to go and do something else. I wondered, What am I going to do next to get that feeling of being worthy? Then I would find a new activity. But I never felt worthy within myself. My worthiness always had to come from some accomplishment, and even then there wasn't a real sense of self-worth inside—just a very temporary feeling of having accomplished something outwardly. I've never really felt worthy, and so I've always been trying to do things to feel worthy.

T: What would it be like to accept being unworthy, to feel, I'm unworthy and that's okay. I don't have to become worthy.

C: [After a long pause] It's a relaxing thought. If I could just relax and say that it's okay. It's like the game is over; I can just sit back and relax. I can feel that! What a relief! That is a real pleasant thought. I don't have to say anything or defend myself or be better than you or be anything else.

T: You seem different.

C: I can just settle into that thought. It's like a reprieve. It feels so good. I wonder how long I could be unworthy.

T: How long?

C: Would it bother me? I'm looking at it like a vacation.

T: How about if you accept your unworthiness for a week and then reevaluate it? I wonder if you could feel unworthy and let the people around you know that you are unworthy.

C: I don't know how I could do that. I spend too much time showing them that I am worthy. How could I do that?

T: How about wearing a sign that says "I am unworthy."

C: Then I would have to explain to everyone why I'm so unworthy. The people at the office would think that I'm crazier than a loon, and that sign is the final proof. They would probably insist that I wasn't unworthy. I would say to them, "You think that I'm worthy, but I'm not. I've been feeling unworthy for years and now that I'm finally content with that feeling, you're trying to ruin it." That's very interesting. I might even get to feeling worthy. If I accept my unworthiness, there won't be anything to feel unworthy about, so I'll feel worthy.

A week later, this client returned to say:

What I was viewing as a flaw and a disturbing thing turned out to be something entirely different. The minute that I quit battling it and was willing to just let it be as it is, the most remarkable thing happened. My lifelong foe turns out to be my long-lost brother. I can throw off my armor and embrace it. It was a really remarkable and exuberant experience when its clothes came off and it wasn't what I thought it would look like at all.

In such ways the yoga therapist may use paradoxical interventions to help a client get in touch with and accept unwanted aspects of himself. He may instruct the client to accept, advertise, or increase the very behavior that the client wishes to eliminate. This type of intervention may loosen the hold that a particular polarity has over the client. Here is another example of such a strategy:

C: No matter what I accomplish, there is still that image down deep of being second-class, and I don't know how to get rid of it.

T: I wonder if the first step might be to accept it. You say that you've been trying to hide it.

C: Accept it? I don't want to be second-class.

T: Perhaps you could become more aware of how you feel second-class in various situations. Maybe each day you could deliberately do something that is second-class. Let someone know that you are second-class and then study that.

C: What?

T: How about eating the leftovers?

C: I usually do eat after everyone else, and I get the leftovers.

T: You could consciously do one extra thing every day that you consider second-class.

C: Any other suggestions?

T: Maybe there is even third-class. You might explore being third-class.

The yoga therapist encourages the client to befriend the unwanted aspects of himself and to recognize the useful function that they serve. Whereas the medical model focuses on the suppression of symptoms, in yoga therapy one's suffering is the open door that can lead to significant growth. It is the signal that something is wrong and a clue to the source of the disturbance. If the signal is successfully suppressed, the growth process will be delayed until the signal erupts again, perhaps with greater force or in another aspect of one's physical or mental functioning.

If one's doorbell rings, he usually answers the door; he does not cut the wires to stop the bell from ringing. However, in dealing with signals from within, many people try to interrupt the signal, so the message that something is wrong does not get through. For example, if a person has a headache, he takes aspirin so that the pain that is signaling that he needs to slow down, or that he has eaten overly rich foods, or that he has made himself tense and worried, no longer reaches consciousness. As a result, he never deals with or corrects the underlying disturbance. Perhaps other symptoms will appear, such as shakiness or heartburn. If those are also repeatedly treated with symptom-suppressive drugs, the underlying problem will finally express itself in the form of a more dramatic signal, such as a heart attack, which leaves increased structural damage. Now the message "Change your lifestyle, the way you deal with your body, your work, your relationships" gets through for a short while, until the palliative effects of pharmaceutical agents again establish a false sense of reassurance, and one falls back into the old habits.

By contrast, if one works with a yoga therapist, he will be encouraged early on to pay greater attention to his suffering rather than avoiding it, to become aware of the situations and inner attitudes that bring on the suffering, and to change those aspects of himself that lead to suffering. From a yogic perspective, all suffering is regarded as having a positive, valuable function. When faced directly, pain and suffering can be seen as the greatest of blessings. Paying attention to pain and tracing it to its source makes one aware of areas of existence that need to be attended to. One grows little from outward success, for a person falsely clings to success as a source of security, and as a result becomes stagnant. On the other hand, suffering, when acknowledged and traced to its source, creates the greatest opportunity for growth. The presence of pain motivates one to correct imbalances within himself and in his relationship to his environment.

This is not to say, of course, that it is necessary or advisable to seek out suffering. Clearly, a prime goal in life and the purpose of all therapy and of yoga is to eliminate suffering. But this cannot be achieved through suppression or denial and subsequent displacement. Suffering can be eliminated only by becoming fully aware of what the pain is signaling. The message that pain bears is often so surprising or startling to our limited ego-consciousness that we have extreme difficulty comprehending where the message originates and what it is actually saying, and so we do not know how to respond to the distress we are experiencing. Only by truly understanding the nature and source of suffering, and acting on that understanding, can we eliminate suffering from our lives.

Frequently it is our petty ego, our unnecessarily delimited self-definition, that is the source of pain. Our ego's refusal to accept certain aspects of experience causes us to feel that we are suffering. By changing our attitude, by viewing things in a different light, by accepting the world as it is, we eliminate our distress. For ultimately it is not life that needs to be changed, it is only our attitude. A situation or experience that we have been viewing solely as a source of misery can, by a change of attitude, come to be seen as something positive and good. The following two case histories help to illustrate this principle.

The first involves a middle-aged man who was a professional violinist and who had had his arm crushed by an automobile that struck him as he was crossing the street. He was depressed and embittered when he consulted the therapist a few months later. He could not understand why such a fate would befall him. During the first interview, the therapist asked him whether anything positive might result from the accident. The client questioned how the therapist could entertain such an absurd notion. As the sessions continued, the therapist occasionally introduced similar questions about the positive changes that might come about as a result of the injury. The client gradually began to comment on the leisure time he now had to pursue neglected interests, in contrast to the hectic pace of his life before the accident. As therapy progressed, he began to recognize that his life had been stagnant for a number of years. He had long fantasized about moving to a warmer climate and beginning a new line of work, and he recognized that now he was in a better position to make those changes. He began taking exploratory trips to the South and made plans to settle there. Six months after the start of therapy, he acknowledged that despite the pain and suffering it had caused him, the accident had led to significant growth in his life, and indeed was one of the best things that had happened to him in years.

The second client was a lawyer who began therapy just after he had been fired for embezzling money from his firm. He sobbed during the therapy hour as he described his fear that his career was ruined. Getting caught embezzling seemed to him to be the worst thing that ever could happen to him. During the first few weeks of therapy he explored his motivations for embezzling and reported that ever since he was a teenager he had wanted recognition from his father, who was a highly successful businessman. Each time he had accomplished something, he had turned to his father for acknowledgment, but his father always found fault with what his son did. The son thought that if he showed his father how successful he was by having an expensive house and car and other costly possessions, he would finally win his father's approval.

This client began to realize how much significance he was giving to his father's opinion of him in many aspects of his life, even in choosing a mate. In further sessions he began to explore other avenues for experiencing that he was lovable and competent. Gradually he began to divest his father of the power and authority he had been giving him. He came to recognize that being caught embezzling was a turning point in his life, for had he not been caught he would have gone on living with the same desperation. But being fired freed him from repeatedly seeking his father's approval. He even began to recognize ways in which he had made it quite easy for others to discover his theft, as though he had deliberately designed the course of events as a way out of his predicament.

These two situations illustrate how a situation or experience that is initially regarded as negative can be turned into a positive force in one's life by understanding its value and the potential it has for helping one to grow. Yoga psychology takes this perspective in regard to any situation, no matter how awful it may initially seem. Each situation is an opportunity for one to make great strides in his growth toward improved interaction, transcendence of ego-identification, and a more comprehensive consciousness.

The Experiential Basis of Yoga Therapy

The client in therapy ordinarily identifies with the thoughts and feelings he experiences during the therapy hour; he becomes swept up in the dramas that his thoughts and emotions create. He takes himself all too seriously, losing all sense of playfulness and joy. He may wallow in complaints, disappointments, fears, or self-deprecation. The yoga therapist is a neutral witness to the postures of the client and the melodramas in which the client is entangled. He encourages the client to disengage from the melodramas and to give up his posturing, so that together they can discover what lies behind the role and the character that the client is assuming.

The client expects the therapist to take his melodramas seriously. When instead the yoga therapist remains lighthearted or amplifies and exaggerates the client's predicament, the client may complain that the therapist is making fun of him. The yoga therapist may acknowledge that, in fact, he does not take as very real or exciting the client's attempt to gain sympathy and his feigning ineptness, confusion, or victimization. There is something beneath all the client's acts, however, that he does take very seriously. He is waiting patiently to share at a more intimate level than is possible when the client remains identified with a particular role.

At times the therapist may be more than a witness. He may choose to be playful, to cajole, or to share his own fantasies and craziness. The therapist thereby helps the client to value the client's own "craziness." The following dialogue between a therapist and a client who was himself a graduate student in psychology illustrates the way in which the yoga therapist may playfully challenge the client's assumptions. This may initially frustrate the client who is trying to make the world fit his assumptions, but eventually such dialogues may lead the client to break out of his limited perspective and become more spontaneous and alive.

C: The first session was my gripe session and this is my second session. Let's get into prescriptions. Let's spend this session more directed so that I can walk out of here and feel some kind of direction that is different or unique. I want to know what you can do for me.

T: I think that the question is: What can you do for you?

C: Okay, fine, I see that, but can you tell me some things about myself? In lectures you talk about chakras and energies and things like that. Can you make some interpretations of my behavior or personality makeup?

T: How would that help you?

C: I'd then have more of an understanding about myself; I would know what I need to work on.

T: It seems you know a lot conceptually already.

C: I guess I need to confirm my suspicions about myself. You don't give at all. You answer questions with questions, and you do a good job of getting me frustrated.

T: Do you feel frustrated?

C: I went to this other therapist and he made an interpretation about my problems and the flow of energy in my body.

T: How did that help you?

C: I can keep my mind focused on my personality structure and on what I do and how I do it in terms of my personality type.

T: What type do you want to be? If you had a diagnostic label, you wouldn't have to be yourself. You could say, "What can I do? I'm this particular way, and that's simply the way I am."

C: Then I would deal with my limitations more.

T: Exactly. That's what I'm saying. But maybe you don't have limitations.

C: I don't?

T: Just the ones that you impose upon yourself in your fantasies.

C: So how do I change? What will change me? How will I change myself?

T: How do you want to change yourself?

C: I want to hear you talk, to feel like I'm getting my money's worth.

T: I already gave you more than your money's worth.

C: Why do you say that?

T: Your money isn't worth that much. It's not worth as much as you are.

C: How much am I worth?

T: What do you think?

C: I don't know. I guess that is what I am trying to discover. Well, if I were a therapist, I would have something in mind for my patient; I would have some general precept for what was going on.

T: Maybe I'm just trying to drive you crazy. Maybe that's all there is to it.

At times the therapist may be playful; at other times, he may assume a more serious attitude toward the client, but he does not become identified with the role of helper or teacher or adopt a pose of solemnity. If a client says the opposite of what he means, it is sometimes necessary for the therapist to do the same, so that they can get together and realize that they understand and accept one another. Some of the most meaningful moments in therapy occur when client and therapist are able to share their craziness.

The heart of yoga therapy consists of a Socratic-like dialogue, a meeting between two human beings. The yoga therapist has oriented his life around the monistic perspective, while the client is operating from a different model of the universe. The client's assumptions lead him to experience addictions, aversions, and conflicts within and between himself and others, as well as emotional turmoil, insecurity, and lack of clarity about the meaning and purpose of his life.

The yoga therapist does not base his response upon theories or methods he has learned secondhand from books; rather, he uses his own experience gained in dealing with and overcoming suffering in his own life. He does not try to impart his experience by didactic teaching; instead, he opens himself to take in and respond to the experiences of the client. In this process the client will sometimes describe experiences that are foreign to the therapist, not because the therapist is unfamiliar with those experiences, but because they grow out of an entirely different set of assumptions than those from which the therapist functions. The therapist seeks to comprehend what the client is saying in terms of his (the therapist's) model, but finds that it just does not fit. As a result, he may stop the client in midsentence, confronting him with his duplicity. For example, a client will typically describe his behavior with such expressions as "I should," "I have to," "I can't," and "I'll try." These words reflect an inner split between one part of him that is making a demand and another part that is reacting to the demand. This reaction may take the form of compliance, resistance, feigned compliance, panic, fear, immobility, or some other response.

Concepts like "I should," "I have to," and so on are not part of the world view of a therapist functioning from a monistic perspective. They make absolutely no sense to him, so he lets the client know this. He encourages the client to explain what he means by such verbalizations, for they do not exist in any dictionary written from the therapist's perspective. The therapist may say to the client, "What do you mean by saying 'I'll try'? That seems dishonest. To me, trying implies merely making a show of effort. It is a posture of nonsuccess. Is trying something that you do in order to remain as you are?"

On the other hand, the yoga therapist remains open to the client's phenomenology rather than automatically interpreting the client's experience according to a preordained framework. He is willing to let go of any preconceptions, including those formulated in this book, in the face of the client's experience. While fully acknowledging the client's experience, the therapist also remains sensitive to and accepting of his own experience. The therapist does not allow himself to become identified with the client's scenario and to take the role that the client has scripted for him. The yoga therapist may confront the client if he experiences attempts by the client to confuse, mislead, or distract him, or if he experiences a diminution in spontaneity or directness in their relationship. The therapist's challenges to a client are based not so much on conception as on his own experience. Though he may verbalize his experience within a conceptual framework, his experience of himself and the client is primary.

Therapists like to go to workshops to learn methods and techniques, but these are actually superfluous in psychotherapy. If one is living from the perspective of the dualistic or monistic paradigm, all techniques will inevitably evolve out of the assumptions of that paradigm and out of the therapist's experiences. He need not learn methods developed by another therapist.

To the extent that the therapist is genuinely self-accepting, he will provide an environment in which the client can discover self-acceptance. Techniques often camouflage and create diversions to hide the therapist's lack of self-acceptance. The self-accepting therapist is more likely to respond with spontaneity and innovation in his encounter with a client, forging a unique intervention that is suited to the moment rather than rummaging through an old bag of tricks.

The client typically enters therapy with certain assumptions about himself and his life. These may include:

1. Someone or something else is responsible for my condition and circumstances.
2. Somewhere out there in the world is what I need to be happy.
3. I want something different from what I am getting.
4. The predicament I am in is very important, serious, and real.
5. I *have* to do certain things, and I *should not* do other things.

To the yoga therapist, these assumptions are not valid. They are based on a frame of reference and logic that is foreign to him. It is as if the client were saying, "I walk on my head in the sky." The therapist tries to make sense out of what the client is saying. He asks, "What do you mean by that?" He may offer his own alternative assumptions to the client, not as truths to be believed, but as a different set of working hypotheses with which the client can experiment. Especially in the beginning, the assumptions of the therapist functioning from the nondual paradigm may well be antithetical to those of the client. The assumptions of the nondual therapist include:

1. I am fully responsible for my own condition and circumstances.
2. What I need to be happy is already here within myself.
3. I am getting exactly what I want, and when I begin wanting something different, I will get that.
4. Any predicament I seem to be in is self-created in order for me to learn to let go of addictions. If I let go, I will find that my perceived predicament is not so serious, important, or real, and I will begin to treat it in a playful way, which will open up all sorts of positive possibilities for responding to it.
5. I *choose* to do certain things. I *choose not* to do certain other things.

As the relationship develops, the client has the opportunity to encounter the assumptions of the therapist, to apply them to himself, and to observe their effects. The yoga therapist is not a guru or a fully enlightened being. He is merely another person seeking freedom from suffering and awareness of his true self. He offers what he has learned and invites the client to experiment with new attitudes toward himself and others.

The relationship is far from one-sided. The therapist who is open to what the client is experiencing may learn from the client as much as or more than the client learns from the therapist. Perhaps the client will also challenge the therapist's limiting assumptions. At times the client's model may be more conflict-free than that of the therapist. A client may present a way of experiencing that calls attention to the therapist's insensitivity or lack of awareness and points out an area in which the therapist has yet to grow. The yoga therapist opens himself to the client's wisdom and uses the meeting as a growing experience for himself. Clients may teach the therapist about compassion, fortitude, humility, serenity, and any number of other qualities that may not be well developed in the therapist. The therapist may often wonder who is teaching whom. He may hear words of wisdom and see expressions of admirable qualities that provide examples that help him grow. Even the less admirable qualities that the client expresses can make the therapist aware of the many facets of himself. The therapist often finds that the process of helping the client to deal effectively with his problems is also helping the therapist to deal effectively with his own.

Chapter Ten

The Collective Unconscious from the Yogic Perspective

Chakras and Archetypes

In helping a person to bring unconscious contents and modes of experience into awareness, yoga therapy includes but goes beyond the personal unconscious. It works extensively with a deeper layer of the unconscious, where universal archetypal themes have their play. This layer of the psyche, which Jung called the collective unconscious, plays a far greater role in motivating a person than does the personal unconscious.

Tantric philosophy and psychology offers a comprehensive model for understanding the archetypal themes around which human life revolves. This model refers to specific centers, each of which creates a unique mode of experience. These centers are called *chakras*. The English words "circle" and "circus" are derived from the Sanskrit word "chakra." A circus is a circular arena with tiers of seats in which public entertainment takes place. Similarly, each chakra is an area in which a particular form of entertainment or drama occurs. Typically, one is involved in the drama, but if one develops his powers of self-observation, it is possible to become a spectator of the grand show that occurs at each chakra. The word "circus" also refers to a circular area where many streets intersect. In the same way, each chakra is a center at which many forces intersect in a human being. Each chakra may be likened to the hub of a wheel, with spokes radiating outward from the center. The forces that radiate out from each chakra affect one's physical, emotional, and psychical functioning.[1]

Jung pointed out that

the *chakras* are symbols. They symbolize highly complex psychic facts which at the present moment we could not possibly express except in images. The *chakras* are therefore of great value to us because they represent a real effort to give a symbolic theory of the psyche. . . .

243

> . . . we are studying not just consciousness, but the totality of the psyche. The *chakras* . . . become a valuable guide for us in this obscure field. . . .
>
> . . . They are intuitions about the psyche as a whole, about its various conditions and possibilities.[2]

In the system of chakras, the archetypes that are considered primary are organized into an evolutionary hierarchy, ranging from those that are predominant in more primitive modes of experience to those that come to the fore only in the more highly developed modes of consciousness. The manner in which consciousness evolves through the archetypal modes of experience is reflected in both phylogenetic and ontogenetic development and in the structure and organization of the human organism. According to tantra, there are seven primary modes of consciousness, each quite distinct from the others. Each mode of consciousness has a corresponding physical center. The most primitive form of consciousness is related to energy and physical processes that take place at the root of the spinal cord. As consciousness evolves, it is localized in progressively higher centers along the spinal cord and brain, culminating in the seventh chakra at the crown of the head (see figure 1). Jung noted that "the chakras of the Tantric system correspond by and large to the regions where consciousness was earlier localized, *anahata* corresponding to the breast region, *manipura* to the abdominal region, *svadhistana* to the bladder region, and *visuddha* to the larynx and the speech-consciousness of modern man."[3]

There is a well-known story about a man who finds himself standing in front of two closed doors. Behind one door is a beautiful lady and behind the other, a tiger. The experience awaiting him behind one door is dramatically different from the experience awaiting him behind the other. Now imagine that a person is standing before seven closed doors. However, instead of the doors being all on one level, they are arranged one above the other, with a spiral staircase connecting the different levels. If the person were to open any one of the doors and enter the environment within, his experiences, his way of thinking, his emotional states, and his way of relating to others would be entirely different from what they would be were he to ascend or descend the staircase and cross the threshold of any other doorway. This is analogous to the different modes of consciousness of the seven chakras.

The Chakras

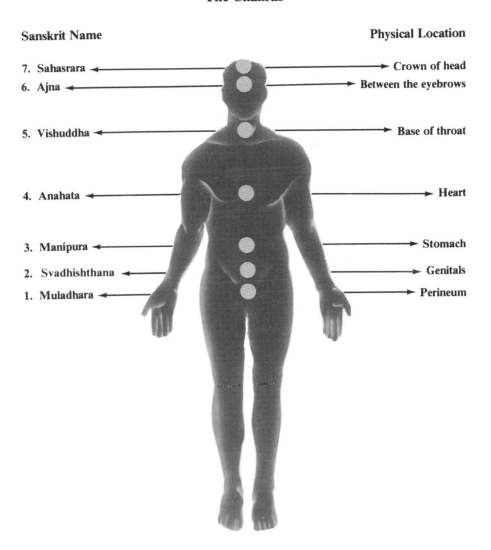

Sanskrit Name	Physical Location
7. Sahasrara	Crown of head
6. Ajna	Between the eyebrows
5. Vishuddha	Base of throat
4. Anahata	Heart
3. Manipura	Stomach
2. Svadhishthana	Genitals
1. Muladhara	Perineum

Figure 1

A similar metaphor is employed by the Pueblo Indians:

> There is a Pueblo myth according to which man was generated far down in the earth in a pitch black cave. After untold ages of dormant and absolutely dark worm-like existence, two heavenly messengers came down to them and planted all the plants. And finally a sort of cane grew up which was jointed like a ladder and long enough to go through the opening in the roof, and so mankind could climb up and reach the floor of the next cave; but it was still dark. Then after a long time they climbed up in the same way and reached the third cave. And then again, ages later, they climbed up to the fourth cave, and there they reached light, but an incomplete and ghostly light. That cave opened out upon the surface of the earth; but it was still dark. At last they learnt to make a brilliant light, out of which the sun and the moon were finally made.
>
> You see this myth depicts very beautifully how consciousness came to pass, how it rose from level to level. Those are *chakras*, new worlds of consciousness of natural growth, one above the other.[4]

As Jung noted, "each *chakra* is a whole world."[5] Each is a different realm of one's internal environment with its own decor, textures, mood, and atmosphere creating a unique mode of experience. Within that setting, there are particular story lines and interactions. The dramatizations of each chakra consist of a dance around a particular polarization and are based on an attempt to come to terms with a basic polarity in the world of names and forms, for each polarization creates an interaction, and the chakra is the focus of that interaction. At each chakra a primary archetype is expressed in the form of a dramatic representation. Each chakra has its unique scenario involving a protagonist, a foil, and supporting characters. These parts have been enacted from time immemorial in myths, fairy tales, recorded history, and the theatrics of everyday life.

In disturbed functioning, one becomes mired down and continues to repeat the same lines and the same scene again and again. Psychotherapy is a means for freeing a person from his fixation upon particular lines so that the drama can complete itself and reach a resolution. When one is under the spell of an archetypal realm, he becomes identified with and loses himself in the roles created by that archetype. Resolution occurs when he becomes aware that the polarities created by the enactment are insubstantial and he ceases to identify with the dramatization, becoming free from his entanglement in that mode of experience.

At each chakra, the same archetypal drama is enacted time and again by countless people in various times, places, and costumes. Although there may seem to be an endless variety of enactments, they are actually variations on a single theme. The apparent differences are the result of changes in setting and costume rather than changes in the basic plot. In the same way that motion pictures may stage the conflict between good and evil as a Western, a modern-day big-city police story, a futuristic science fiction drama, a pirate adventure, or any number of other possible forms, so the playing out of an archetypal drama may be clothed in various garbs and embellished with a large variety of subplots. Superficially the drama changes with every enactment, but the essence is ever the same.

Table 1 presents a synopsis of the archetypal themes that are enacted at each chakra. The table may be thought of as an evolutionary ladder. At the bottom is the most primitive mode of consciousness, and at the top is the most evolved.

Each archetype exists within each person, along with all the characters and enactments that unfold from each archetype. However, most people are especially involved with a particular chakra and a specific part. They may at times enact parts in dramas from other chakras, but they return again and again to the role that dominates them, whatever that may be: rebellious child, mother, seductress, second best, outsider, hero, coward—any of the innumerable roles that exist in human life. Those parts that one does not consciously adopt remain in the unconscious and are also projected out onto the world, where they are observed second-hand.

The archetypal themes that are acted out are impersonal and universal, but a person usually identifies with the part he is embodying and thinks that he is acting as an individual. He thinks of himself as actually being the character he has assumed; he does not realize that the role he plays on the world stage is not his true identity. An important goal of psychotherapy is to have the person cease to identify with the part and the drama that he has taken as his own. Jung warned that

> you must not identify with the unconscious. You must keep outside, detached, and observe objectively what happens. . . .

TABLE 1
Chakras and Archetypal Themes

Chakra	Mode of Experience	Ideal Representation(s)	Polarities Experienced	Examples
7—Sahasrara	Unitary consciousness	No representations; beyond form	none	Shankara, Meister Eckhart, Shiva in meditation
6—Ajna	Insight, witnessing	The sage	sage/fool objective observer/deluded participant	Socrates, Lao-tsu, Immanuel Kant, the Wizard of Oz, the Delphic Oracle, Merlin
5—Vishuddha	Devotion, receiving nurturance and unconditional love, surrender, trust, creativity, grace, majesty, romance	The child	object of devotion/devotee mother/child found/lost trust/distrust	Christ Child with Madonna, St. Teresa of Avila, Hanuman, Sri Ramakrishna, Don Quixote
4—Anahata	Compassion, generosity, selfless loving, service	The mother The savior	rescuer/rescued liberator/liberated	Blessed Virgin Mary, Jesus, Mother Teresa of Calcutta, Albert Schweitzer, Gandhi, St. Francis
3—Manipura	Mastery, domination, conquest, competition, inadequacy, inferiority, pride	The hero	gain/loss success/failure dominance/submission blame/praise	Alexander, Napoleon, Hamlet, Prometheus, Superman, all sports and military heroes, corporate presidents, political leaders
2—Svadhishthana	Sensory pleasure	The hedonist	pleasure/pain male/female	Bacchus, Eros, King Henry VIII, Ravana, Salome
1—Muladhara	Struggle for survival	The victim	predator/prey life/death	Movie monsters and their victims, Hitler and the Jews of the Holocaust, The Inquisition, Hansel and Gretel and the Witch

> The idea of an impersonal, psychical experience is very strange to us, and it is exceedingly difficult to accept, because we are so imbued with the fact that our unconscious is our own—my unconscious, his unconscious, her unconscious—and our prejudice is so strong, that we have the greatest trouble to dis-identify.*[6]

The various forms of psychotherapy are aimed at freeing human beings from their identifications with particular enactments and from the limitations, distress, and suffering that result when one identifies with any part or dramatization. However, psychotherapy typically leads a person to free himself from one part in an archetypal drama only to replace it with another. For example, one may gradually cease identifying with the role of the incompetent bungler and instead begin acting in a self-confident manner. This substitution of a new part which enjoys greater rewards seems to be a means of leaving behind the limitations of the less desirable part. However, new limitations, conflicts, and distress will soon be experienced in the new part as well. One continues to remain in the same drama despite the switching of roles.

Beyond Sublimation

The way a person can transcend the conflicts engendered by his absorption in a particular chakra is to stop identifying with that realm entirely and to become absorbed in a chakra further along on the evolutionary ladder. Then the polarities and conflicts that were so absorbing will be left behind. By evolving to a higher chakra, one achieves a new world view, and the old conflicts are transcended. From the perspective of the higher chakra, the former conflicts will be seen as illusory distinctions with no real significance. One will experience new polarizations, but these will be more subtle. As one moves up the ladder of evolution, the polarizations encountered become increasingly less conflictual and less absolute. There is a progressive decrease in the experience of opposition and an increasing awareness of the complementary and supportive nature of polar qualities, culminating at the most

---

*Jung's view that there is a single universal or collective unconscious that is being expressed through many people may appear to be similar to the conception in Vedanta psychology that there is only one consciousness. But for Jung, the universal unconsciousness stands in juxtaposition to the individual ego, which is the center of consciousness. By contrast, Vedanta psychology asserts that the universal consciousness alone exists.

evolved chakra with the realization that all polarities are the illusory manifestation of unitary consciousness.

The view that energy may be transformed and expressed in less conflictual ways is also found in modern depth psychology. According to Freud, the more primitive modes of experience are primary, but primitive drives can be channeled or sublimated into more constructive modes of expression. This conception of sublimation reflects Freud's reductionist bias. Jung, on the other hand, did not regard any instinct to be primary. He believed that psychic energy finds a number of different channels of expression; it can be expressed through any archetypal model with no mode being inherently more fundamental than any other: "For Jung the concept of *libido* has a different or rather a wider meaning than it had for Freud. It comprehends the sum total of the energic life processes, of all the vital forces of which sexuality represents only one area. Jung speaks of libido as an energy value which is able to communicate itself to any field of activity whatsoever, be it power, hunger, hatred, sexuality or religion, without ever being itself a specific instinct. In other words, the psychic functioning is understood as taking place within a number of relatively autonomous areas each of which is invested with a certain amount of energy."[7]

Jung himself offered the following metaphor:

> In physics . . . we speak of energy and its various manifes-
> tations, such as electricity, light, heat, etc. The situation in psy-
> chology is precisely the same. Here, too, we are dealing primarily
> with energy, that . . . can appear in various guises. If we conceive of
> libido as energy, we can take a comprehensive and unified view.
> Qualitative questions as to the nature of the libido—whether it be
> sexuality, power, hunger, or something else—recede into the
> background. . . . I see man's drives . . . as various manifestations of
> energic processes and thus as forces analogous to heat, light, etc. Just
> as it would not occur to the modern physicist to derive all forces
> from, shall we say, heat alone, so the psychologist should beware of
> lumping all instincts under the concept of sexuality. This was Freud's
> initial error which he later corrected by his assumption of "ego-
> instincts."[8]

From this perspective "all religions as well as cultural expressions become an authentic point of psychic existence and cannot be regarded as derivative. Hence the concept of sublimation becomes void. In its place we find the concept of *transformation.*"[9] Transformation, in contrast to sublimation, implies that no particular mode of psychic energy is primary, but that one mode can be changed into another.

Freud viewed the developmental process from the perspective of one who looks upward from the lower rungs of a ladder. He believed that the lower rungs formed the foundation but that one could climb upward from this starting point. In Jung's metaphor of the transformation of energy, primacy is not given to any mode of energy expression. Monistic psychology takes a third position that appears to be the complement of Freud's view: it looks at the evolutionary process from the top of the ladder. As Jung noted, the chakras "symbolize the psyche from a cosmic standpoint. It is as if a super-consciousness, an all-embracing divine consciousness surveyed the psyche from above."[10] In the monistic view, the unitary mode of experience is primary and expresses itself in progressively more gross and materialistic forms as it descends through the chakras. From this perspective, evolution does not consist of sublimating the basic energy, but of progressively freeing consciousness from its entanglement in the illusory forms manifest by each of the chakras, beginning with the most primitive. Only when one is identified with a particular archetype does that mode of consciousness seem to be primary.* When one moves to a more evolved mode of consciousness, the perspective changes, and what had seemed to be important and real becomes insubstantial and unimportant. The conception that a conflict can be resolved by embracing the perspective of a more evolved chakra has a parallel in modern psychology in the conception of second-order change, which involves, as previously noted, "a quantum jump . . . to a different level of functioning."[11]

Yoga leads one to leave his absorption in one chakra and to reach a higher perspective, and then to leave the new perspective behind for a still more evolved mode of consciousness. One passes through a series of evolutionary changes. Each time he awakens from one dream, he finds himself enmeshed in a more subtle dream. This process continues until he reaches unitary consciousness.

---

*It is because of such identification that Freud gave preeminence to the sexual drive and that subsequent theorists emphasized other archetypal modes of experience.

Survival

In the most primitive mode of consciousness on the evolutionary scale, an animal or human being remains absorbed in coping with life-threatening situations. In order to survive, he preys upon other life forms and avoids being preyed upon himself. This preoccupation with survival is found most dramatically in animal life, in some primitive societies, and in uncivilized conditions where law and order has not been established or has broken down, such as in the "Old West," in war, prison life, and street gangs. This mode of consciousness is also predominant in large-scale or private catastrophies, such as floods, tornadoes, serious automobile accidents, and medical emergencies. But the experience of this archetype is not reserved for primitive or catastrophic situations: concern with survival is part of the fabric of modern life. If one glances at the headlines of a daily newspaper or watches the evening news on television, he is repeatedly reminded of the nuclear arms race, armed conflicts, disease, automobile and airplane accidents, mass unemployment, economic concerns, and brutal muggings and murders. One carries with him an ongoing concern about his safety and his ability to survive.

As if those concerns weren't enough, we also seek out fictional dramatizations in which threats to survival are central. Some of the most popular motion pictures focus on this theme. There are countless medical, disaster, war, and crime movies in which one vicariously experiences the struggle for survival. Many motion pictures vividly portray the brutal murder of one human being by another. Horror movies abound in which primitive, powerful, animal-like creatures maim and murder innocent victims. The popularity of such movies indicates the degree to which human beings are haunted by the fear that a primitive, uncontrolled savage beast within or without will rise up and destroy them. Perhaps watching such movies and emerging from the theater unharmed provides one with a sense of mastery over the threats to his life. Many people also seek out situations that are or appear to be dangerous in order to assure themselves of their invulnerability. Race-car driving, hang gliding, or going on thrill rides at an amusement park are examples of such experiences.

The mode of consciousness in which one is preoccupied with survival is experienced in the *muladhara* chakra, the lowermost chakra, located at the base of the spine. *Muladhara* is a Sanskrit word meaning "root support." This chakra is related to solid matter, or earth: "In *muladhara* . . . we are rooted in the soil."[12] Here one has a materialistic perspective; he identifies with his physical existence. A young man who was serving a prison term for rape provides an example of the world view of a person living within the compass of this archetype:

> I like to live with animals. That is how I base my life. People don't realize it, but I stalk them like an animal to see how they react. An animal stalks and sees what the prey will do. If the prey runs, then the animal goes after it. He kills to survive; I fight to survive. No matter what, I'll survive.

One role in this dramatization is that of the aggressor—the murderer, rapist, predator. The reciprocal role is that of the potential victim who fears being attacked. Below, two women in psychotherapy who are absorbed in this role describe their experiences:

C1: When I was a young child, I remember having terrible fears. I couldn't go down from the second floor to the first floor without my father at one door and my friend at the other. My back would be against the wall, and I'd be running, panic-stricken all the way. I was terrified of the dark. I did get locked in the basement once. Now I won't shut a door, let alone lock it. I was terrified of death. If I saw anything on TV about death, I was horrified. I've had a terrible fear of being raped, even though I've never even come close to it.

C2: When I got home from group last week, my husband hadn't left the porch light on, and I was really scared. I ran into the house. I'm afraid of dying a violent death, of being tortured to death. I read the other day where this woman was coming home from a job, and three men picked her up and raped her. I have a fear of that happening to me. There are so many things that do happen, people being killed or raped. That's all you see in the paper. If I hear a noise in the house, maybe it's just a creak or something, I start imagining that somebody is trying to get in. I lock my bedroom door when I'm alone, and if there was a fire, I don't think that I would ever get out because I have so many locks.

Such themes often appear in psychotherapy sessions.

In yoga therapy, there are various means of helping a person transcend his identification with a particular part in an archetypal dramatization. The yoga therapist helps the client to see the drama that is being enacted in a more comprehensive context. This may be accomplished by leading the client toward awareness of how the theme that preoccupies him has been enacted in other settings and with many variations. The client may be encouraged to read stories, myths, or other descriptions of the archetypal drama and to understand it as an archetypal enactment. He may also be encouraged to alter the script. For example, he may be directed to exaggerate his part, making it more extreme; to seek out additional opportunities to play the part he is already playing; or to experiment with different roles and outcomes.

A person with a phobia may be instructed to purposely exaggerate his fear or to experiment to determine whether he can intentionally create the situation he fears. For instance, a claustrophobic client was afraid of being trapped in a subway train after it lost its power or in an elevator stuck between floors. Whenever he rode the subway or stepped into an elevator, he would become preoccupied with thoughts that the car might stop at any moment. This client was asked if he believed in "mind over matter," if he thought it might be possible to will the car to stop. When he agreed that this might be possible, he was asked to carry out an experiment each day that week when he rode the subway. He was instructed to will the car to stop with his thoughts, for no more than ten seconds. As he carried out this prescription, his uncontrolled panic reaction was replaced by new responses that were under his conscious direction. His fear diminished. Another client was afraid of fainting on the street. She was encouraged to pretend to faint and also to make herself faint on purpose, with a similarly beneficial result. Of course, this paradoxical approach of encouraging symptomatic behavior and bringing it under the conscious control of the client is not unique to yoga therapy. But when this approach is used in yoga therapy, it is done in the larger context of helping the client to understand the purpose and value of his symptomatic behavior.

Such paradoxical prescriptions often lead the client to see the humor in his scenario, to take his part less seriously, and to realize that it can be modified. In some cases, the client who is identifying with the victim role may be encouraged to take the reciprocal role—to imagine that he is the perpetrator or predator—and to experience the world from that perspective. This helps the client get in touch with the complement of his usual role, to become aware of the polarization he is creating, to transcend his identification with one part, and to reach a reconciliation between the reciprocal roles. An even more effective means of helping one out of the fear and paranoia created when he enacts this archetypal theme is to lead him to the perspective of a chakra further up in the evolutionary hierarchy. From that new perspective, the creak in the house or the stranger one encounters will not inevitably be experienced as a cause for alarm.

In the first chakra, polarization is most extreme: one's opposite is experienced as a threat to his very existence. At the next chakra, one's opposite is experienced as both threatening and alluring; here one seeks one's opposite instead of running from it or trying to eliminate it. At the third chakra, one's opposite is seen in a competitive light. As one progresses further up the ladder of evolution, he increasingly experiences the two sides of a polarity as supportive and complementary, finally reaching the zenith of the evolutionary journey, in which the two poles are experienced as illusory manifestations of one unity. The system of chakras traces the transition from reductive to dualistic to monistic modes of experience (see table 2, p. 256). Indeed the paradigms result from the experiences of specific chakras. Each of the various psychological models takes the perspective of a particular chakra and explains the human being from that perspective.

Pleasure

When one enters the realm of the second chakra, *svadhisthana,* he leaves the concern with survival behind. At this chakra, one is dominated by the pleasure principle: he desires to attain and maintain pleasurable experiences through all sensory channels and to avoid unpleasurable experiences. He may be consumed by his desire for sensory or erotic pleasure. Considering physical sensation to be primary, he lives a materialistic and hedonistic life. He identifies with his physical body and fears growing old or dying and losing his capacity for sensory experience.

TABLE 2
Chakras and Psychological Models

Chakra	Mode of Experience	Psychological Theorists or Models
7—Sahasrara	Unitary consciousness	Advaita Vedanta
6—Ajna	Insight, witnessing	Yoga, Buddhist psychology
5—Vishuddha	Devotion, receiving nurturance and unconditional love, surrender, trust, creativity, grace, majesty, romance	Jung
4—Anahata	Compassion, generosity, selfless loving, service	Rogers, Fromm
3—Manipura	Mastery, domination, conquest, competition, inadequacy, inferiority, pride	Adler, Ego psychology
2—Svadhishthana	Sensory pleasure	Psychoanalysis, Reich, Bioenergetics
1—Muladhara	Struggle for survival	Primal scream therapy

Believing that the sources of pleasure are to be found outside himself, a person operating from this center seeks a sexually attractive partner, delicious foods, stimulants, physical comforts, or any other object or experience that he imagines will give him sensory pleasure. He is ruled by desire for the objects that give him sensate pleasure, and spends most of his time and energy pursuing such objects. All other goals become secondary. When under the sway of this hedonistic mind-set, one may be willing to sacrifice security, prestige, friendship, acceptance by society, and perhaps even his very life in order to attain pleasure.

In his pursuit of the objects of pleasure, one experiences considerable unrest. The chase often ends in frustration or disappointment. Even if one attains his goal, he may find that the experience of pleasure is insufficient and fleeting. For instance, after his sumptuous meal is finished, he will begin searching for another pleasurable experience. He will become addicted to those objects that give him pleasure and will frantically attempt to recreate experiences that have given him pleasure in the past. When he is not able to recapture a pleasurable experience, he will become frustrated and angry, and if someone else attains the object of his desire, he will experience jealousy. The pursuit of pleasure gives rise to a number of scenarios that are repeatedly portrayed in soap operas and in real life.

Today in our society, many people lead a life in which they are preoccupied with the pursuit of pleasures of various sorts. They spend their free time indulging the senses through eating, drinking, sexual activities, the use of drugs, and other means of attaining sensory gratification. Some experience a sense of emptiness or incompleteness in this pursuit. Others are torn by conflict between the pursuit of pleasure and needs that arise from other archetypal modes of experience. Here is a woman who is experiencing just such a conflict:

Yesterday I got up at 6:00 a.m. and meditated and did hatha yoga. I ate well, and later in the day I jogged. Today I'm smoking two packs of cigarettes and I'll probably go to a bar and get drunk. I love to smoke and drink together. There's something about having cigarettes and drinking that's real nice. But it's not what I want to do. I can feel what it's doing to my body.

There are two distinct parts of me: the part that would love to sit in a monastery, and the part that could do a lot of drugs and go to bars every night and pick up men. If I do everything I want to do for three or four days, the next day I'll feel even more like going to the opposite extreme. Somebody told me once, "You can't be a whore and a nun at the same time. Make up your mind." Well, I can say that I want to be the whore and it's real fun—all this drinking, partying and stuff—but it's not satisfying to me. There's always that part of me that's saying, "This is not taking you to a place you want to go."

I've slept with so many guys and smoked lots of dope. I've had my share of booze and partying, and that doesn't make me happy. There's no lasting value to me doing all that stuff, any more than indulging in an ice-cream cone; it's good for just while you're doing it. But if you tell people that you don't smoke, you don't do drugs, and you can't stay up late because you want to get up early in the morning to meditate, they don't understand. They think you're very weird.

Just as there are many people who are preoccupied with the pursuit of pleasure, so conversely there are many people who believe that pleasurable sensations are wicked and that they should not allow themselves to experience sensory pleasure. Although they may have intense desires for sensory gratification, they place severe constraints on themselves. But repressing one's desire for pleasure only gives it increased power and significance. If this mode of experience is not allowed expression, a hysterical disorder or some other form of psychopathology is likely to occur. Such reactions were prevalent in the Victorian era and prompted Freud to focus on the pleasure principle as the chief motivating force in human beings. Freud analyzed human experience and behavior in terms of the second-chakra mode of experience. For Freud, the pleasure principle was primary; all other motivations and modes of experience were seen as secondary elaborations of the urge to experience pleasure.

Wilhelm Reich and Alexander Lowen also view human existence from the perspective of the second chakra. Their psychologies emphasize the capacity to experience sensory pleasure as the measure of a human being's fulfillment. They emphasize the positive aspects of this mode of experience and assert that a human being should fully experience his capacity for orgasm. Their therapies focus on removing muscular and characterological blocks and inhibitions in order to increase one's experience of pleasure. The methods they use can help one achieve that end, but their therapies neglect to look beyond the pleasure principle to recognize the significance of other realms of experience.

According to yoga psychology, the loosening of blocks to this mode of experience is an intermediate goal. Once one has realized his capacity for pleasure and also the limitations of this mode of being, he will be ready to turn his attention to still other realms of experience. For while the second chakra brings one pleasure, it does not lead to lasting satisfaction but only to temporary appeasement. During periods in which sensory stimulation occurs, one experiences pleasure, but at other times he experiences unrest, frustration, and other unpleasant states. The desire for pleasurable experience is like a fire that can never be quenched. The more one feeds the flame of desire with the fuel of objects that gratify the senses, the more intense the flame of desire becomes. The more one enjoys, the greater becomes his desire for continued and more intense enjoyment. If one experiences repeated enjoyment, he eventually tires of that experience and seeks out variations that will engender new pleasures. His desire makes him restless; it leads him onward to seek new sensory experiences. In this mode of experience, one ordinarily feels a lack within himself and searches outside for that which he believes will give him pleasure. Only when he finds that object and incorporates it into himself does he temporarily experience pleasure.

In trying to attain pleasure, one creates tension within himself that actually diminishes his experience of pleasure. The most intense sensory pleasure actually occurs when one gives up all pursuit and relaxes his entire body. For most people, that relaxation occurs only after having attained the sought-after object. But if one learns to relax and experience his own organism rather than pursuing something outside himself, he will find that the experience of pleasure is inherent in that relaxed state. Then he will experience that intense sensory pleasure that is already a part of one's being and is not dependent upon uniting with an external object. Reich was aware of this. In his therapy, he emphasized the relaxation of chronically tense muscles and the capacity to experience intense sensory pleasure throughout one's body, independent of external objects.

In yoga therapy, one may learn techniques that lead him to very deep states of relaxation and to a feeling of inner comfort and pleasure. If one learns and practices the extended series of progressive relaxation exercises, he can relax the body to such a degree that he experiences sheer delight. Sensory pleasure is an adumbrated form, an imperfect expression, of that delight. It points the way to a more complete and fulfilling ecstasy. One can learn to luxuriate in a degree of pleasure that is greater and more comforting than that which is found through temporarily merging with an external object of desire. The delight experienced through yogic progressive relaxation is like basking in the warmth and comfort of an inner sun. One feels that he is living in the lap of luxury. That subtle yet intense pleasure experienced within is itself only an imperfect approximation, a prefiguring, of the ecstasy that can be experienced as one carries relaxation beyond his musculature to ever more subtle aspects of his being, including relaxation of the mind.

Mystics throughout the ages have described such ecstatic states but have usually offered little in the way of systematic means for attaining those states. In most instances, the mystics had little ability to control their experiences. They were overwhelmed by states of ecstasy that came upon them for no reason that they could discern. However, yoga science systematically teaches one how to regulate his states of consciousness. Yoga relaxation can progressively lead to the state of *yoga nidra,* in which the body is in an extremely relaxed state comparable to that of deep sleep while the person remains conscious in a state of bliss.[13] Though that experience is attained only by a fortunate few who have mastered the yogic techniques of progressive relaxation, even those who master the beginning techniques of muscular relaxation will come upon an inner state of inherent pleasure, the existence of which they had not previously known.

In order to know those states, one must learn to turn inward, to experience the joy radiating within. That joy is ever so subtle compared with the coarse, dense, noisy experiences that come from contact with the external world. As one relaxes, quiets himself, and learns to tune in to his inner state, that dim, far-off radiance will shine with ever greater intensity, until one finds himself at the center of radiant bliss. He will attain a state of ecstasy many times more intense than the pleasure that can be experienced through sensory channels.

One cannot turn inward toward that internal ecstasy unless he lets go of his preoccupying desire for external objects. Thus the yogic teachings encourage one to give up desire and thereby experience joy:

> When a man dwells on the pleasures of sense, attraction for them arises in him. From attraction arises desire, the lust of possession, and this leads to passion, to anger.

> From passion comes confusion of mind, then loss of remembrance, the forgetting of duty. From this loss comes the ruin of reason, and the ruin of reason leads man to destruction.

> But the soul that moves in the world of the senses and yet keeps the senses in harmony, free from attraction and aversion, finds rest in quietness.

> In this quietness falls down the burden of all her sorrows, for when the heart has found quietness, wisdom has also found peace.

There is no wisdom for a man without harmony, and without harmony there is no contemplation. Without contemplation there cannot be peace, and without peace can there be joy?[14]

Tantra philosophy and psychology emphasizes the second chakra as a motivating force. In the tantric system, one's latent energy (*kundalini*) is depicted as a coiled serpent that has its home at the second chakra. Tantra recognizes the importance of respecting this archetype rather than suppressing its expression. In tantric practices, one's latent energy is awakened, made available to consciousness, transmuted, and expressed through more evolved centers. In less evolved tantric schools, one may engage with the objects that ordinarily lead to the experience of sensory pleasure. While maintaining contact with the objects, he learns to stop identifying with the sensate pleasure and to thereby experience more subtle forms of ecstasy. Through this process one becomes a master of the sensory realm rather than its captive.

Yoga is not puritanical; it does not lead one to deny the second-chakra mode of experience. Rather it seeks to refine that mode of experience, leading one to more profound and complete experiences of joy and ecstasy. The sensory channels are limited in the degree and type of pleasure that they can transmit, but the capacity of one's consciousness to experience bliss knows no limit.

Mastery

At the first and second chakras, one ordinarily identifies solely with his physical body. Since the body is fragile and subject to injury, disease, and death, suffering is inevitable when one is enmeshed in those modes of experience. At the third chakra, *manipura,* one extends his territory to include what he owns and that for which he is responsible. The scenarios at this chakra are created from one's absorption in defining, maintaining, and expanding his territory and achieving control over his dominion. Here one replaces the pursuit of pleasure with concerns about mastery and power. He views others as adversaries or rivals and becomes absorbed in such issues as success and failure, dominance and sub-mission, heroism and cowardice, conquering and being conquered.

This third mode of consciousness is the realm of the ego. One seeks to prove himself by outdoing others and by gaining power, prestige, and recognition. He is absorbed in politics both in his personal life and in his relationship with the world at large. Manipulation, coercion, and conniving are characteristic behaviors in the scenarios created out of this archetype. A person operating on this level is goal-oriented; he has difficulty being in the present moment. From his perspective, even spiritual experiences are attainments to be achieved and gloated over by the ego.

Psychological theories, rather than being objective descriptions of the functioning of the psyche, are created by human beings and reflect the biases and limited perspectives of their creators. Every theory reflects its founder's personality, conflicts, scenarios, and preoccupations. Thus if the founder of a theory is himself thoroughly enmeshed in one particular archetypal realm, his theory will describe the psyche in terms of that mode of functioning: "We can . . . discern a dominant archetype underlying the doctrines of the various . . . psychologists. When Freud sees the beginning and principle of everything that happens in sexuality, Adler in the striving for power, these two are ideas expressing . . . archetypal representations."[15]

Thus it is not surprising that psychological theorists who look at the world from the perspective of the second chakra do not consider the development of the ego to be a positive step in one's evolution. Indeed, one of the founders of bioenergetic therapy, Alexander Lowen, so highly values the experience of sensory pleasure that he has written: "The domination of the personality by the ego is a diabolical perversion of the nature of man. The ego was never intended to be the master of the body, but its loyal and obedient servant. The body, as opposed to the ego, desires pleasure, not power. Bodily pleasure is the source from which all our good feelings and good thinking stems."[16]

By contrast, theorists such as Alfred Adler, Robert W. White, and other ego psychologists consider ego development to be the measure of man. Those theorists take the perspective of ego-consciousness, and they lucidly describe the psychology of one who is absorbed in the ego archetype. They are able to understand the dilemmas, anxieties, and preoccupations of such a person, but they may have considerable difficulty in understanding someone who is functioning from another archetype. Their therapies help one to build his ego, to replace submissiveness with assertiveness, failure with success, and a sense of inferiority with the experience of being capable and competent. Such changes occur within the framework of ego-consciousness. They lead to the substitution of one role with its reciprocal within the same drama. The plot remains focused on failure and success, competence and in-competence, top dog and underdog, master and slave.

Those who are functioning in this mode and who play the role of being powerful, successful, dominant, or heroic are not likely to find their way into the therapist's consulting room. If the egoist experiences internal conflict, he is likely to avoid psychotherapy. He likes to tackle problems on his own, and looks upon those who go to a therapist as weak. Because of his felt need to assert control and authority, when and if he does find himself in psychotherapy or marital counseling, it will likely be for only a short time.

It is the person at the other end of this polarity—he who is timid and insecure, who feels inadequate in jousting with the world—that tends to seek the support, encouragement, or guidance of a counselor or psychotherapist. Such a person is caught up in a vicious cycle. He feels inadequate, so he becomes preoccupied with gaining approval from others. He is afraid that if others find out how inadequate he is, they will reject him. So he hides. He neither expresses his inner feelings nor acts. He remains frozen. As a result, he fails to get the acclaim he seeks and is often snubbed by others, who find him to be lacking in vitality and spontaneity. His feelings of inadequacy are thus confirmed, leading to further self-doubt, hesitation, and ineptness. Here are two examples of this mode of being:

C1: I have this inhibition. I'm not able to go on a date and feel comfortable. I always want to make sure that my date has a good time. I want to keep an image. I'm also afraid that she might gossip; she might say that I'm boring or dull. I want others to have positive reactions toward me. I'm always trying to please.

C2: I want to be able to take risks, like getting up in front of a group and feeling that it's okay to mess up. But if I were to screw up, there would be a lot of people that would laugh or gossip. I even feel that way when I'm with a group of friends and it's time for me to leave. I feel that I'm on the spot and I have to really produce. I have to get up and say goodbye to them. I want to make it look a certain way. I want to have control and I want to impress the person I'm saying goodbye to. But I'm afraid that I might screw it up.

I was going to call a girl on the phone last night. All of a sudden, there she'd be on the phone and I'd have to talk to her, so I was hesitating. The week before, I saw her at a bar and I wanted to meet her. I was in a little panic. Then after my friend introduced us, I tried to talk, but my mind was thinking, Don't blow it. Don't say the wrong thing. Don't lose control. Don't panic. I was afraid that I would mess up. It's pretty hard to carry on a conversation with all those thoughts going through your mind. My heart was pounding, and I wanted to run away.

Some people feel a greater sense of adequacy, but have not yet learned to assert themselves. The following client, who is attempting to overcome her timidity, is such a person:

At times at work, someone will criticize what I'm doing—my boss will make some kind of negative comment about something that I've done. Sometimes he'll be accusative, which I suppose has certain benefits for him: he keeps in control and power. I'm usually timid about responding.

I'm always surprised in situations where people take advantage of me. I'm generally taken aback without knowing how to respond. But I'm learning to be more assertive. This week I had a talk with my neighbor. She's been playing her stereo very loud for months. I finally told her it disturbed me. She said, "Okay, I'll keep it turned down." I feel a need to be more assertive. I have always let my husband deal with neighbors up until now. This is the first time that I have said anything. I walked right up to her door and I talked to her. And she said, "I don't blame you. I would be angry, too." I feel more responsible and have more respect for myself.

In this mode of consciousness, one is concerned with establishing, maintaining, and expanding what he regards as his territory. Two common character types that epitomize this way of being are the entrepreneur and the bureaucrat. The bureaucrat primarily seeks to maintain his territory, while the entrepreneur seeks to take over more territory. When a person operating from this level of consciousness believes that his territory is being threatened or invaded, he typically reacts with anger. Here is an example:

> When I was in the hospital, I asked to have no visitors. Everyone respected that, except the woman I work with. She walked right into the hospital room. I was furious. It was an invasion of my privacy and disrespectful. I had made it very clear to everyone: "no visitors." The door was closed, which I thought gave me some control over who would walk in. But she walked in anyway, so I felt that I had lost control. She does the same thing at work: I'm in a room with the door closed and she just bursts in. I become enraged.

Many people fail to distinguish between aggression and assertiveness. Their characteristic response to being invaded or verbally attacked is to retaliate, to answer tit for tat by calling names or in some way attacking the other person. Some people, however, afraid of their own aggressiveness, hold back their anger for fear of losing control. In yoga therapy, one learns to distinguish between assertiveness (moving the other person out of one's territory) and aggressiveness (invading another's territory).

Children are often taught that expressing anger is unacceptable, so they learn not to express it. As adults they may habitually keep their anger to themselves, and also discount and devalue their emotions and other feelings. Such people value what others think and feel above their own experience. Wanting to be accepted even by a person who is being invasive, they do not express their anger or defend their territory. Many of these people have so successfully cut themselves off from their anger that they are not even aware of their own physiological and emotional responses to the invasion of their territory.

Many approaches to psychotherapy help clients to get in touch with their anger. The client may be encouraged to experience the depth of his rage and to express it both physically and verbally in therapy. While it is important to recover emotions that have been repressed, this is only an intermediate step in the expansion of consciousness. Identifying with one's anger can also leave one mired in a particular plot line and closed to other ways of being. Yoga therapy does not encourage one to be passive or to deny his emotions; it helps one to recover repressed anger, but it also goes further to help one gain a perspective on the anger rather than identifying with it. The following client, who suffered from an asthmatic condition, is struggling with this issue:

C: My mother-in-law came to visit and she started to change my plans around. I had promised to help someone, but she wanted to go shopping. I did rearrange things, but the whole day was negative; everything that came up I was against. I couldn't seemingly do anything about it. Evidently, I was very resentful and angry that I had to change my plans.

T: You say you *had* to?

C: I didn't feel that there was anything I could do. It would have been much easier for me if I had been able to express my anger. I didn't do that. I didn't know how to do it without somehow becoming involved in the anger. I still am not able to look at a situation that makes me angry rather than being right in it. I can't get above it and see it objectively. I was angry that she was invading my space. I don't think that she realized that she was imposing on me.

T: Did you tell her that you felt invaded?

C: No, I really didn't know how to go about approaching her and saying, "You are invading my space." Not get angry, but just say it without causing more problems because of my emotions.

T: I just thought of an interesting phrase: "getting it off your chest." It seems to me that if you would assert yourself when you first sense someone invading or taking over, you wouldn't be nearly as emotional. But if you let it go on, it seems that your emotions intensify. This situation showed you that you can't escape from your anger. If you don't express yourself, it's going to come out another way—through negativity or through physical symptoms. In a sense, you got it off your chest by being negative.

C: Yes, but I really didn't, because that wasn't satisfying. The only thing that would have helped was to withdraw myself completely.

T: I wonder if that would really help. I think it would be better to say directly what it is that is bothering you as soon as you become aware of it. Then you wouldn't be holding on to the anger and turning it into resentment and tension for yourself. Then perhaps you could resolve the issue and move on.

From the perspective of the more evolved archetypes, the territorial boundaries drawn in the first three chakras do not really exist. However, the majority of people in modern society experience the world primarily through the first three chakras, so it is important for them to deal with territorial distinctions effectively. Instead of being mutually invasive and waging internecine war, two individuals can learn to respect each other's personal autonomy. Eventually they may recognize themselves as part of a more comprehensive system in which they share common goals, rather than experiencing themselves as adversaries or combatants. This sort of shift in perspective occurs when one moves from the third to the fourth mode of consciousness.

The development of ego capacities, including the ability to assert oneself, is a necessary step in the evolution of consciousness; it is important that a person be able to function competently in the world. However, difficulties arise when one identifies with his accomplishments, just as they do when he thinks of himself as inadequate and incompetent. One can remain stuck in this mode of consciousness at either end of a polarity.

Lowen has pointed out that egoistic consciousness may stifle one's capacity to experience pleasure. He encourages a way out of identification with the ego by regressing to the pleasure principle and asserting its sovereignty over the ego. Yoga therapy offers another path, not well trodden in modern psychology: it encourages one to move forward to a more evolved mode of consciousness, in which preoccupations with such questions as success and failure, top dog and underdog, are left behind, while the capacities of the ego for mastery are still retained. Lowen is correct insofar as he asserts that the capacity for pleasure is not to be abandoned with the development of ego-consciousness; and in a similar way ego capacities are not to be abandoned as one becomes absorbed in the next archetype. Instead, as one reaches a more evolved mode of experiencing, he becomes able to play the various roles generated in the less evolved modes with increased mastery and greater flexibility.

The yoga therapist encourages and assists those who need to develop and strengthen their egos to do so; however, if a client becomes identified with this archetype to the exclusion of higher modes of awareness, the therapist will lead the client toward the experience of those other realms. For while this third archetypal mode of experience represents a step forward in the development of consciousness toward greater rationality, mastery, and responsibility, it is only an intermediate attainment.

Modern society encourages one to become identified with the first three modes of consciousness. The focus on first-chakra concerns in the news and in movies has already been mentioned. The emphasis that society places on the second-chakra desire for attaining sensory gratification through sex, eating, intoxicants, and other means of stimulating the senses is obvious, as is its accentuation of the third-chakra focus on acquisitiveness, control, competition, gambling, self-aggrandizement, and so on. These three modes of being lead one to experience considerable discomfort, anxiety, and distress, along with the more positive experiences of security, sensory pleasure, and mastery. In comparison with the more evolved modes of being, the degree of joy, harmony, and fulfillment experienced in these realms is quite limited. Yet these lower modes are integral aspects of the overall design of being and do have their value in leading one up the ladder of evolution to greater consciousness of oneself and to ever more self-responsibility. Even at further stages of development, they may continue to remain meaningful realms of experience in the service of more evolved modes of being.

Psychosomatic Disorders

The system of chakras helps one to understand how particular mental-emotional states are directly related to and experienced in specific parts of the body. A disturbance in a bodily function can be understood as a physical manifestation of a disturbance in the psychological functioning related to a specific chakra; that is, an archetypal theme being enacted at a particular chakra can lead to a disturbance in the part of the body that corresponds to that chakra. Many psychosomatic and physical disorders can be better understood and treated more successfully if the therapist is aware of the archetypal theme that is being played out through a somatic dysfunction. For example, colitis, diarrhea, and other bowel problems can occur as a result of the fear and anxiety experienced in the first-chakra mode of consciousness.

Likewise, any of a number of various stomach disorders can result from one's involvement in the egoistic mode of consciousness. One who is preoccupied with self-worth, who experiences jealousy and envy of those who have what he does not, or who has difficulty in establishing or maintaining his territory, is likely to experience ulcers and other stomach problems. Many stomach disorders are a result of liver dysfunction, and in this regard the Greek myth of Prometheus is highly instructive. In Greek mythology, Prometheus symbolizes the egoistic consciousness of the manipura chakra. Prometheus stole fire for mankind from the realm of the gods. Instead of assuming a devotional attitude and acknowledging the superiority of the heavenly realm, Prometheus attempted to make man an equal of the gods. As retribution for this hubris, he was chained to a rock, where a vulture ate at his liver. This myth is, among other things, a symbolic explanation of the psychical origin of liver dysfunction. It informs us that one who lives by his ego and fails to acknowledge that which transcends the ego robs himself of nourishment from the heavenly realm. This is expressed even at the physical level, where the malfunctioning liver at the navel center does not allow the nutrients ingested at the throat center, the center of nurturance, to be assimilated. A person who identifies with his ego, who seeks to control others, who is demanding and easily angered if his demands are not met, may well experience a liver disorder. Indeed, the word "jaundiced" refers both to one who is embittered, hostile, and envious, and to one who has a liver dysfunction.

The person whose liver is not functioning properly may consume a great deal of nutritious food and yet feel undernourished. He may even come to believe that he has a tapeworm that consumes the nutrients he needs. And in a sense he does: his ego is the tapeworm. The ego is a parasite that derives its sustenance from the Self. Although it draws its nourishment from the Self, the ego has no regard for its host. It attempts to assert its sovereignty, and in so doing deprives the person of the nourishment that flows from the Self. In many cases, liver dysfunction can be ameliorated by rising to a more evolved mode of consciousness. At the heart center, one is transformed from a parasite to a servant, and the liver no longer plays a central role in his life drama. If one rises to the level of vishuddha consciousness at the throat center, he experiences the nourishment that was lacking in manipura consciousness.

Asthma is another condition that results from a disturbance at manipura. Whereas the person with a bilious or choleric temperament aggressively asserts his ego, the asthmatic is likely to be at the other extreme, not asserting himself sufficiently. The asthmatic typically takes no corrective action when he feels pressed or suffocated by another: he neither flees, nor does he fight to defend the autonomy of his territory. He does not allow himself to fully experience the resentment or anger he feels; he doesn't "get things off his chest." This way of being is reflected in a disturbance of physical functioning at manipura. For an asthmatic, the adrenal glands, which are located in the region of the manipura chakra, do not secrete enough adrenalin. This hormone helps to energize an animal or a human being, and its secretion is integral to the fight or flight reaction. The asthmatic lacks the charge of energy that the adrenal glands provide. In some cases cortisone, another hormone from the adrenal glands, is used to treat asthma.

Other conditions related to disturbances in the third chakra include anorexia nervosa and bulimia, which are also related to issues in the fifth chakra. The personality of the anorexic clearly reflects a third-chakra mode of being: anorexics are frequently described as controlled, perfectionistic, stubborn, and conscientious. Their symptomatic behavior often begins when they feel inadequate because life changes are requiring new skills with which they are unfamiliar. Anorexics deny themselves the experience of being nurtured.

Bulimics exhibit a conflict between feeling helpless and a need to be independent, between the wish to surrender to a source of nurturance and a distrust of that source. They are hungry for nurturance, but they find that no matter how much they gorge themselves, they are never satisfied. A bulimic craves parental love and acceptance, but is likely to have experienced repeated rejection and thus feels unlovable. Though the parents of a bulimic may verbally express their love for their child, the child is convinced that they actually have little or no love for him. As adults, bulimics continue to feel that they are despicable, and their behavior reflects and perpetuates this self-concept. For such people food symbolizes the love and acceptance they long for, but they can no more stomach the food they ingest than they can stomach their parents' protestations of love, which they experience as insincere. The bulimic both craves food and rejects it as though it were poison. He vomits up the poisoned nurturance and then again compulsively gorges himself with more, only to vomit it up once again.

In helping a client to correct these and other physical and behavioral disorders, the yoga therapist leads the client to become aware of the underlying psychological disturbance and its symbolic aspects and to modify the scenario that is perpetuating the disturbance. He may ask the client to do mental exercises in which the client concentrates on the chakra that is related to the disturbed functioning. Concentration on a particular center helps to energize that center and bring the disturbance to the foreground of one's consciousness, where it can be more readily resolved.

Service

The first three modes of consciousness lead to the various unpleasant emotional states experienced by human beings, such as fear, anxiety, frustration, anger, jealousy, envy, greed, and depression. At the fourth chakra, *anahata,* those emotions are left behind, and the egocentric perspective of the third chakra is also transcended. At the fourth chakra, one comes out of the underworld and into the light. He undergoes a revolution of perspective: leaving the realm in which struggle, secrecy, conniving, and self-aggrandizement prevail, he comes into the warm, radiant sunshine of caring for others. He now lives by the principle which is the complement of that found in the first three chakras. No longer either fearing that something will be taken away or striving to attain and hold on to what one thinks he needs, he experiences a sense of fullness within himself and seeks to share his abundance with others. Grabbing and clutching are replaced by generosity. At the more primitive chakras, one feels in need and is concerned for himself alone, but at anahata, one does not care for his needs. Instead, he feels the needs of others and becomes salve to their hurts. He is truly a friend or parent to all.

The fourth chakra, at the heart center, is midway in the journey toward unitary consciousness. At the three more primitive chakras that lie below this center, one involves himself in and identifies with the material forms. As one evolves through the chakras, he first learns to cease identifying with the most gross or material existence, and then to progressively let go of his identification with ever more subtle forms and to draw nearer to the experience of unitary consciousness. At the heart center, one moves from preoccupations with his body, senses, and territory to a new focus on that which transcends the individual.

When a person whose consciousness is at muladhara encounters someone else, his thoughts revolve around survival issues; when a person functioning from svadhisthana meets another, he is interested in whether he can receive pleasure from the other; when a person operating from manipura interacts with another, he is concerned about who will have power and control. Such people are concerned solely with their own needs and desires; they are interested in and concerned for others only insofar as others can help them obtain their own wants. But a person functioning from the heart center has a different way of relating to others. When he encounters another person, he asks himself how he may serve that person. Instead of being absorbed in his own needs, he is interested in meeting the needs of others. At the heart center, one becomes transformed from a person who takes to a person who is generous. In giving, he finds a greater joy than he experienced in taking, for a person who takes carries the attitude that he is incomplete and in need, while in giving one comes in touch with that which he has.

The word "love" is often used in describing one's experience at this chakra. But this word has been misused so often and debased so much that it is not adequate to convey the emotion experienced at the heart center. As one moves from one chakra to another, each symbol or concept is reinterpreted and given an entirely new meaning. When one is functioning at a lower chakra, he interprets the words used to describe higher-chakra experiences in terms of the perspective of his level of functioning. For example, a person functioning at muladhara explained that he followed the golden rule, which he interpreted as, "Do it to them before they do it to you." Similarly, those who are functioning at a lower center misunderstand love in terms of the consciousness of that center. For example, the word "love" is often used to express the sensory desires of the second chakra. We say, "I love ice cream" or "I love the way silk feels." The word "love" is also used to express the acquisitiveness characteristic of the third chakra. Here one "loves" his possessions. In these modes of consciousness, one has expectations of that which he "loves." One "loves" another person or an object because it fulfills his needs. If the person or object does not meet his expectations, such "love" can easily turn to hatred or indifference.

One may do something for another, claiming that he is doing it because he loves that person, but actually doing it because he expects the person to do something for him in return. If his expectation is not met, he complains, "Look what I did for you, and you couldn't even do this one thing for me." Such doing with expectations is not love as it is experienced through the heart center. Such actions are based on an implied contract: "If I do something for you, you will do something for me." An agreement of this sort has its place, but it is unfortunate if one takes such an exchange to be love, for then he is missing the genuine experience.

The word "love" as it is used by those functioning at the lower chakras focuses on what the object of love is doing or can do for the person who "loves" that object. But in love as it is experienced at the anahata chakra, there is no thought of receiving. Such love is giving, giving, giving. One dissolves his sense of separateness in giving, so there is no thought of return. When functioning from the lower chakras, one feels incomplete and seeks something to make him feel complete, but at the anahata chakra, one's fullness overflows to nourish others.

The sun is a symbol of the heart chakra, for the sun nurtures all living things on earth. It radiates continuously in all directions and does not discriminate in any way; all living things receive its life-giving light. And what does the sun seek in return for the energy and warmth it gives?

So far no one has ever received an energy bill from the sun. Neither has the sun sent a message threatening that it will not shine unless everyone bows down, worships it, and lives according to its dictates. The sun radiates energy and light and nourishes us because that is its nature, that is the way the sun expresses itself.

Most people place limits on the extent to which they give. They are concerned that if they give too much, they will become depleted. And if they do give, they are interested in what they will receive in return. Such "giving" is not an experience of the fourth chakra, but rather a bargain made in the insecurity of a lower mode of experience. One is concerned that he will be taken advantage of if he gives too much or does not get something in return. If he does not receive something of a material nature, he will seek recognition or appreciation from others or will praise himself for being a kind person.

In the way of the heart center, however, one has no such concerns. He is interested in providing what is needed and does not want appreciation or recognition. He may even prefer to give anonymously. At the heart center, the lower-chakra feeling that one is lacking what he needs is replaced with the experience of abundance. The more one freely gives, the more abundance he experiences, and in turn, the more he is able to give.

This way of being makes no sense to the person living within the perspective of the third chakra. He is convinced that the person who gives so abundantly will eventually become depleted or break down. He does not consider this to be a viable way of living in the modern world. He thinks that those who function from the heart center will be hurt and abused; he believes that one must of necessity be "tough" in dealing with the harsh world he perceives.

In the first three chakras, the two sides of a polarity are experienced as being distinct from or in opposition to one another, but at the heart center, one begins to understand the complementary relationship between the two sides of a polarity. Instead of projecting his opposite, as in the first three chakras, at anahata one becomes aware that the distinction between himself and others is artificial and unreal. He realizes that in giving to others, he is giving to himself, that in treating others, he is treating himself. He experiences warmth and joy in giving, but only uneasiness and discomfort in grasping and holding on.

Those who have not reached this center are unaware of the paradoxical twist in the nature of giving and taking. Genuine giving never depletes itself, whereas no matter how much one takes, he will never feel satisfied. Giving never empties itself; taking never leads to feeling full. The only way to experience fullness is to give everything.

When a person remains in the lower chakras, he continually seeks to maintain or enhance himself. He may want to take in pleasurable experiences, to possess more and more, or to have increased power over others. But he actually depletes his energy on all levels through worries, preoccupations, nervousness, and emotional turmoil. He remains in a state of confusion and agitation, caught in a vicious cycle. For the more one is oriented toward self-advancement and self-aggrandizement, the more he notices what he needs and does not have, the more upset and emotional he becomes, and the more he feels the need to take in order to be satisfied. But at the heart center, this vicious cycle is replaced with a cycle that leads to abundance: the more one gives, the more joy, fulfillment, and completeness he experiences, and the more he has to give.

One need not give up egoistic functioning as he ascends to the heart center. He can continue to use that mode of consciousness as a tool in the service of the more evolved mode of being. For example, one who genuinely wishes to serve may find it helpful to have a building to care for others, to train assistants who work under his guidance, and to have an organization in order to carry out his work more effectively. One may adopt a provisional egoistic perspective in order to function competently in serving others.

When individuals functioning through the less evolved archetypes predominate in a society, that society is characterized by such qualities as brutality, promiscuity, coercion, competition, politicking, and outsized bureaucratic structure for maintaining security. Such societies, no matter how much they may esteem themselves for their apparent accomplishments, have not yet developed a genuine concern for human beings. Humanism dawns when consciousness reaches and is expressed through the heart center. A society composed of individuals functioning at this center will be interested in the welfare and self-actualization of all its members.

At the heart center, the humanistic paradigm comes to the fore. One values human well-being and is concerned with nurturing human potentials. Carl Rogers, with his emphasis on empathic understanding and unconditional positive regard, has developed an approach to psychotherapy founded on this mode of experience. Rogers's person-centered approach helps to free therapists from a more authoritarian third-chakra orientation. Likewise, Erich Fromm's teachings focus on the transition from a preoccupation with mastery and power to the expression of love. Fromm encourages the development of such qualities as a willingness to give up all forms of having, in order to fully *be;* a joy that comes from giving and sharing, not from hoarding and exploiting; an ever-developing capacity for love; and a shedding of narcissism.[17]

In many cases, a client's conflict and dissatisfaction result from dwelling on himself and what he perceives as his unfulfilled needs. Such a person believes that he will be happier when he finds a way to satisfy those needs, but such satisfaction is never attained. As long as one is oriented in this way, he will always find needs that are not met, and he will continue to feel unfulfilled. The only way out of this predicament is to cease to be concerned about one's needs and to become interested in the needs of others. The following two clients who have been in yoga therapy describe such a shift from an acquisitive third-chakra orientation to a loving, nurturing way of being:

C1: I want to quit dwelling on myself. There has been a feeling in me of wanting to hold and retain what I have, a fear of letting go. I've been very fearful of giving what I have. But I experience a certain sense of freedom and gladness when I help people. When I have experienced giving, I've liked it. There seems to be a change in my attitude from deficiency, feeling I might be depleted, to the feeling that I have plenty left over for me and others, too.

C2: I want to use my knowledge in a way that is not egotistical but is worthwhile to other people. As soon as I start doing that, I'll feel that I'm a useful member of this universe instead of constantly being on my own trip and feeling like a self-centered unity, locked up in this box I call "me." Until I do that, I'm not going to be satisfied. I've been very self-centered; I've done very little in terms of really being out in the world and giving. And until now, when I did give, I'd expect something in return—to know that someone would think well of me. But I don't want to give in that way. Giving should be sufficient in itself. I want to move away from my self-centeredness. I want to develop more of a sense of selflessness and doing service.

Until now, I've been insecure. I've felt that unless I attained certain things, I would have nothing to give. I would think, Unless I'm this and this and this, how can I possibly give? What do I have to give? But I'm beginning to realize that there is always something to give; you can never run out of things to give. There are a lot of things a person could do even without some special qualifications, like being a big brother or just doing something for your neighbor or your wife just for the sake of giving. I want to do more of that type of thing. The more I love, the more I'll be in touch with love, and the more I'll have to give.

Family life teaches one this giving and caring mode of being. It requires the sacrifice of one's own desires, service to others, and the development of empathy. When one finds himself with children to care for, he learns to be generous and self-sacrificing. Many people are transformed from an absorption in the third-chakra mode of consciousness to a fourth-chakra perspective through their relationships with their children.

When one begins to function from the heart center, his way of relating with others undergoes a dramatic reversal. Thus, whereas two people functioning from the perspective of the third chakra might fight each other because they both desire the same object, two people operating from the fourth chakra would each be concerned with the other's welfare, and not their own. In this regard the story is told of a young man and an elderly man who, during a famine, were arguing on the street over a loaf of bread. A third man approached them to intervene. He said, "Shame on you, fighting over food. Can't you share it?" The young man replied, "I don't want to share it. I'm strong and can go for days without food. This man is old and very weak from hunger. If he doesn't eat, he may die. I insist he take this loaf of bread." Whereupon the older man retorted, "He is young and has many years before him. It is better that he eat and live. I will die soon anyway. Please convince him to take this loaf."

This story conveys the attitude of the heart chakra. There are many shining examples of those who have sacrificed self-interest—in some cases, even their lives—in order to nurture others. Living a life of service to others, they have experienced a peace and joy that is found only in this mode of consciousness. Mother Teresa of Calcutta is a contemporary exemplar of one who has experienced the fullness of giving.

The songwriter Bob Dylan has noted that even those who are most identified with mastery, power, and ownership are involved in service in some aspect of their lives. One of his songs states:

> You might own guns,
> And you might even own tanks;
> You might be somebody's landlord,
> You might even own banks—
> But you're gonna have to serve somebody,
> Yes, you're gonna have to serve somebody.[18]

During the course of a day, most people perform many services for others. For example the mailman, bus driver, garbage collector, politician, accountant, assembly-line worker, all serve many people each working day. But many of these workers remain oblivious to the service they are performing. They are working for a reward: their paycheck and the objects and experiences it will buy. If their job is routine, they may feel little sense of accomplishment or self-worth. Thus they perform their work with inattention and carelessness while dwelling on fantasies of pleasure or attainment. If, however, they were to focus on the service they are performing, even the most menial job would be experienced as meaningful and of great worth.

The view that some work is more significant and of greater worth than other work is an attitude of the third chakra, where weighing and comparing are important. At the fourth chakra, one has no interest in such comparisons, for his energy and enthusiasm are directed toward being of greater service. The bus driver or mailman operating from the perspective of the anahata chakra will take care to serve his patrons as best he can. He will be concerned for their interests rather than his reward. Working with this attitude, he may be surprised to find himself doubly rewarded where he sought no reward at all: he will be rewarded by the joy he experiences in serving and also by the unsought material rewards that are likely to accrue when one does his job well and with care.

There are various yogic practices that cultivate the modes of being found in the fourth through the seventh chakras. Karma yoga, the yoga of action, leads one to experience the fourth archetypal mode of consciousness. In karma yoga, one is taught to do actions as a service.[19] The Bhagavad Gita teaches: "Do thy work in the peace of Yoga and, free from selfish desires, be not moved in success or in failure. . . . Even as the unwise work selfishly in the bondage of selfish works, let the wise man work unselfishly for the good of all the world."[20]

This way of being is not imposed on the student of yoga, for inculcation of selfless precepts is ineffective and even harmful if one is not ready to make the transition to this mode of consciousness. Far too many children have been taught by parents, educators, and religious teachers with the best of intentions that self-interest and assertiveness is bad and that they should be selfless, giving, and loving. Rather than being encouraged to grow through the stage of ego development, they have had a more mature perspective forced upon them before they have been ready to assimilate it. As a result, it becomes necessary for them as adults to retrace their steps and acknowledge and accept those egoistic qualities in themselves that they had long denied. For one must learn to establish boundaries and a territory and to assert himself before he can move to later stages in the evolution of consciousness. He must first define himself and take responsibility for himself before he can give himself in serving another. If he does not, he will merely develop an outward persona, a false front, of being loving and generous; he will mimic this way of being while inwardly remaining in that earlier mode of consciousness that he was not allowed to develop. Yoga therapy assists at each stage in this evolutionary journey. It helps one to recover emotions, to develop assertiveness and ego capacities, and then to progress beyond identification with the egoistic mode of being.

Although identifying with the fourth-chakra mode of consciousness leads to a more radiant and loving life, it is still far from the most evolved state of consciousness. One operating from the heart center still may experience incompleteness and discontent. Though one is reaching beyond himself, he still experiences the world from a dualistic frame of reference. The scenarios that are played out at the anahata chakra require a helper and a person who needs aid, comfort, and nurturance. For one to experience and enact those dramas, discomfort and suffering must exist in the world, so that one can provide aid and comfort and partially alleviate suffering. In still more evolved states of consciousness, those limitations are also transcended.

One may believe that the love he shares emanates from him, that it is his love. But when this mode of being is used in the service of the more evolved chakras, one comes to understand that he is merely an instrument for the love that is flowing through him from a more comprehensive center of being. By emptying himself of his egoistic concerns, he makes himself a clear channel through which the love of the Supreme may flow unimpeded.

Chapter Eleven

Spiritual Aspects of Psychotherapy

At the fourth chakra, the heart center, one begins the transition from egoistic consciousness to a new mode of being that recognizes and is guided by a far more inclusive center of organization than the ego. In the first three modes of consciousness, one learns to define himself as a distinct being and to function in terms of his limited self-definition. As the ego develops at the third chakra, it helps to lift one out of the elemental fear and impulsiveness that can plague one in the first two modes of consciousness; the unfoldment of the ego enables one to cope in the world. However, the ego itself can become an obstruction to further progress. It stands as a barrier at the threshold of the evolutionary phase of development. When the ego attempts to assert its supremacy, it restricts one from consciously reorganizing around a more comprehensive center.

Modern psychotherapy, for the most part, is oriented toward the development and strengthening of the ego, and this is quite appropriate for those who are struggling to free themselves from the preoccupations of the more primitive levels of consciousness. As we have seen, yoga therapy also helps one who is functioning at those levels to develop his ego capacities. However, current models of psychotherapy generally neglect to help one reach beyond identification with the ego, whereas yoga therapy is especially beneficial in this latter phase of development.

A person typically identifies with the ego and the extremely limited attributes that the ego has taken upon itself; he considers himself to be, for example, good-looking, shy, lazy, competent, absentminded, and so on. Psychotherapy helps one modify his definition of himself; attributes that are considered to be more positive or that fit more closely with the demands of the social or natural environment are gradually substituted for those that have caused acute distress. As a result of psychotherapy, a person may begin to define himself as capable and lovable or in terms of other attributes that are considered to be positive. But even an ego that identifies with positive attributes remains fundamentally insecure and seeks to bolster itself by manipulating the external environment. One acquires possessions and power, yet he continues to suffer as a result of demands, expectations, frustrations, disappointments, and various emotional states. Changes in the attributes associated with the ego may temporarily diminish one's sense of unhappiness to a limited degree, but such surface modifications have no effect on the underlying cause of unhappiness. Human suffering cannot be eliminated by this process.

According to the dualistic and monistic paradigms, all human suffering is ultimately the result of spiritual impoverishment, that is, nonawareness of transcendent being. Psychotherapies that do not foster this awareness are at best a means for temporarily holding suffering at bay. Therapies that help to strengthen the ego are fine in their place, but therapies are also needed that lead a person beyond identification with the ego and that help him become aware of a more integrative center of consciousness. The therapist who is unable to help the client recognize this dimension of life is severely restricted in his ability to help his client grow.

Many aspects of life that are difficult for clients to face are dealt with in the accepting atmosphere of the therapist's consulting room. For instance, many clients learn to come to terms with their sexuality or aggression. Yet strangely enough, the open exploration of spiritual concerns still remains taboo for the majority of psychotherapists. A number of clients who had previously been in psychotherapy have told me that when they tried to deal with spiritual concerns, the therapist was unable to work with them in a way that respected and affirmed the spiritual aspect of life. There are a significant number of people who feel a need for psychotherapy but who do not seek out a therapist because they believe that the typical therapist has little regard for spirituality. Many of these people also avoid pastoral counseling because they do not want to be directed toward a particular religious dogma. They find themselves in the dark limbo between reductionist psychology and religious insti- tutionalism, limited to a choice between psychotherapy that ignores the spiritual dimension of life and counseling that incorporates religious dogma. It is important that psychotherapeutic approaches be developed that encourage one to explore and discover for himself his relation to transcendent being.

There is a legitimate concern among psychotherapists that a clear distinction be maintained between psychotherapy and religion. It is unfortunate, however, that most psychotherapists have not yet learned that it is possible to deal with spiritual issues outside the context of religious institutionalism. It is possible to develop a spiritually based psychotherapy that respects the client's own developing awareness of transcendent being without imposing belief in a particular form of God, means of worship, or religious dogma.

In yoga therapy, a consideration of the spiritual dimension of life is the foundation of the therapeutic process; it is the substratum upon which all the therapeutic work is based. In this form of therapy, work with the body, breath, habits, the unconscious, and interpersonal relations all focus on clearing up obstructions, preoccupations, and divisiveness in order to free one to experience the unity that underlies all apparent conflict within and without. The client learns to overcome discord, to reach beyond his limitations, and to experience an ever more en-compassing unity, while at the same time maintaining his integrity as a conscious being. The therapist who himself has an appreciation of unitary consciousness will gradually help the client to let go of his absorption in each of the polarities of his life and thereby come closer to the experience of unity. In the process of therapy, identification with the ego is transcended and consciousness of the Self as the most comprehensive center of integration dawns.

Yoga therapy does not involve itself with any religion, the worship of any particular deity, or devotion to any religious or charismatic leader. It is an experimental and experiential quest, in which one gradually increases his capacity to be an unbiased observer. Its experiments are not limited by either the dogmatism of the mechanistic scientific paradigm or the dogmatism of religious belief. In this quest, one becomes a voyager within. There are maps and guides, but one must experience and find out for himself what is true and what is mere fancy or fantasy.

One's spiritual evolution takes place in three stages; the three highest chakras lead to progressively more encompassing experiences of spiritual unfoldment. At the first of these, the fifth chakra, *vishuddha,* the ego surrenders its authority to a universal nurturing center of love and wisdom. One remains identified with the more circumscribed ego, but the center of his interest is now some aspect of universal consciousness, which becomes the object of his devotion. At the sixth chakra, *ajna,* further disinvolvement with the limited perspective of the ego takes place. One becomes a neutral observer of the melodramas of life, experiencing an underlying unity of being. Finally, at the seventh chakra, *sahasrara,* one passes beyond all involvement with form and realizes the highest state, nondual consciousness.

Surrender

We have seen how the first three chakras draw one into the involutionary phase of the unfoldment of consciousness. One becomes entangled in the world of names and forms as he becomes addicted to the objects of his desires and then identifies with the ego and the scenarios the ego creates. The heart chakra is transitional, and the fifth chakra, vishuddha, brings the evolutionary phase of the journey into prominence.

At the stage of transition, the heart center, one leaves behind the distrust, desire, and pride of the lower three chakras and begins to experience a greater sense of unity with others. In the egoistic mode of consciousness, one remained focused on himself. He established the boundaries of and defended his territory, came to believe in his own capacities as an individual ego, and also became aware of his limitations as a separate person. Now at the anahata chakra, he experiences abundant love that radiates outward toward others. But we may wonder, Is it possible to love so genuinely and completely unless one has received such abundant love himself? To answer this question, we must climb still higher on the ladder of spiritual evolution, to the vishuddha chakra. Here one finds the complementary experience to that which occurs at anahata. When one's heart is his center, he nurtures others; at vishuddha, the throat center, one receives nurturance.

At the anahata chakra, one gives up his egoistic preoccupations and, looking outward across the horizontal plane of his existence, becomes concerned with the needs of others. At vishuddha, one's outlook changes: at this center one looks upward toward that which transcends himself and humanity; he calls upward toward the heavens. While the heart center leads to the experience of humanism, the throat center awakens one to theism. At vishuddha, one gives up the ego as his center; he turns toward a more transcendent center and experiences the nurturance and guidance that flow from that center. He becomes enthralled with one or more of the glorious forms of God.

Educated people in modern society, for the most part, have not reached this perspective. They are functioning from the orientation of the egoistic or humanistic center. Modern psychology, with a few exceptions, does not appreciate the validity of the vishuddha perspective but considers the expressions of a person in this mode of consciousness to be an indication of regression to a more primitive mode of being. To the present-day societal establishment, the perspective of vishuddha seems irrational, mystical, other-worldly, impractical, naive, childlike, and irresponsible. Jung has noted that "collectively we have not crossed the distance between *anahata* and *visuddha*. So if one speaks of *visuddha,* it is of course with a certain hesitation. We are stepping into the slippery future when we try to understand what that might mean. For in *visuddha* we reach beyond our actual conception of the world, in a way we reach the ether region."[1]

In the vishuddha mode of consciousness, one realizes the majesty and grandeur in all manifestation, from the colossal to the most minute. He recognizes the archetypes that lie behind the world of names and forms as it is ordinarily experienced and becomes aware of divinity present in and sustaining all existence. Finding that he is loved and supported by the divine source from which all is manifest, he becomes like a trusting child and feels guided and protected. He experiences being fully accepted and forgiven, no matter what he has done or may do.

Devotional prayer, chanting, adoration of a divine form, and other devotional acts are means of surrendering one's absorption in his personality, desires, and egoistic concerns and turning toward the divine beloved. Becoming absorbed in the beloved instead of in his own desires or the cares and concerns of his ego, he begins to experience the limitless stream of love, compassion, and understanding that flows from the Mother or Father of this universe. He realizes that he is loved unconditionally and begins to accept himself unconditionally. Thus it is through experiencing divine love that one becomes truly able to love. The divine milk that is taken at the throat chakra flows through one's heart to nurture others. The great lovers of humanity have never felt that it is their love that is being expressed; they feel as though they are merely a conduit for the expression of divine love. They have succeeded in the most difficult of human undertakings: to surrender one's petty concerns and turn oneself over to that which is universal, to become a channel for the ever-flowing love that emanates from the fountainhead of life.

Creativity

Physically, the throat serves the dual purpose of enabling one to take in sustenance and to express oneself. Although these may seem to be unrelated functions, they actually complement one another in forming the experience of the vishuddha chakra.

One's voice is a vehicle through which he shapes his experiences. By speaking in a derogatory or doubting manner, one can create negative experiences in himself and others, whereas by speaking loving words or chanting with devotion, one can create a heaven. In fact, the throat chakra is the center through which the individual creates his environment and his relationship to it; vishuddha is the center of creative expression in all forms.

One's creative abilities have the power to raise him to the heavens, but most people use their speech and creative powers in the service of the ego and the lower chakras. Modern works of art often lead both the creator and the experiencer to greater identification with worldly desires. Such use of our artistic capacity, instead of uplifting us, keeps us mired in the more primitive modes of consciousness. In the modern world, we have to a large extent lost our connection with the spiritual realm. Today, as Jung observed, "our conscious idea of God is abstract and remote, one hardly dares to speak of it; it has become tabu, or it is such a worn-out coin that one can hardly exchange it."[2]

Whether he is aware of it or not, one does not create through his ego alone. The ego has a severely limited scope of concern. Most creative artists describe their inspiration as coming from a more transcendent source; for one must surrender to a higher and more encompassing fountain of inspiration if he is to pour forth new insights or forms. The source from which guidance and inspiration flows to the artist has historically been called the muse; in the modern world, it is often called the unconscious. When another person experiences an inspired work of art, he also feels connected to that which transcends his egoistic focus. The vishuddha mode of experience may be summarized by the word *surrender*—not surrender to another person, to desires, to some cause or ism, but surrender to the divine. One surrenders to a higher power and only then does creative expression flow forth.

It is by directing his voice and creative powers upward that a human being establishes a relationship with divine forms. Chanting, prayer, and devotional art enable one to surrender his egoistic perspective and preoccupations and become aware of his connection to that which sustains him and the entire universe. Through surrendering one's egoistic concerns in devotional exercises, one brings his consciousness into relationship with the divine; he comes to feel that he is the child or beloved of that transcendent consciousness. Through this process, he opens himself to become aware of the divine nectar or ambrosia that has always been flowing to him and through him. He becomes aware that he is being looked after, guided, and loved by the supreme consciousness at all times, no matter how mischievous he may be, no matter how much he may at times ignore, turn away from, or deny that love.

From this center, one calls the divine down from the heavenly realm to nurture and sustain him. This mode of being has been evoked by the mystics throughout history. The Psalms of the Old Testament convey this experience. They sing:

> The Lord is my shepherd; I shall not want.
> He maketh me to lie down in green pastures: he leadeth me beside
> the still waters.
> He restoreth my soul: he leadeth me in the paths of righteousness
> for his name's sake.
> Yea, though I walk through the valley of the shadow of death, I
> will fear no evil: for thou art with me; thy rod and thy staff they
> comfort me.
> Thou preparest a table before me in the presence of mine enemies:
> thou anointest my head with oil; my cup runneth over.
> Surely goodness and mercy shall follow me all the days of my life:
> and I will dwell in the house of the Lord for ever.[3]

The vishuddha chakra is not only the center and source of creation within the individual; it is also the center through which one experiences the creative process in the macrocosm. When consciousness is centered here, one becomes aware of the primordial or archetypal forms and powers from which the universe is manifest. The truly great artists and spiritual leaders throughout history are those who have opened themselves to the experiences of those transcendent forms and have made the experiences available to others through their words and artistic expressions.

Seeking Unconditional Love

The chakras depict the various motivations that a human being may have. Man is motivated by the survival instinct, the desire for sensory pleasure, mastery and power, and he is motivated to love and nurture others. But the attainment of all that one seeks in the first four modes of consciousness still leaves one incomplete and unfulfilled. More significant than any of those motivations is the desire to be loved and accepted unconditionally. If one experiences unconditional love and acceptance, all prior motivations lose their compelling quality.

Every client who comes to therapy feels he has been deprived of unconditional love and acceptance. Under the guise of attempting to resolve conflicts and problems, the client enters therapy to find unconditional love and acceptance in the therapeutic relationship. In the unique and artificial structure of psychotherapy, the therapist may provide a greater degree of unconditional acceptance than the client has been able to find anywhere else in his life. But every therapist has his human limitations. The therapist who is conscious of the vishuddha chakra may help the client to become aware of a more profound source of nurturance and love than even the therapist can provide. The following interchange with a young woman who had been experiencing insecurity and moments of panic is an example of a yoga therapist leading a client in this direction:

T: As you were talking, I was imagining you in a place where everything that you needed was being provided. I wanted to say, "Don't panic; there is nothing to panic about. Everything you need is here; there is nothing for you to be afraid of." Then I imagined you experiencing all that you need being given to you. Whatever you needed in terms of nurturance, or comfort, or feeling good was given.

C: That feels real good. That is the way I felt the other morning in meditation, that I was really loved and cared for. Every time I think of that I just feel so warm. I don't have to be aggressively seeking it. It would be there if I just surrender.

Throughout the course of history, human beings have directed their devotion toward a deity. They have worshiped God as Father or as Mother and have felt nurtured, guided, and accepted by that form of transcendent consciousness. Today, for many educated people, the belief in divinity is absent. One searches about like a homeless orphan for a refuge in the restless storm of modern life.

Life today is filled with interpersonal politics and competition. Many people have learned to be distrustful of others, of institutions, and of religious and secular leaders. Such a person develops an egoistic attitude, asserting, "I can take care of everything myself." He does not allow himself to relax and experience support and nurturance. He has not learned to acknowledge weakness, uncertainty, or vulnerability within himself and has yet to experience the comfort of surrendering his egoistic identifications.

The neck, an extremely vulnerable part of the body, is where the jugular vein is located. Certain species of animals expose their necks in play or in a fight as an indication of surrender. People who lack trust and are unable to experience surrender may complain of a tightness and constriction in the neck and throat. In our everyday parlance, a "stiff-necked" person is one who is stubborn, obstinate, and unyielding. Such a person may attempt to protect himself and hide his vulnerability. Rather than exposing his neck, he may wear stiff, tight-fitting collars, ties, or turtleneck shirts.

The yoga therapist may help the client to experience trust and vulnerability and to establish a connection to transcendent or ideal forms. He may guide the client in this direction without influencing him to adopt any particular religious belief. The following group therapy session illustrates this aspect of the therapeutic process:

C1: I fight any kind of assistance or help from outside myself. I don't like to accept help from other people.

T: Are you saying that you have difficulty trusting another person or the group, that you stand by yourself rather than trusting?

C1: I think that's part of it. (Crying) Last week I had some glimpses of being taken care of. Once in a class, you said something about divine nurturance, and I asked you what that was. You talked about being taken care of by the Divine Mother, but I couldn't really understand. It wasn't something I could internalize or believe myself. It was something that I would have liked to believe, but I couldn't at the time.

I never had a clear concept of what God is. But last week after the group, I went home and lay down to sleep. I was thinking about my relationship with my husband and how I get to these points where I don't know what to do anymore. I surrendered myself to the Divine Mother. While I was doing it, I could hardly believe it. It was a revolutionary thing for me; I felt almost embarrassed even to myself. It didn't fit in with the way I was or the way I believe. It was such a good feeling for me to surrender like that, to feel as if some invisible person was holding me like I hold my son. It was such a powerful experience for me.

I've had trouble falling asleep after our weekly group meeting because so much comes out in the group. But that night I was able to fall asleep and sleep soundly all night. I've had a similar experience almost every night since. I feel embarrassed about telling you this; if I would tell my husband, he'd laugh at me and would think I was really kooky.

C2: This week I made a conscious effort to mentally picture myself being taken care of, just like I would take care of my child. I'd run the thought through my mind that I was whole and complete and cared for and loved by whatever God is. It's something I need to do.

C3: I can really identify with what you are both saying. A few weeks ago when I was home alone, I lay down and I was crying. There was a fear that I had gotten in touch with, and there was that feeling of not trusting; I had to be in control and to be tight and cautious and careful. Then I thought, "Who do I think I am? I can't control everything." If I would just trust and let go, just trust life. Not that I give up all responsibility: I do what I have to do, and at the same time, I'm aware that it's okay. Then I remembered an experience I had once in which I knew with my whole being that I would always be taken care of. I thought, "How could I go back to not trusting?" It's a very slow process. I know it all involves trust.

A person ordinarily expects his parents to be ideal rather than human. When his parents fail to live up to the ideal projected onto them, when they are not able to provide unconditional love, nurturance, and refuge from the travails of life, he may become cynical and untrusting. If he does not receive the love he seeks, he may blame himself and carry a sense of unworthiness and inadequacy into his adult years.

Clients in psychotherapy frequently report that they have tried unsuccessfully throughout their lives to gain acceptance from their parents. A client may come to the realization that he will never win his parents' approval, but that does not necessarily free him from feeling worthless. As long as he invests his parent with archetypal significance, considering his parent to be his basic source of love and acceptance, he will continue to feel unworthy and inadequate. However, if he is able to separate the archetype from the parent and find a more adequate expression of that archetype, his experience of being rejected can be replaced with the awareness that he is loved unconditionally.

In some instances, clients are made aware of this transference of the ideal onto a human being through direct confrontation, as is illustrated by the following dialogue:

C: I was constantly rejected by my mother. I was never accepted. I can't remember ever being hugged by her when I was little or hearing the words, "I love you." I didn't get that from my father either.

T: What if I were to tell you something that will sound really absurd?

C: What's that?

T: That your father and mother aren't really your father and mother. That they don't really have the authority that you think they do.

C: Then I don't have anybody. Then I'm like an orphan; I'm lost and all alone.

T: Might you have another father and mother? (Pause) In telling you this, I'm sharing my own experience of how I relate to my parents.

C: How's that?

T: I don't experience them as really being my father and mother. They have shared with me what they have been able to share; they've taken care of me, guided me, and loved me the best they know how; but their understanding and their capacities are limited. I don't expect the unconditional love and acceptance I seek to come from them, but from another source.

Another client described her response to a similar confrontation:

In our initial session together, I spent a lot of time complaining about my parents and other relatives. You told me that it is always frustrating to expect things from people that they simply aren't able to give. You said I might be better off looking toward my "real parents." I think you were talking about a supreme consciousness, a more complete and reliable source of nurturance and support. I realized that this change of focus could ultimately enhance my relationships with the loved ones I was complaining about. I'd need less from them. I'd be more capable of allowing them to be as they are.

That seemed like a terrific idea, but it was too big for me to deal with directly at the time, so I put it on the back burner to simmer. Now it seems to be spilling over into my life almost without effort and without my thinking about it. For example, often now when I'm angry, afraid, frustrated, or even simply bored, I don't stay very long in that frame of mind. I experience that there is a power I can call on so that I can do things in the world more smoothly than if I use my mind, ego, and emotions alone. I don't yet have a real understanding of what this power is or where it is, but I do know that I can use it.

The recognition of expressions of the parental archetypes other than one's natural parents does not depend on belief in a religion or belief in God in a particular form. But there is a shared assumption between client and therapist that some transcending, divinely nurturing force exists, and that if one opens oneself to that source, needs that cannot be adequately met in human relationships can indeed find fulfillment.

The source of nurturance can mistakenly be projected onto objects as well as people. Those objects that have accompanied the experience of being loved may themselves be sought out as though they could provide love and acceptance. For example, in childhood the experience of receiving unconditional love and acceptance is closely related to being fed. One unconsciously makes the connection even as an adult. Hence when one is anxious or fearful or feels inadequate or unloved, he may substitute physical nurturance for the love and acceptance he would like. In our society, many people overeat in order to eliminate the emptiness, hollowness, insecurity, or anxiety they experience when they do not feel loved and accepted. But food will not provide the comfort and security that one seeks. The following statement by an obese woman who had come to the United States from South America as a teenager describes the lack of nurturance she experienced upon coming here and the way in which she turned toward sweets to take the place of affection:

> I stayed in a house in the suburbs, and it was quiet all the time, just like a cemetery. Where I grew up, all the windows were open and you heard people talking. Merchants went around making loud noises, and there were always people in the house. Food was always cooking. But here I was isolated. It just felt dead to me. There were no trees and the homes all looked alike. The house where I lived was so cold and the kitchen was always so neat and clean. I just couldn't believe two white pieces of bread and a thin piece of bologna between and that was lunch. I was used to lots of rice and beans and tasty potatoes, a whole meal. I didn't feel fed at all. It wasn't just the food. I was starved for love and warmth. Somehow affection has gotten tied up with food. At home, I never had candy bars or cakes or things like that. When I came to the United States, there were vending machines at school, which was strange to me—machines standing there all day and night. You put money in and a candy bar or some ice cream came out. I turned toward sweets.

In the course of therapy, this woman had become aware that her longing for sweets was a compensation for the nurturance she was not receiving from others. In a later therapy session, she realized that neither her parents nor food can provide the degree of nurturance and protection that she seeks, that she must turn toward a transcendent source to experience that sustenance:

C: I was home alone and I wanted to forget about my problems and enjoy eating. I let myself act out my feelings to see what it is that I'm so attached to. My first reaction was that the food was security. I wanted to be held by the orange. I could see how silly it was.

T: Don't you find that kind of nurturance apart from food?

C: I don't recall being held by my mother. Sometimes even now when I go to visit my parents, I would like to kiss and hug them, but instead we sit and enjoy my mother's food. I'm looking for something more than food and kissing and hugging. When I kiss a couple of times, it gives me joy, but then I become tired of it.

T: How can you maintain that feeling?

C: I don't know. I think that food is going to give it to me, and it does for the first few moments, but then comes the depression.

T: Could that urge be satisfied by turning to some spiritual object?

C: Yes; once instead of eating, I called for God's help. Then I started crying and just let it out. I don't know why I was crying.

T: I wonder if it would help even more to visualize God nurturing and loving you.

C: Is there a female God?

T: In the Christian tradition, there is Mary, Christ's mother. In some Eastern traditions, she is called the Divine Mother.

C: You know, when I call "Mother" when I'm feeling pain, I'm not actually calling for my mother, for her as a person. Usually I feel relieved and cry.

In the vishuddha mode of consciousness, one experiences in a theistic way; he experiences relationships to ideal forms. If he does not find an adequate carrier for his ideal, he projects the ideal onto people, institutions, and objects and eventually experiences disappointment. The therapist's function here is to help the client find adequate symbols through which he can establish his relationship to the ideal forms. In some cases, leading the client to a relationship with symbolic expressions found within spiritual traditions serves that purpose.

Many psychologists would react negatively to this viewpoint, arguing that the therapist is encouraging the client to substitute benign fantasies for the "hard reality of life." Reductionist therapies do not offer the possibility that the longed-for relationship can be fulfilled. The sought-after love and acceptance is interpreted as a primitive wish fulfillment that does not square with the reality of the adult world. According to this view, maturity comes when one gives up the wish for unconditional acceptance and understanding.

By contrast, yoga therapy, as well as other therapies that acknowledge the archetypal level of human experience, offers the possibility of establishing a relationship with the ideal nurturing parent and with other ideals. In these therapies, one learns to respect his need for unconditional love and acceptance and develops a conscious relationship to those symbols and forms that embody the archetypes of the nurturing parent. One is encouraged to withdraw his projections from objects, people, and institutions and to direct his longing toward symbols and forms that can adequately express the archetype without leading to disappointment.

In the course of yoga therapy, one learns that even the ideal forms, which may be experienced as divinities existing outside oneself, are really projections of one's inner being. Ultimately, this process leads to the experience of a transcendent core within oneself. As one progresses in spiritual awareness, he is encouraged to realize that the source of nurturance and acceptance is not external but is at the center of one's being. This is perhaps the most important contribution of meditation and the Eastern spiritual traditions. As the following client indicates, this realization may be difficult for those who are taught to believe in a god that is forever external to oneself:

C: It sometimes scares me to believe in divinity within myself. It is so different from what I am used to.

T: What are you used to?

C: The notion that God is out there and we are here in misery. He is there to help us when we need help, but the only things that we have are the things that are down here. These are in our domain, and God is out there somewhere. The challenge of this new perspective seems to bring me more to life: I am not depending on God out there to take care of me or to give me paradise. I can take responsibility for the spirituality also. In the old way, we could take care of the physical aspect, and the emotional was ours too; but once you got to the spiritual, that was always left to God.

Another client expressed a growing awareness of a transcendent center of consciousness within:

> You are the first therapist that I have come to not just for psychological or emotional problems, but to deal with spiritual concerns as well. Somehow I connect religion with my old experience of God as being someone outside of me. In order to learn about God, I had to learn it from other people. And they taught that He was out there and up there, and the only way to get there was to go through them. My experience in the past few years is that God is within; the way to understand God is to understand myself and to go within. When I have meditated with that attitude, it works.

In psychotherapy the client may develop a positive transference, projecting the archetype of divine nurturance onto the therapist. Some therapists, in order to raise their own sense of worth and esteem or to manipulate the client, may encourage such transference reactions rather than encouraging the client to relate to the archetype through spiritual symbols or forms or to experience the archetype within himself. Such encouragement leads the client to become dependent on the therapist and eventually to become disappointed. The following description by a client of her relationship with her former therapist illustrates the way that the archetype of the nurturing, all-accepting parent may be projected onto the therapist with the therapist's encouragement. The client then expects the therapist to extend that relationship into their personal life outside of the therapy session. Disappointment, frustration, and anger are the inevitable results.

> In Dr. K's presence, I felt protection and care, but even more. Through him, I had a sense that not only was I provided for and

loved, but all things were watched over and taken care of. The amphetamines and antidepressants that I had previously required to fight my despondency were no longer needed. I felt happy and alive again. Through this doctor, I felt reconnected to the source of life from which I had been cut off.

I began to mistake his kindness and concern as a personal response to me. The desire for union became very intense. I longed for us to be together and fervently believed it would be so. I associated with him all the childhood dreams that a young girl formulates and still carries around with her as an adult. I projected all those hopes onto him, conceiving of a life of relative simplicity, shared with him in love and reverence.

When the unreality of my dreams hit me, I suffered an unendurable sense of loss. I experienced tremendous grief and pain; I felt totally abandoned and alone. It was not that a certain kind of love and caring didn't still exist, for it did, but it was not directed toward me in the very special way I had imagined. I felt only the absence of all I had hoped for and lived for. Along with the pain, there was anger too, directed toward this doctor who had let me misdirect myself so completely and for so long. I felt I should not have been allowed to make that error and that he could have prevented it.

This client terminated therapy, and later entered a more spiritually oriented therapeutic process. During the course of that therapy, she withdrew that which she had been projecting onto her first therapist and came to experience a more fulfilling center of nurturance within herself.

When the sense of protection was withdrawn from the person whom I depended upon for it, it slowly emerged from sources within. I had definite, clear experiences where I felt led, directed, and guided from deep within. Gradually, the feeling of protection and guidance became more constant, and I felt wholly enveloped by loving care. As I felt this love and care more, I also found myself more loving and caring. My whole life changed.

One may also project the archetype of the ideal nurturing parent onto one's mate, as the following excerpt from a therapy session illustrates. In this session, the therapist helps the client to become aware that what she is seeking outside is really to be found within herself.

C: Ever since my teens, I have been preoccupied with a fantasy somewhat like the story of Cinderella. The charming prince comes and takes care of me. He is powerful and he gives me a sense of worth by caring for me. He is supposed to be perfect. My husband had some of the qualities I was looking for, but I augmented the whole thing, making a perfect being out of him in my mind. I saw my husband as some type of savior. I had the illusion that once we were married, there would be happiness forever. But after we had our daughter, he started to have some psychological difficulties himself. That really shocked me. I wasn't ready to have my Prince Charming have any psychological problems.

T: It seems that the sense of worth in your fantasy doesn't belong to you, that you see it as being out there. The prince has all the self-worth and he can dispense it. Where is Prince Charming getting his power?

C: He has it. He is all-powerful.

T: And you are just recognizing it in him, you are just recognizing what is already there?

C: Yes.

T: And your husband lost his power?

C: (Pause) I guess he never had it. I put it there in my fantasy.

T: So the power and sense of self-worth belong to you, and you give it to Prince Charming in your fantasy so that he can give it back to you?

An executive in his early forties gave the following account of his therapy:

Last year I saw a conventional therapist for about six months. That process seemed to have a circularity and opaqueness which failed to yield any insights that I considered significant. My motivation for going was the conflicts I was having with my parents. I came out of that therapy experience without understanding the real nature of my contribution to that conflict. I determined to find a new psychotherapist who combined psychology with spiritual practice, knowledge, and insight.

I had been intently seeking acceptance in the outer world. I wanted desperately to please my wife all the time, to have her never become angry at me, and I wanted to feel that my parents love and accept me. This search drove me to try to find ways to meet their conditions.

After I described a conflict I had with my wife last week, you asked if I felt she accepted me without any conditions. Clearly not; there were definite conditions. Then you asked a question which triggered dramatic personal insights: "Is there *anybody* who accepts you unconditionally?" I thought, Certainly my wife loves me deeply, and yet sometimes she places conditions on her acceptance of me. Family? Each parent definitely has expectations of me and does not fully accept me unless the expectations are met. Friends? Same thing. Myself? Do I accept myself unconditionally? Definitely not. My mind is the least accepting of all. It has an endless string of conditions for accepting me. I work hard to meet one, and before I've finished, five more conditions jump into my consciousness.

You asked again, "Is there anybody who accepts you unconditionally?" Then I felt a wave of emotion sweep through me. The Supreme accepts me unconditionally. I felt unconditional acceptance flood through my heart. The awareness flowed as direct feeling, no longer as a mental idea. For so long, I had sought unconditional acceptance in the outer world—from friends, family, job, my own mind. Whenever conditions arose, I tried hard to meet them. But I never experienced unconditional acceptance.

I realized then that the drawing force of my life is a continual search for unconditional love and acceptance. I am a seeker of unconditional love, and I can receive it only from the inner world—from the Supreme. All I have to do is open myself to it, and the feeling flows into my awareness—because it's already there. There is no way I can ever get unconditional acceptance from anything in the outer world or from my mind, with all its confusions. Only the Supreme can give this unalloyed love. For me to focus my seeking on my wife or parents rather than on the Supreme is to place an impossible burden on them. It's unfair. And yet for all my life, that's exactly what I had been doing. Now I feel like my life is permanently centered. And my need to look for this unconditional acceptance from others and from my mind is much less.

In my relationship with my wife, there have been no recurrences of our past conflicts. I can accept her nonacceptance of me when it occurs. I acknowledge to myself at such times that the Supreme loves me unconditionally, that I can't expect my wife to, and that it's okay.

When one experiences such a relationship with the transcendent, he no longer relates to others in terms of demands that he be loved and accepted, for that fundamental need is already being fulfilled. He can relate more fully and spontaneously to another person without distorting his experience of that person because of his own needs. That enables him to become more responsive to others.

Transference may extend beyond one's relationship to parents, mate, or therapist. A person may idealize a movie star, musician, hero, political, religious, or cult leader, or any figure who is portrayed as an ideal, and direct his devotional feelings toward that person. Or he may surrender to a political, religious, or cult movement with similar zeal. If he becomes enraptured with an ideal as it is projected onto the worldly sphere, he may go to any lengths for that ideal. He may become caught up in intensely melodramatic experiences in sacrificing himself for a cause rather than establishing objectivity to observe the grand archetypal themes being played out around him. Far too late, he is likely to find that his idol or cause is not all that he or it claimed to be.

If one's devotion is directed toward a cause, he may find guidance and nurturance from that movement and surrender his decision making, his responsibility, his territoriality, even his possessions, to the cause or its leader. It is important to distinguish surrender to a form that claims to be an ideal from surrender to that which genuinely symbolizes the ideal. Many people are so eager to find support or parental figures that they surrender themselves to a leader or institution that they believe will rescue them from their unhappiness. They are prepared to follow almost any charismatic figure. Such people are merely surrendering to the ego of another and are ready to believe any nonsense that may be put forth by the leader or institution.

One of the most important qualities to be developed in yoga therapy is discrimination (*viveka*), the ability to distinguish between that which is unreal, insubstantial, and illusory, and that which is real, substantial, and abiding. The world contains many allurements and attractions that promise one fulfillment but that ultimately lead to disappointment if one surrenders to them. One must learn to distinguish between those allurements and that which stands behind and manifests the alluring forms that enrapture human beings.

As a person evolves, his experience of surrender also evolves. Surrender is initially linked with experiences at the more primitive chakras: a person may surrender in a battle for survival and be slain; one may surrender to a person or object that gives him sensory gratification; he may devote himself to someone who has more power and authority than he—he may identify with the person or institution to which he is surrendering and thereby feel a greater sense of power himself. All these forms of surrender are adumbrations: they prefigure surrender to a state of consciousness that transcends the ego's subject-object mode of being. Ultimately, one must learn to surrender egoistic consciousness to a mode of consciousness that is far more comprehensive. That is the experience of the vishuddha chakra. One must be careful not to stop short by merely surrendering to a cause or to the ego of another.

It is at the throat chakra that one also experiences romance; the romances of ancient and modern times are expressions of this mode of consciousness. As Cervantes' Don Quixote shows us time and again, anyone or anything can become the object of one's romantic inclinations. If the object later turns out to be unworthy of one's investment, he will become disillusioned, but the longing for romance will not cease. For one's unrelenting quest is to find an object that is not merely a receptacle for his projected ideal but actually is that ideal. One need not create romances out of fantasy. If he simply empties himself of all imagined romances, he will find that there is a substratum to life that is the basis and the fulfillment of all romances—a realm more alluring, majestic, and splendorous than he could ever envision in fantasy. All romances conjured up by the human imagination are merely adumbrations, imperfect imitations, that point the way to a realm where fulfillment of one's ideals can be experienced.

Yantra

When one is unaware of the archetypal level of his being, he unknowingly acts out archetypal themes. He is not free to choose his own attitudes and actions. At the vishuddha chakra, one becomes conscious of the various archetypes; he learns to appreciate the majesty that underlies even the most ordinary occurrences. To the extent that he is able to remain a neutral observer of the archetypal enactments, he also becomes free from the power and dominance of the archetypes.

Yoga assists one in becoming aware of the archetypes as they function in his life and in freeing himself from their dominance over him. Each yogic practice, from the hatha yoga postures to the use of mantra in meditation, helps one to become aware of the archetypal themes being played out in the dramas of everyday life. In yoga therapy, one may come to know the hero, the wise old man, the divine mother, the fool, the trickster, or numerous other ideal forms. He becomes aware of the archetypes within himself as well as in others, and of the dramas that evolve from them. He learns how his identification with a particular archetypal expression restricts his awareness and freedom, and he undergoes a process of leaving behind his identification with each archetype and its limitations in order to experience all his possibilities. The yoga therapist may use dreams or artistic expression to help the client become aware of the ideal forms. He may also ask the client to concentrate on a particular form that symbolizes a divine state of being in order that the client may align his consciousness with that transcendent state of consciousness.

Both Sankhya and tantra psychology, upon which much of yoga therapy is based, lead one to an awareness of underlying archetypal principles from which the phenomenal universe is manifest. Sankhya is based on the science of numbers, and according to this science, each number symbolizes a mode of experience. For example, the number two represents polarity and all experiences of a dualistic nature, while the number three introduces a new perspective that comprehends polarity. Sankhya describes the many psychological, philosophical, and practical meanings and implications of each number. The science of yantra is a branch of tantra which is concerned with geometric archetypal forms—the point, line, circle, triangle, square, and so on—which are the basic building blocks of the phenomenal universe. In tantric practices, one gains mastery over the archetypal forms and thus mastery over the manifest world.

In yoga meditation, most students concentrate on a sound form called a *mantra*. As the student's ability to focus the mind is strengthened, he may also be given a *yantra* or visual form upon which to focus his attention during meditation. A mantra is the expression of the ideal in the realm of sound, whereas a yantra is its expression in the visual realm.

A yantra is a particular type of mandala used in the yogic tradition. It is made up of basic geometric forms arranged in a prescribed manner. The yantra usually has a central point (*bindu*) around which triangles, circles, squares, and other shapes are ordered. The prescribed arrangement is a symbolic depiction that elicits the experience of a particular archetypal mode of consciousness. The arrangement reflects an underlying order within the psyche and the underlying organization of some facet of the universe. A yantra is a kind of mathematical formula expressing basic laws of the universe, similar to an equation like $E=mc^2$, but using geometric forms rather than arabic numbers or roman letters as the means of expression. The yantra expresses a very high order of unity and integration and is also the expression or embodiment of an extremely evolved state of consciousness. The yogic practitioner may focus his attention on a particular yantra for many minutes each day in order to experience its nature and significance. He may gaze at the form or sit with the eyes closed, visualizing the form within.

Jung was very interested in the use of visual images in psychotherapy and frequently had his patients draw or paint visual representations of their emotional and psychological states. Typically, the painting would reflect the patient's inner turmoil and discord. But some paintings produced by patients were remarkably similar to the mandalas or yantras of the Eastern meditative traditions. Jung noted the similarity, concluding that the more harmonious forms were produced by patients as the more integrative aspects of their unconscious came forward. To the degree that a patient was in touch with the deeper levels of integration within, forms similar to the Eastern mandalas and yantras spontaneously appeared in his artistic expressions.

Further comparison of the way that mandalas are used in Eastern

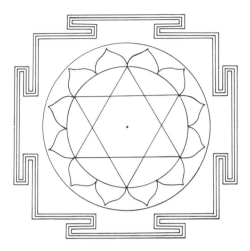

Yantra of the Anahata Chakra

meditative traditions and in Western psychotherapy leads one to become aware of a striking contrast between the methodologies of most Western therapies and the process of self-transformation in yoga. In analytic therapy, forms are analyzed as representations of one's inner state. Mandalas are considered to be expressions that arise from the unconscious and that betoken a rearranging of the personality and a new centering. It is the exceptional client who is able to bring forth these forms that express order, balance, and wholeness. Contrastively, the Eastern methodologies "anticipate the natural course of development and substitute for the spontaneous production of symbols a deliberately selected set of symbols prescribed by tradition."[4] In the yogic tradition a yantra or mantra is *given* to the student as an object of concentration. The student is asked to spend considerable time each day concentrating on the integrative form of the mantra or yantra. He is taught not to be swayed by the many distractions the mind produces but to center his consciousness ever more completely on the unifying form of the mantra or yantra. He has simply to still himself rather than wandering about in his thoughts, fantasies, daydreams, and remembrances. In order to focus his mind on the ideal form, he must withdraw his attention from the conflicts, disharmonies, and melodramas of his life. During the periods of focused awareness, he identifies with the archetypal form of the mantra or yantra. As the process is repeated each day, the old preoccupations of his mind are increasingly replaced with the divine form of his object of con-centration. In this way the object of concentration leads him to an ever more complete awareness of the underlying order of his psyche and to a more universal mode of consciousness.

Modern therapies, for the most part, do not have comparable methods that draw one toward highly evolved states of consciousness.* In modern therapy, one gropes and meanders along the path leading to self-understanding, but in the yogic tradition one is pulled toward the goal with the aid of the evolved forms. One increasingly lets go of his identification with his personality and worldly melodramas and embodies and expresses the unifying order of the universal form in accordance with which he is shaping his mind. Through repeated concentration on the given form, his old discords are gradually left behind and are replaced with the harmonious form of the mantra or yantra.

Jung understood the value of using such forms in this way. He wrote that he was "in complete agreement with the Eastern view, [that] the mandala is not only a means of expression but also produces an effect. . . . Through the ritual action, attention and interest are led back to the inner, sacred precinct, which is the source and goal of the psyche and contains the unity of life and consciousness."[5]

In analytic psychology, there is also a movement toward integration and unity, although final integration is never achieved. The mandalas drawn by patients never fully reach the degree of integration achieved in the Eastern mandalas. In summarizing Jung's view, his close student Jolande Jacobe wrote:

> The mandalas with their mathematical structure are pictures, as it were, of the "primal order of the total psyche," and their purpose is to transform chaos into cosmos. For these figures not only express order, they also bring it about.
>
> Meditation on Yantra images . . . aims precisely at the creation of an intrapsychic order in the meditator. Naturally the mandalas of analysands can never achieve the artistic perfection and finish, the "traditionally established harmony," of the mandalas of the East,

*Exceptions are found in psychosynthesis, which is derived from yoga philosophy, and in other schools of psychotherapy that use guided visualization techniques to help clients experience archetypal expressions. In these therapies the client may be asked to visualize a wise old man, a source of radiant light, or some other ideal form and to receive guidance or nurturance from that archetypal form. However, such techniques lead to only a dim recognition of the archetypes.

which are not spontaneous products of the psyche but works of conscious artistry. We have cited them only as parallels in order to show that they rest on the same psychic foundations and therefore disclose striking similarities.[6]

In yoga therapy, concentration on a mantra or yantra outside of the therapy session may be integrated with an exploration of the unconscious within the session. These are not exclusive processes, but can complement one another in the growth process. Concentration on a mantra or yantra helps to lead consciousness in a particular direction, while the exploration of the mental contents in therapy can help to clear up the involvements that keep one absorbed in the world drama and unable to fully concentrate on the ideal form.

Yantras and mantras may also be used to help one deal with unresolved issues related to a particular chakra. Each chakra has a unique yantra and a particular mantra that are the visual and sound symbols of that chakra. One may concentrate on the symbol of a particular chakra or on the physical location in the body that corresponds to that chakra. Such concentration helps to bring one's consciousness into that field of expression. As a result, one's involvement with a particular archetype may become intensified. Regular meetings with a yoga teacher or therapist are often helpful in enabling one to deal effectively with the unconscious material that surfaces as a result of such exercises.

Beyond Archetypes

If one is fortunate enough to penetrate behind the veil of materiality and to know the subtle majestic ideals from which the world of form is fashioned, he encounters another danger: he must be careful not to become enraptured even by the ideal forms. Attachment to archetypes can hold one back from still greater vistas, and identification with an archetype can lead one to lose his stability. It is important to maintain a neutral center of consciousness in order to experience the archetypes without being taken over by them. Here one needs the aid of a still more evolved mode of consciousness.

Jung and his followers developed a psychology based on the vishuddha mode of experience. In Jung's psychology, the ideals are regarded as existing within the psyche. Jung explored the realm of vishuddha in depth throughout the course of his life, and he left valuable maps and charts describing this realm that is so foreign to ego-consciousness. Few modern psychologists have reached this heightened understanding of the psyche. Nevertheless, Jung's psychology is limited, for he did not enter into the realms that lie beyond vishuddha. Jung repeatedly criticized Freud for his reductionism, for Freud understood the realms of the higher chakras in terms of the primitive chakras. Yet Jung's psychology may also be considered reductive, though not nearly to the degree of psychoanalytic psychology. Jung elevated psychological phenomena, for he interpreted the lower realms in terms of the mode of experience found at vishuddha. He nevertheless understood still more evolved modes of consciousness and interpreted more comprehensive realms in terms of this fifth chakra rather than appreciating them in their own right. This mode of consciousness is a rung on the ladder of evolution, but it is not the final step, for it is still a dualistic mode of consciousness. There is a subject and an object that is experienced—for instance, a devotee and an object of devotion—whether that object is gross or subtle, whether it is experienced as being outside or within oneself.

Archetypal forms lead one to the experience of majestic, transcendent ideals from which the world of the senses is formed, but ultimately one goes beyond involvement with all forms and becomes aware of that source from which they are manifest. Before unitary consciousness can be fully experienced one must take two more steps beyond vishuddha. Yoga psychology goes on to explore those modes of experience found above the realm of archetypes.

Self-Observation

At the ajna chakra, the sixth mode of consciousness, located between the eyebrows, one gains distance from the archetypes and from the dramas created in the other chakras. One becomes the objective observer, the witness who does not identify with the world of names and forms. One whose consciousness is fully absorbed in this realm may be called a seer, a sage, a visionary. His understanding reaches beyond ordinary intellectual knowledge, for he sees into the subtleties of the hidden laws and principles of the universe. At vishuddha the subtle principles are experienced as symbolic forms, but at the ajna chakra one attains a still greater power of understanding that goes beyond those forms. The Sanskrit word *ajna* means "the lotus of command." Here one has command over the phenomenal universe. According to the yogic tradition, all knowledge can be found within, through absorption in the ajna chakra.

As a result of the awakening to this mode of consciousness, some people may experience psychic powers. If this happens while the egoistic mode of consciousness is predominant in the personality, one will use such insight for his own aggrandizement. Others may experience this mode of consciousness in a partial and distorted way, for one may be intellectual and detached from the emotional involvement generated at the lower chakras without having attained clarity of understanding. The intellectual remains absorbed in the illusory problems and conflicts of the world. Jung said of modern man: "Our *ajna* is caught in this world. It is a spark of light, imprisoned in the world, and when we think, we are thinking in terms of the world."[7]

For most people, the ajna mode of consciousness is used in the service of a less evolved sphere. For example, one may use his intellect to avoid a disaster, to attain something he desires, to prove his self-worth, to criticize, or to compete with or manipulate another person. Many people who are caught up in the third chakra struggle to prove their adequacy through intellectual accomplishments or through amassing a great deal of information. A person who feels vulnerable and of low self-worth may attempt to cover over his experience of inadequacy with his intellectualizations. Rarely will such a person be able to see beyond his intellectual preoccupations; he will be bound to his worldly concerns and thus will not penetrate to the source of wisdom and understanding. To reach that source, one must cease to identify with the mind and its thoughts and develop the ability to witness the mind. One must become a quiet, still observer rather than being swept along in the intellectual process.

From the perspective of yoga psychology, consciousness is not an attribute of the mind; rather, the mind is an instrument of consciousness. As long as one identifies with the mind, his consciousness seems to take on the limitations of that instrument. If one further identifies with the thoughts that run through the mind, consciousness becomes even more constricted. In order for the unrealized potentials of consciousness to become evident, consciousness must disengage from its instrument and the contents of that instrument.

One can use a computer to accomplish astounding feats of information storage and computation, but the computer has obvious limitations. It can take in only certain kinds of information; its structure and the programs that direct it allow it to calculate only in certain ways. The mind is useful for experiencing and dealing with the phenomenal world, but it too has limitations. It is limited by the way it receives information, the range of information it can receive, and the way it processes that which it receives. There are limitations that are imposed by one's "programs" or habits of reasoning, and limitations of the instrument itself. For example, the mind is incapable of calculating with the speed of a modern computer.

Just as a computer can be turned off or unplugged, so too the mind can be stilled. Most people imagine that when the mind is stilled, nothing occurs for the individual; they imagine that the state of mental stillness is one of unconsciousness, deep sleep, or death. But advanced practitioners of yoga who have learned to turn off the mind report a quite different occurrence. Instead of going to a state of unconsciousness, they experience a vastly expanded consciousness that is not encumbered by the instrument called mind and its contents.

Meditation is the means of disengaging from the mind and its contents, thereby enabling one to experience alternate modes of consciousness. Through meditation one can cease identifying with thoughts, emotions, and desires, and the tendencies toward action that arise out of those thoughts and desires. Meditation is also a means of ceasing to identify with one's past and with the melodramas of life that arise out of the lower chakras. Meditation helps one learn to live more fully and spontaneously in the present rather than being so completely encumbered by the programs and memories that reside in the unconscious mind. Meditation and the application of its principles in the conduct of one's life are central to yoga therapy.

In yoga meditation, one is given a mantra on which to concentrate his mind. Holding the same thought in the mind over a considerable period of time helps to disengage the mind from the thinking process, from the subject-object mode of experience, and from sequential or cause/effect reasoning. If one's concentration is interrupted by the unfinished business of the mind—memories, desires, daydreams, discomforts, fears, expectations, and so on—the tendency is to become absorbed in the melodramas that result from those mental perturbations. But the meditator learns to remain a witness, to neutrally observe the activities taking place in his mind. To the extent that he is successful in the endeavor, he frees himself from the conflict, dissatisfaction, and unrest that ordinarily result from mental turmoil.

Meditation is a means of letting go of one's preoccupations and complexes and living more fully in the present. The meditator's increased ability to focus his attention on the intended object carries over to his life in the external world. He becomes better able to concentrate on the task at hand without distraction, emotionalism, and daydreaming. As a result of regular periods of meditation, one becomes more effective in carrying out the tasks of everyday life.

In psychoanalysis and related psychotherapies, one's personal history is considered to be weighty and significant. One spends many arduous hours rooting through complexes, conflicts, and entanglements in order to disengage himself from distortions that he has been superimposing on his current life situation. As he recalls experiences from the past, he scrutinizes them carefully in order to understand them more objectively. He takes his story to be very serious indeed. One client told me:

I've been frustrated in previous therapies I've been in because of the limited goal. Finding out about the unconscious and whatever has been repressed is blown out of proportion. That has never been satisfying to me. It's so seducing that you get lost in bringing it out, as if that were the thing to work for and there was nothing else beyond that, beyond what we call the person, conscious and unconscious.

In yoga psychology, one's personal history is considered to be relatively superficial—a cover for one's true identity. From the very beginning, one learns not to identify with his past, for it is not considered necessary to scrutinize one's life history in order to lessen its effect in the present. Complexes that have resulted from past experiences are worked out in one's present interactions without focusing so extensively on their causes. One may explore the way the past has led to his present problems, but finding causal links is secondary to dealing with current conflicts. Part of the client's problem is that he already takes his personal history too seriously, identifying with his story and ignoring his true Self. In the course of yoga therapy, the therapist will help the client to gain a more detached, objective, and neutral view of his past and to appreciate aspects of himself that transcend his personal history. He will not lead the client toward a causal explanation or historical rationale for his current way of being but will instead focus on modifying the client's way of being in the present.

Meditation is the yogic technique for dissolving one's identification with his personal history. In meditation, one learns to neutrally observe his thoughts, memories, emotions, and desires. Ordinarily, one identifies with his thoughts, and a thought with which one identifies then leads to desire and finally to behavior. One acts out the thought, and a scenario develops. Beginning with a single thought, an entire drama is created. But in meditation, one becomes a detached witness to the spectacle taking place in his mind and personality. When a thought arises in the mind during meditation, the meditator learns to observe the thought disinterestedly. Without personal involvement, the thought cannot lead to desire, action, and a consequent scenario. As one learns to watch each thought without judgment, evaluation, interest, or aversion, he becomes free from any compelling quality that the thought might otherwise have over him.

Clients in yoga therapy are encouraged to meditate daily outside of the therapy session, but half an hour to an hour of meditation each day will not in itself lead to the resolution of one's problems. It may lead to some degree of objectivity and neutrality in confronting the turmoil going on within and without, but one may still feel overwhelmed by the ever-new conflicts, predicaments, and disappointments that arise in the course of each day. A small island of calm may sometimes be reached during meditation, but afterwards one soon becomes swept up in the frantic activity of modern life and loses awareness of that calm center within. In order to progress further toward peace and equanimity, one must also learn to deal with the thoughts, sensations, and external demands that occur as one acts in daily life. Therefore, one must learn to practice meditation in action. In this practice, one applies exactly the same principles that are used in meditation: he observes his thoughts and desires rather than identifying with them. He also witnesses his mental and emotional responses to external stimuli and demands.

The following excerpts from a series of group therapy sessions highlight the development of a neutral, observing attitude toward thoughts and emotions. The sessions from which these excerpts are taken occurred approximately eight months after the start of weekly group meetings. In the first excerpt, the client becomes aware of her tendency to analyze and pass judgment on her thoughts:

> During the week, a little thing that someone would say would set a whole cycle of thoughts and emotions going in me. I was interested in watching this process. At times, I would find myself wanting to analyze my experiences. I'd ask myself, Why do you feel this way? or I'd think, I know what's happening here. But it would just complicate the experience. The more I tried to figure out, the more I would get emotionally involved with the thought or feeling.
>
> Most of the time I'm passing judgment on what I'm thinking or feeling, analyzing it or having some kind of mental reaction to the thought or feeling. This reaction creates more thoughts; it seems to generate a whole new scenario to be replayed. But neutrally observing my thoughts doesn't generate any new thoughts; it settles me down.
>
> It's not easy for me to watch my thoughts and emotions. I find it's nearly impossible for me not to have some kind of judgment on what I'm thinking or feeling. There's almost a constant stream of judging of whether it's right or wrong. And as soon as a judgment is passed, there's an additional thing to deal with. Passing a judgment seems to create a whole new flood of thoughts. For instance, if I believe I'm thinking something good, then there's usually a whole barrage of thoughts that generates a feeling of pride.
>
> Sometimes I'll be lying in bed and thoughts will be coming. I'll see myself beginning to get attached to the thoughts or involved with

them. Then I'll remind myself, Don't get attached; just look at them, watch them.

In a later session, this client further described her increasing awareness of how she ordinarily reacts to thoughts and how these reactions lead to an intensification of emotions:

I woke up in the middle of the night. It was two in the morning, and the thought was in my head, What if someone got into the apartment? Then I reacted to that thought. I started to tighten up and I could feel my heart pumping faster. Then came different thoughts. I was remembering something I had read about a rapist breaking into a house and chopping off his victim's arms. Then I started to feel angry and my stomach began to knot up. All these emotions came. Ordinarily, if I didn't watch the process, I would get real caught up in the emotions.

There's a constant stream of thoughts in my head. Most of the time, it seems like a vicious cycle. I have thoughts and react to them; this brings more thoughts and I react to them, too—like the thought that someone is in the apartment. I'm in the habit of reacting to that thought with fear, and that leads to further scary thoughts, and I react to those with more fear. I find myself wondering how it would be to let all the thoughts go and not react to them.

As therapy progressed, this client began to discriminate more clearly between her emotions and the witnessing consciousness. She also became aware that in order to give up her identification with "negative" thoughts and emotions, she would have to give up her identification with those thoughts that she considered to be "positive" as well.

This week I was observing emotions in myself rather than identifying with them. I would notice anger, anxiety, fear—the things I consider to be negative. I would notice those things, but I'd disidentify with them. I would say, That's Sue. See how she's so fearful. See how she's so caught up and worried. But I am just a neutral observer. I would find myself observing and saying to myself,

See how involved she is in being angry, and Did you notice how she . . . ? Of course, a lot of times I would just be caught up in what I considered to be negative emotions, but as soon as I became aware of them, I would stop identifying with those emotions. I would observe the anger, the anxiety, or the frustration, and I would say, I'm not that anxiety; I'm not that fear.

After I did that for a few days, I was watching my children as they were going to school. I thought, They're such nice kids; I just love them so much. And it dawned on me that if I wasn't the negative emotions, then I wasn't the positive emotions either. That was kind of a shock to me. That wasn't as easy as saying, I'm not anger; I'm not proud or depressed. I thought, If I'm not the negative things, I'm not the positive things either. I began thinking, You can't be one without the other; the opposites come together like a set. You're going to have to be both of them or neither. If you're not a hater, then you're not a lover; and if you're not impatient, then you're not patient either. You can't be one without the other.

It was a funny feeling because I've always wanted to be rid of all those things that I consider negative, but I always wanted the positive things to increase. Later, I watched myself feel that I was very kind or friendly to someone. I would say to myself, I'm not that friendliness; I'm not that kindness. Everything that went through my mind, I would say that I wasn't that. I must be something that's removed from all those things, but I don't yet know what it is.

In the following weeks, Sue also began to watch her emotional reactions to other family members. The skill that she was developing in being a witness to her emotions and thoughts helped her to remain centered and to cope more effectively with situations that previously had led to emotional conflicts. The following excerpt from a group session illustrates this point:

C2   (another member of the group): I used to deny a lot of the emotions that I considered negative, like anger and jealousy. I'm more aware of them now. But going around expressing the anger seems to be as much of a trap as denying it.

T: Could you accept and experience those emotions without acting them out and without identifying with them?

C1   (Sue): When I feel angry with my kids, sometimes I show it—I yell! If they're fighting, I'll feel myself getting angry and I'll scream, "You kids are always yelling at one another! I'm sick of everybody around here fighting!" That gets everybody around me going. Suddenly my husband is mad, the kids are mad, and the dog hides 'cause she's frightened when anyone yells. And I think, God, what a crummy day; I hate days like this. I blame it on the day.

But today I had a great experience in applying what we've learned here. When the children came in the door for lunch, the big one came falling in. He had been pushed by the younger one. Then they proceeded to fight all the way through lunch, kicking each other under the table and saying, "I hate you!" "You're such a dummy!" "You pig face!" I thought, God, I've been meditating and my day has been very peaceful, and here they go again. I suppose they're going to fight all day. Then I thought, I don't have to get into it. I had been starting to get angry, but then I just began to watch them. I thought, It'll just pass like everything else, and my anger just drifted away. I didn't express my initial anger, but at the same time, I didn't think to myself, You shouldn't be angry. I was just not in the mood to get all riled up. So I thought to myself, Oh, so you're angry, Sue. That's all right. And it just went away.

In the next meeting, Sue told the group:

This week I tried to watch my thoughts and emotions. I'd notice a thought or subtle emotion and I'd describe it to myself and clarify what it was. I would say, Now see how you were angry right there. Did you notice how the anger was building up and how you can feel it going now?

One day we were sitting at the dinner table. My husband and son were planning to go to a baseball game. I said, "Maybe I'll go along, too." And my son replied, "Oh, I wanted to go just with Dad." The first thing I was going to say to him was, "Well, that's not a very nice thing to say!" It was just about to come out of my mouth. Then I wondered, Why do I think that's not a nice thing to say? That implies that the nice thing would be not saying how he feels. He would grow up thinking that when he has feelings like that, they're not nice. I was thinking about how much of that must be programmed into me and how that judgment must affect the way I look at everything. The judgments I make about my thoughts cause a lot of the conflict that goes on inside of me. It's not so much the thoughts themselves, but there's judgment that goes along with just about everything I think: It's not nice; It's not good; or, It's not healthy.

It was interesting to see those feelings come up inside myself. I also remember thinking, They'll go and have a good time and I'm going to be home bored. I was getting all involved in those thoughts, starting to feel real sorry for myself. It was strange to see how one thing can trigger so many thoughts and feelings.

Then I watched to see when the day came. They did indeed go off to the baseball game. I was remembering how I had projected that I would be real sad all by myself, but that didn't actually happen. That had only existed in thought, and yet while I was experiencing those thoughts, I started to feel down: "poor me." It was all because of what I was thinking. It didn't turn out that way at all. I see that the thoughts that come through my mind and the judgments that I make are what cause me trouble, not what's actually going on in life moment by moment.

These excerpts show that developing a neutral observing attitude can be valuable for dealing effectively with the practical matters of everyday life. The observing consciousness is able to see through the self-created fantasies, dramas, conflicts, and emotional reactions that occur day to day. It stands as a center of stability for the individual as he is tossed and turned by the tumultuous mind and external world. As one identifies ever more completely with the observing consciousness, he increasingly appreciates the order, lawfulness, and harmony that underlie the confusion and discord in the world of names and forms. At the ajna chakra, the world of polarities is all but transcended. The witnessing consciousness does not identify with the world of distinctions and polarities it observes. It remains aware of the multiplicity but does not react to it, for it is also aware of an underlying unity. It is a transitional state between the dualistic consciousness of the vishuddha chakra and the nondual consciousness of the seventh chakra, sahasrara. At the ajna chakra, one witnesses the illusory forms, but at sahasrara, the insubstantiality of the forms becomes fully apparent.

Interaction Among the Chakras

In observing another person, one can easily be misled as to which archetype is predominant. Certain behaviors or aspects of life may seem to represent a particular mode of experience, but the person involved in that activity may be experiencing something quite different. For example, if a couple is in a sexual embrace, it may appear that they are absorbed in experiencing sensory pleasure. But in actuality one of the pair may be preoccupied with dominating and controlling the other; he, for instance, may be using sexual activity to assert his ego or to prove that he is adequate. Or, alternatively, he may be absorbed in the experience of love or devotion for his partner, rather than focusing on sensory pleasure.

A religious institution, such as a church or synagogue, stands for or represents experiences of the heart and throat chakras. The stated purpose of such institutions is to help one transcend the ego by serving others and surrendering to God. But the actions carried out in the name of a church or synagogue may actually foster another mode of consciousness. For instance, a self-styled holy crusade may lead many people to become absorbed in the muladhara chakra. The following psychotherapy excerpt illustrates the way religion may foster muladhara consciousness in a child:

I've been incapacitated by fear my whole life. Fear is still there, and it's done terrible things to me. I was especially unhappy during my grade-school years. I was frightened and anxious. I was very afraid of going to hell. My religion concentrated on sin and evil and on the consequences of that, and there was a really heavy emphasis on that in my home. I was always afraid of doing the wrong thing and of going to hell, which was always described very vividly. I was taught that if you committed a mortal sin and you died, you would go straight to hell. Well, there were a couple of times when I was a kid that I thought I had committed a mortal sin, and let me tell you, I went through hell without even dying. I got so sick I couldn't go to school. I was vomiting, and just from fear. When I think about it now, I just get so angry that . . . (crying) To do that to a little child . . .

A person may also distort spiritual practices on his own and use them to maintain a less evolved mode of consciousness. For example, as in the following instance, yoga practices may be subverted by the ego to reinforce one's egoistic orientation rather than being used to establish a higher mode of consciousness:

> When I started yoga and meditation, I decided that I was on a spiritual quest. I began eating differently, being disciplined, getting up early and doing hatha yoga and meditation. I thought I was being spiritual, but I really wasn't. I would think, I'm a meditator; she's not a meditator. I don't eat meat; he does eat meat. It was a way of saying, I'm a little better. It was just the same old thing that I had done all my life: I went to college and you didn't; I don't drink and you do. Now I realize that spirituality is beyond such distinctions.

For simplicity's sake, the chakras have been described separately in this book, but that is not meant to imply that a particular experience necessarily represents only one mode of consciousness and no other. Most experiences consist of dramas being carried on at more than one level simultaneously or in rapid succession. For example, sexual teasing may involve both sensory pleasure and experiences related to dominance and submission; and while eating food, one may experience sensory gratification as well as nurturance.

The third and fifth chakras functioning together lead one to establish an ego ideal. In this mode of functioning, one projects ideal or archetypal qualities upon his own ego as he would like it to be. Such projection may lead one to feel buoyed up. It may, however, have the opposite effect, as the following client has discovered:

> I get attached to an image of how I'd like to be. I can see that I'm attached to some ideal. I ask myself how I would appear to be if I were

enlightened. I envision myself as being very softspoken and gentle, as having a sense of depth in my eyes, as being someone who is not affected by another person's anger, someone who can absorb negative things and can say something to help people, who is understanding and who radiates a sense of warmth. There is a real attachment to that image. I think, Why can't I be like that? I see myself falling short of that ideal, and so I get into a rut, putting myself down because I'm not there.

Examples have already been given of a more evolved chakra being used in the service of a less evolved mode of consciousness. For instance, it was noted that the objectivity, understanding, or psychic experiences attained through the ajna chakra may be usurped by the ego to demonstrate one's superiority. A less evolved mode of experience may also be used in the service of a more enlightened mode of consciousness. For example, one who has acquired wisdom and understanding through the ajna chakra may wish to build an organization in order to teach and guide others. To accomplish his goal he may use the egoistic mode of consciousness, but he will not regard the organization as a possession or remain identified with or judge his self-worth in terms of the organization's accomplishments.

Nondual Consciousness

At the seventh chakra, sahasrara, at the crown of the head, one experiences a state of pure consciousness, unencumbered by any instruments or limiting forms. The mind-created grid of time, space, and causation is transcended. All polarities are united and all forms dissolved. One awakens from the illusory world of distinctions and multiplicity. "Sahasrara . . . is the center beyond duality."[8] Here one experiences "a union that is simultaneously the fulfillment and dissolution of the worlds of sound, form, and contemplation."[9] At sahasrara there are no longer any melodramas or scenarios; even the realm of archetypes is left behind. Having reached this center, there is nothing more to be attained, nothing more to be known. One knows himself as the All in all; he realizes himself as the atman (Self) or unitary consciousness.

Since reductive psychologies do not acknowledge the existence of the Self or pure consciousness, and dualistic psychologies do not recognize that one can attain consciousness of the Self, those psychologies offer no methods for reaching this mode of consciousness. Dualistic psychologies can at best offer means for attaining glimmerings of the Self through its symbolic expression. Archetypal psychologies have studied symbols of the Self as found in dreams, myths, and spiritual traditions. They are capable of helping clients to recognize what may be called messages from the Self that may guide the ego and lead one to experience greater harmony and integration, but they do not conceive of the possibility of directly experiencing the Self. By contrast, all the methods of yoga are meant to lead a person step by step to the realization of his true nature as pure consciousness. According to yoga psychology, the realms of consciousness experienced at lower chakras are all preparatory to self-realization. The first six chakras are the way stations on the road to realization of the Self, and the various practices of yoga are designed to facilitate the journey.

Yogic practices have traditionally been divided into distinct branches, each of which develops a particular mode of consciousness.[10] A person may follow one or more of these paths, according to the qualities that he wishes to cultivate within himself. In the practice of karma yoga, one learns how to perform actions in the service of others without concern for reward. Karma yoga leads one out of the primitive modes of consciousness to the experience characteristic of the anahata chakra. Bhakti yoga is the yoga of devotion. In this path, one chooses a particular ideal or divine form and develops an intimate relationship with that ideal through devotional practices. All of one's emotions are directed upward toward that divine form, and one's entire life becomes an expression of surrender to that ideal. The practice of bhakti yoga brings one's consciousness more fully into the vishuddha chakra. One then enjoys that free-flowing sustenance that has been referred to as divine nectar, ambrosia, manna, and the fountain of youth. Raja yoga is a more comprehensive, objective, and systematic approach to human evolution. It includes systematic practices that culminate in concentration, meditation, and samadhi. Through those practices, one becomes a neutral observer of the dramas of life. He eventually learns to stop identifying with the dramas, and approaches awareness of himself as pure consciousness. He becomes absorbed in the ajna chakra.

Finally, the practices of jnana yoga and laya yoga lead one to the unitary consciousness of sahasrara. Laya yoga is the yoga of dissolution. In following this path, the student dissolves all identification with the world of names and forms so that the Self alone remains. Jnana yoga uses contemplation to help one realize that everything that exists in the world of form is insubstantial and illusory. Both laya yoga and jnana yoga use the method of negation, which involves the rejection or dissolution of all that is false until there is nothing more to be discarded. One need only let go of all limiting conceptions and identifications to realize his true nature as unitary consciousness.

There are many ways of following the path of negation. In one practice, the aspirant sits quietly and repeatedly asks himself the question, Who am I? When a response to the question arises in the mind, such as "I am a male," he does not accept that limited polarized identification. He lets go of that thought and asks again, Who am I? Each subsequent response is discarded, for every answer to the question implies limitation. One continues to ask and to reject all the definitions that he ordinarily applies to himself. This is not an intellectual process—one is not merely rejecting a thought about oneself for the moment. The aim of the process is to fully realize that one is not a male as distinct from a female, a good person as distinct from a bad, that he need not identify with any particular qualities and reject others. One may practice this method daily, often going over and rejecting answers similar to those given the day before. Very gradually, one comes to experience that he is not any limited quality he has attributed to himself. The limitations of self-imposed attributes begin to fall away from his thoughts, desires, and actions. The following client described her experience with this practice as it has been adapted in mime:

> When we start our performance, we go through a process very much like contemplation in yoga. I slowly walk up to the stage, and with the first step, I ask myself, Who am I? And I consider the first thing that comes to mind: "Janet, a married woman," and everything that means to me. I take a good look at it and then I try to move one step closer to who I *really* am, which is the universal Self. I leave that married Janet back there and again question, Who am I? and I deal with the next thing that comes and then take another step. I keep

taking steps, trying to reach a more universal Self, and when I feel that I have reached as far as I can go for the day, I pause and just let the movement evolve from within myself.

If one follows this method within the yoga tradition, one may eventually be able to wholly cease identifying with all limiting attributes, achieving a breakthrough in which he truly recognizes that he is beyond any of the distinctions that make up the world of names and forms. There are in yoga various other methods of attaining this end, but they all involve a similar process of negation and dissolution. For instance, in the practice of meditation one learns to disentangle himself from identification with the thoughts that come before his mind. In more evolved stages of meditation, one may even give up his identification with the mantra or object of meditation in order to experience consciousness beyond form.

Silence

The practice of meditation involves a temporary retreat from the world of activity in order that one may find a neutral center of observation within, a center unaffected by external events and by one's emotions and thoughts. The experience may be compared to sitting in the eye of a hurricane: all around, there is a frantic whirlwind of activity, but at the center all is calm and at peace. Here one may observe the restless activity without getting swept up into it.

The meditator sits without movement in a quiet place, his eyes closed. He withdraws his senses from the outer world and also withdraws from his identification with thoughts, emotions, and desires, to a neutral observing consciousness. This solitude and silence lead one to that which lies behind and beyond the activity of the body, emotions, mind, and external environment. In that stillness, one experiences a state of great peace and satisfaction.

The restriction of environmental stimulation has been an important part of traditional therapeutic practices throughout the ages. Both the ancient Greeks and the American Indians, among others, put disturbed members of their societies into environments in which they were isolated from external stimulation in order to heal them.

The treatment of the mentally ill by the use of "darkness [which] quiets the spirit" was already ascribed to the ancients in a medical treatise written by a first century Roman, Aulus Cornelius Celsus. It was still the practice in the Middle Ages, along with reduced social and sensory stimulation. As [a] review of the history of psychiatry makes clear, solitude, darkness, silence, immobilization, and other forms of restricted environmental stimulation techniques were frequently recommended and used during the Renaissance, the Enlightenment, the Industrial Revolution, and so on without interruption to today.[11]

The practice of solitude and silence is also an important aspect of yoga therapy, and extends beyond the practice of meditation. Certain clients may be invited to spend from one to ten days in retreat. During that time, their duties and activities in the external world are suspended; external demands and disturbances are minimized. One need not even prepare his food; meals are provided for him. He is asked to refrain from contact with others—except for counseling sessions that may occur daily—and is dissuaded from filling his time by reading books. Instead, he is encouraged to be with himself.

In the absence of external stimuli, one's thoughts and desires take center stage. During the first days of solitude, one typically notices how restless the mind is and how intense and demanding are his thoughts and emotions. Many thoughts and desires that have been in the back of his mind now have the open space to come forward into the light of consciousness. These disturb him and lead him to become restless. However, as the days pass and one maintains an observing attitude rather than acting on his thoughts, fantasies, emotions, and desires, the disturbances become less intense, and gradually dissipate. One feels refreshed and renewed; he experiences an inner calm like that after a storm. His gait becomes more relaxed, his face loses wrinkles, its worried look is replaced by a soft radiance, and he appears younger. He becomes aware of and enjoys subtleties in his environment and in his inner states that he did not experience before. He finds himself becoming more playful and begins to laugh spontaneously and joyfully as he notices the humor in the dramas of life taking place around him.

This is an intense practice undertaken only by those who have prepared themselves. Most people are not ready to be with themselves without distractions. Some clients in yoga therapy would find this practice unsettling; it would be more appropriate for them to attend a short seminar in a retreat-like setting with limited periods of silence. The yoga therapist may also encourage some clients to practice silence periodically while remaining in their normal environments. The client may remain silent for an entire day while carrying on his normal routine, including interacting with others. This practice helps one refrain from reacting to internal and external stimuli and increases his skills in observing himself and others. When one has a desire to speak and refrains from speaking, he may realize that he wanted to speak in order to hide his feelings or boost his ego. He realizes how much energy is dissipated in chatter and becomes aware of the insecurity, defensiveness, and wish to control others that often prompt one to speak. Those who practice silence are often surprised at the joy and spontaneity that can arise as they relate to others without speech.

Occasionally, periods of silence occur during therapy sessions, but many clients feel that they must talk continuously in order to accomplish as much as possible in therapy. They believe that their time is wasted if there is silence. However, according to the monistic paradigm, being silent can be of much greater value than filling all the empty spaces with talk. It allows one to hear the subtle promptings of his deepest self. The following discussion occurred after a ten-minute silence at the beginning of a group therapy session:

C1: I can't stand it! I have nothing to say. I just can't take sitting here in silence.

C2: This is the first time I've been able to sit without becoming uncomfortable. It's kind of nice just to be quiet. I thought of several things that I could talk about, but none of them really seemed that important, so it felt better just to be quiet.

C1: I can't stand it!

T: Is it just here that you're uncomfortable with silence? Do you feel that way at other times?

C1: I do find that if I have a telephone conversation, I can't tolerate it if there's a void. I have to fill it. I always think of something to say, meaningless or not. I feel compelled.

(Two-minute pause)

C1: Do you want me to talk about something important? I'll tell you about my illness. I have this pain in my back.

(Client continues talking about her illness. Therapist stretches out across two chairs. He is about to doze off.)

C2 (to therapist): What are you doing? I've never seen you in a prone position.

C1: Is this too boring?

T: I lost interest when you stole our silence. I felt that you were sharing more in your silence and in telling us your feelings about the silence than in talking about your illness.

C2: Are you really comfortable inside when we all sit here silently?

T: I was today. I don't always feel comfortable in silence. I'm comfortable if I feel there's not an expectation. If I create an expectation, for example, that silence means the group's not performing as it should be or that I should be directing the group, then I get anxious. But if I can just be here and be open, then the silence feels good, and I become aware of a lot of sharing.

C2: There are times when I would like to be able to appreciate silence with others, but unless it's something that's agreed upon ahead of time, unless we've all sat down and said, "Let's all be quiet," it's awkward, even with my husband and children.

C3: I noticed that a program is offered here in which one spends five days in silence. Maybe my life would be simpler if I go through that program and become less cluttered with emotions.

C4: I went through that practice, and I learned that a lot of what I say is not very meaningful. I realized that I often finish other people's thoughts and sentences. If people can't think of a word, I'll be right there to take care of them.

I wasn't completely comfortable sitting here in silence. What I find most difficult is knowing where to look. It's difficult for me to look anyone in the eye. I'll look at someone and then I'll have to look away.

T: What makes it difficult?

C4: It's too intimate, looking directly into someone's eyes. I'm not used to that kind of intimacy. But one day, a very good friend and I went to the park for a couple of hours. I said, "Let's be silent," and it was wonderful.

C2: My mouth has to be flapping all the time, except when I'm alone. I've been wondering what it would be like to be a more quiet person. I wonder what you see when you're more quiet with people. I'm always filling in and jabbering and finishing people's sentences.

T: You could try keeping silence for a day.

C2: I tried one day at home. It was fun. We acted things out instead of talking.

C4: When I practiced silence for five days, I was more in touch with what was going on than I am when I'm talking. When I'm talking, I have a one-track mind. I'm not as aware and attentive to people, to the expressions on their faces or what they're doing or saying. When I'm talking, I'm just busy, and a lot of things are blocked out.

C3: I've noticed that the attitude toward silence seems to vary in different forms of therapy. In meditative therapy, the principle seems to be: Be still within yourself and let things rise up and let them go. In Western therapies, you just sit there and try and talk it out. I've gone through the talking-out bit. I'm not so sure it worked.

Another client had been in psychotherapy for several months. He usually talked nonstop, describing his struggles to change his habitual patterns of living. He wanted to get in as much as possible in the limited time we had together. In the middle of one session, however, he stopped speaking. After some minutes of thoughtful silence, he said:

C: This is the first time that I've been in therapy where I've been able to just stop talking for a period of time and not feel totally threatened. I feel that I should be talking when I'm here because it's through talking that I gain awareness. But I'm beginning to realize that through the talking, I protect myself from another type of awareness that might be too painful to deal with.

(Ten-minute pause)

C: I'm thinking that if I were quiet for periods of time, certain thoughts or feelings might come up which I feel are potentially threatening to me.

(Fifteen-minute pause)

C: The feeling I now have about being silent is that there is a certain amount of comfort, security, and love.

T: Just the opposite of what you were saying before—that in the silence, you felt insecurity.

C: I was afraid of the silence. Things would come up that I was afraid to deal with. But now I feel a sense of calm, not a lot of anxiety about being silent. I was thinking about what the womb would feel like, being enveloped by silence, very secure.

I never thought of therapy as being relaxing. I've had this preconditioned notion that it has to be high-powered and tense. The last thing that I could ever imagine therapy being is relaxing. The structure here, I now realize, is very loose and flexible. It is what I bring to the structure that is limiting. To feel that relaxation and know that I won't be judged or feel embarrassed is really amazing. I was looking for some type of change with a preconceived notion about how I would go about changing, imposing an old structure on an unknown and hoping that something new would come of it.

Because I was able to stop today and just be quiet, I feel I've discovered that new dimension which I was looking for so desperately. It's obvious in a way, and yet what has been most obvious, I have often overlooked.

(Five-minute pause)

C: What do you feel when I'm not saying anything?

T: I feel more in contact than in any other meeting we've had.

C: I realize that in our sessions, I've been beating myself to death. Now I know that I don't have to do that. It has been a refreshing and delightful experience. I expected something terrible to come out of the silence, but I feel good. I feel joy.

Silence and solitude are means of separating oneself from the melodramas of the world. One's inner turmoil then comes to the foreground of consciousness. One must remain still, observing the play of the personal unconscious and the collective unconscious; he must learn detachment from both their alluring and their demonic forms and plots. If one maintains his stillness and silence, he will pass beyond the restless, turbulent, ever-changing forms of the phenomenal world and enter a quiet haven of pure formless being. This state of consciousness is the ground of all being, for all forms arise out of it.

Progressing through each of the first five chakras, one experiences a new and more subtle variation of the game of hide and seek. In each of those chakras, there is a subject that seeks after an object or state that is distinct from it. One may seek security, pleasure, status, the object of his devotion, or countless other goals. At the sixth chakra, the ajna chakra, one recognizes the game for what it is, and at sahasrara, the seventh chakra, the game is over; one is no longer playing hide and seek, for one is found. He has found himself. He realizes that he has been both the seeker and the alluring goal. The years and millennia spent in separation, darkness, delusion, disappointment, in happiness and sorrow, pleasure and grief, are over. One who has so often been weary finally awakens refreshed to find that the entire extravaganza, with all its uncountable forms, plots, attainments, victories, defeats, discoveries, losses, loves, hates, deaths, and births, was all a dream. One's destiny is to realize his true nature as that illimitable, immortal consciousness which is *sat-chit-ananda*—existence, knowledge, and bliss. The Upanishads echo through the ages: "*Tat tvam asi,* 'Thou art That.' Awaken from this dream and realize your true Self."

Notes

CW = *The Collected Works of C. G. Jung.* Edited by Herbert Read, Michael Fordham, and Gerhard Adler. Translated by R. F. C. Hull. Bollingen Series, no. 20. 18 volumes. Princeton, N.J.: Princeton University Press; London: Routledge & Kegan Paul, 1953-80. All references are to volume and paragraph, and are reprinted with the permission of the publishers.

PART I
PSYCHOTHERAPY EAST AND WEST

Introduction to Part I.

1. John R. Harvey, "Behavioral Principles Cast in the Non-Reductionist Context of Classical Yoga Psychology" (Paper delivered at the annual convention of the American Psychological Association, Montreal, September 1980), 4.

2. Ibid., 12.

3. Stephen A. Applebaum, *Out in Inner Space: A Psychoanalyst Explores the New Therapies* (Garden City, N.Y.: Doubleday, Anchor Press, 1979), 281-87.

4. Two popular books on this subject are Fritjof Capra, *The Tao of Physics: An Exploration of the Parallels Between Modern Physics and Eastern Mysticism* (Boulder, Colo.: Shambhala Publications, 1975), and Gary Zukav, *The Dancing Wu Li Masters: An Overview of the New Physics* (New York: William Morrow and Co., 1979).

5. *Encyclopaedia Britannica,* 1970 ed., s.v. "geometry."

Chapter 1. PARADIGMS OF PSYCHOTHERAPY

1. *Encyclopedia of Philosophy,* 1972 ed., s.v. "psychology."

2. Ibid., s.v. "humanism."

3. Albert Ellis, *Humanistic Psychotherapy: The Rational-Emotive Approach* (New York: McGraw-Hill Book Co., 1974), 2.

4. Gregory Bateson, *Steps to an Ecology of Mind* (New York: Ballantine Books, 1972), xvi-xvii.

5. Shankara, *The Quintessence of Vedanta,* 2d ed., trans. Swami Tattwananda (Hollywood, Calif.: Vedanta Press, 1970), 86, aphorism 475.

6. Fritjof Capra, "The New Physics: Implications for Psychology," *The American Theosophist* 68, no. 5 (May 1980): 114, 116.

7. Ibid., 116.

8. Melvin H. Marx and William A. Hillix, *Systems and Theories in Psychology* (New York: McGraw-Hill Book Co., 1963), 169.

9. Frank J. Sulloway, *Freud, Biologist of the Mind: Beyond the Psychoanalytic Legend* (New York: Basic Books, 1979), 63.

10. Ibid., 62.

11. Viktor E. Frankl, *The Unconscious God: Psychotherapy and Theology* (New York: Simon and Schuster, 1975), 20.

12. Kurt Goldstein, *The Organism: A Holistic Approach to Biology Derived from Pathological Data in Man* (New York: American Book Co., 1939), 197.

13. Cited in Frankl, *Unconscious God,* 93.

14. Robert W. White, "Competence and the Psychosexual Stages of Development," in Marshall R. Jones, ed., *Nebraska Symposium on Motivation 1960* (Lincoln, Neb.: University of Nebraska Press, 1960), 97.

15. Gordon Allport, *The Person in Psychology: Selected Essays* (Boston: Beacon Press, 1968), 383-84.

16. Christopher F. Monte, *Beneath the Mask: An Introduction to Theories of Personality,* 2d ed. (New York: Holt, Rinehart and Winston, 1980), 543.

17. Carl R. Rogers, *On Becoming A Person: A Therapist's View of Psychotherapy* (Boston: Houghton Mifflin Co., 1961), 185.

18. Howard Kirschenbaum, *On Becoming Carl Rogers* (New York: Dell Publishing Co., 1980), 257.

19. J. F. T. Bugental, *The Search for Authenticity: An Existential-Analytic Approach to Psychotherapy* (New York: Holt, Rinehart and Winston, 1965), 139.

20. Kirschenbaum, *On Becoming Carl Rogers,* 258-59.

21. Bugental, *Search for Authenticity,* 10.

22. Alexander Lowen, *Bioenergetics* (New York: Coward, McCann and Geoghegan, 1975), 43.

23. Ibid., 30.

24. Ellis, *Humanistic Psychotherapy,* 3-4.

25. Roger N. Walsh and Frances Vaughan, eds., *Beyond Ego: Transpersonal Dimensions in Psychology* (Los Angeles: Jeremy P. Tarcher, 1980), 19.

26. Cited in Walsh and Vaughan, *Beyond Ego,* 19-20.

27. *CW* 9, part 1, 149.

28. Ibid.

29. *Encyclopedia of Philosophy,* s.v. "psychology."

30. *CW* 9, part 1, 149.

31. Ibid., 150.

32. Ibid., 154.

Chapter 2. POLARITIES EAST AND WEST

1. Cited in *Sigmund Freud: Collected Papers,* vol. 4, ed. Ernest Jones (New York: Basic Books, 1959), 187.

2. Ibid., 184.

3. Ibid., 187.

4. Lao-tzu, *Tao Teh King,* ed. Archie J. Bahm (New York: Frederick Ungar Publishing Co., 1958), 12.

5. *Chuang-tzu: Taoist Philosopher and Chinese Mystic,* trans. Herbert A. Giles (London: George Allen and Unwin, 1889), 164.

6. *The I Ching,* 3d ed., translated by Richard Wilhelm and rendered into English by Cary F. Baynes (Princeton, N.J.: Princeton University Press, 1967), lvi.

7. Alan W. Watts, *The Two Hands of God: The Myths of Polarity* (Toronto, Macmillan Co., 1969), 54.

8. Ibid., 48.

9. Cited in Watts, *Two Hands of God,* 47.

10. Cited in Ken Wilber, *No Boundary: Eastern and Western Approaches to Personal Growth* (Los Angeles: Center Publications, 1979), 28.

11. *CW* 16, 219.

12. Watts, *Two Hands of God,* 23.

13. Erving Polster and Miriam Polster, *Gestalt Therapy Integrated: Contours of Theory and Practice* (New York: Random House, Vintage Books, 1974), 61-62.

14. See Edward W. L. Smith, "The Roots of Gestalt Therapy," in *The Growing Edge of Gestalt Therapy,* ed. Edward W. L. Smith (New York: Brunner/Mazel, 1976), 32-35.

15. *CW* 11, 791.

16. *CW* 9, part 1, 174.

17. *CW* 11, 961.

18. *CW* 14, 470.

19. *CW* 16, 330.

20. *CW* 6, 709.

21. *CW* 11, 791.

22. *CW* 12, 22.

23. *CW* 7, 311.

24. Paul Watzlawick, John H. Weakland, and Richard Fisch, *Change: Principles of Problem Formation and Problem Resolution* (New York: W. W. Norton and Co., 1974), 18.

25. Madhu Khanna, *Yantra: The Tantric Symbol of Cosmic Unity* (London: Thames and Hudson, 1979), 67.

26. Shankara, *Crest-Jewel of Discrimination,* 3d ed., trans. Swami Prabhavananda and Christopher Isherwood (Hollywood, Calif.: Vedanta Press, 1978), 137.

27. *CW* 9, part 1, 524.

28. *CW* 16, 400.

29. Cited in Wilber, *No Boundary,* 28.

30. Lao-tzu, *Tao Teh King,* 12.

31. C. G. Jung, *Memories, Dreams, Reflections* (New York: Random House, Vintage Books, 1963), 381.

Chapter 3. PROJECTION

1. Cited in Bernard I. Murstein and Ronald S. Pryer, "The Concept of Projection: A Review," *Psychological Bulletin* 56, no. 5 (September 1959): 353.

2. Cited in Jolande Jacobi, *The Psychology of C. G. Jung* (New Haven, Conn.: Yale University Press, 1973), 92.

3. C. G. Jung, *Psychological Reflections,* ed. Jolande Jacobi (Princeton, N.J.:

Princeton University Press, 1973), 239.

4. *CW* 8, 517.

5. *CW* 9, part 2, 17.

6. *CW* 8, 507.

7. *CW* 16, 383.

8. *CW* 16, 534.

9. *How to Know God: The Yoga Aphorisms of Patanjali,* trans. Swami Prabhavananda and Christopher Isherwood (New York: New American Library, Mentor Books, 1969), 90.

10. *CW* 11, 849.

11. Chapter 4, verse 10.

12. Swami Prabhavananda and Frederick Manchester, *The Upanishads: Breath of the Eternal* (Hollywood, Calif.: Vedanta Press, 1975), 119.

13. *CW* 9, part 1, 7.

14. *CW* 11, 520.

15. Matt. 25: 35-40.

16. C. G. Jung, *Modern Man in Search of a Soul* (New York: Harcourt, Brace and World, Harvest Books, 1933), 79-80.

Chapter 4. TRANSFERENCE

1. *CW* 11, 875.

2. *CW* 7, 67.

3. *CW* 8, 43.

4. Otto Fenichel, *The Psychoanalytical Theory of Neurosis* (New York: W. W. Norton and Co., 1945), 29.

5. *CW* 8, 146.

6. *CW* 4, 679.

7. *CW* 16, 279.

8. *CW* 9, part 1, 159.

9. *CW* 9, part 1, 172.

10. *The Essene Gospel of Peace,* ed. and trans. Edmond Bordeaux Szekely, 17th ed. (San Diego: Academy of Creative Living, 1971), 21-22.

11. For a much fuller discussion of this topic, see Edward F. Edinger, *Ego and Archetype: Individuation and the Religious Function of the Psyche* (Baltimore: Penguin Books, 1973).

12. *CW* 7, 150.

13. *CW* 16, 442.

14. James Hillman, *Re-Visioning Psychology* (New York: Harper Colophon Books, 1977), 47.

15. *CW* 9, part 1, 62. The words in brackets have been added.

16. *CW* 9, part 2, 24.

17. *CW* 7, 297.

18. *CW* 9, part 2, 30-31.

19. Hillman, *Re-Visioning Psychology,* 100.

20. *Self-Knowledge (Atmabodha): An English Translation of Sankaracharya's Atmabodha with Notes, Comments, and Introduction,* by Swami Nikhilananda,

copyright 1946 and 1974, Ramakrishna-Vivekananda Center of New York, Third Printing. Reprinted with permission.

21. For a fuller discussion of this topic, see Marina Warner, *Alone of All Her Sex* (New York: Alfred A. Knopf, 1976).

22. Cited in Raymond Prince and Charles Savage, "Mystical States and the Concept of Regression," in *The Highest State of Consciousness,* ed. John White (Garden City, N.Y.: Doubleday, Anchor Books, 1972), 131.

23. St. Teresa of Avila, *Interior Castle,* trans. and ed. E. Allison Peers (Garden City, N.Y.: Doubleday, Image Books, 1961), 215.

24. Cited in Warner, *Alone of All Her Sex,* 197.

25. Ibid., 197-98.

26. C. G. Jung, "Psychological Commentary on Kundalini Yoga, Lecture II," *Spring: An Annual of Archetypal Psychology and Jungian Thought* 1975: 20.

27. Srimat Swami Saradanandaji Maharaj, *Sri Ramakrishna: The Great Master,* trans. Swami Jagadananda (Mylapore, India: Sri Ramakrishna Math, 1952), 144.

28. Ibid., 242.

29. Prince and Savage, "Mystical States and the Concept of Regression," 127.

30. *CW* 11, 890.

31. Gershem Sholem, *Major Trends in Jewish Mysticism* (New York: Schocken Books, 1961), 235.

32. St. Teresa of Avila, *Interior Castle,* 126.

33. Ibid., 207.

34. *CW* 12, 192.

35. *CW* 12, 43.

36. *CW* 16, 442.

37. Sir John Woodroffe, *Sakti and Sakta* (Hollywood, Calif.: Vedanta Press, 1969), 442.

38. Cited in *A Sourcebook in Indian Philosophy,* ed. Sarvepalli Radhakrishnan and Charles A. Moore (Princeton, N.J.: Princeton University Press, 1957), 509.

39. Eliot Deutsch, *Advaita Vedanta: A Philosophical Reconstruction* (Honolulu: University Press of Hawaii, 1973), 33.

40. Shankara, *The Quintessence of Vedanta,* 2d ed., trans. Swami Tattwananda (Hollywood, Calif.: Vedanta Press, 1970), 85, aphorism 468.

41. Fritz Perls, *The Gestalt Approach and Eye Witness to Therapy* (New York: Bantam Books, 1976), 34-35.

42. Franklin Merrell-Wolff, *The Philosophy of Consciousness Without an Object* (New York: Julian Press, 1973), 159-60.

43. Swami Prabhavananda, *The Spiritual Heritage of India* (Hollywood, Calif.: Vedanta Press, 1969), 288.

44. Shankara, *Quintessence of Vedanta,* 91, aphorism 495. The words in brackets have been added.

Chapter 5. GENERAL SYSTEMS THEORY AND BEYOND

1. Magoroh Maruyama, "Toward Cultural Symbiosis," in *Evolution and Consciousness: Human Systems in Transition,* ed. Erich Jantsch and Conrad H. Waddington (Reading, Mass.: Addison-Wesley Publishing Co., 1976), 208.

2. Ernest R. Hilgard, Rita L. Atkinson, and Richard C. Atkinson, *Introduction to Psychology*, 7th ed. (New York: Harcourt Brace Jovanovich, 1979), 284.

3. Ludwig von Bertalanffy, "General Systems Theory—A Critical Review," *General Systems Yearbook* 7 (1962): 8.

4. Paul Watzlawick, Janet Helmick Beavin, and Don D. Jackson, M.D., *Pragmatics of Human Communication* (New York: W. W. Norton and Co., 1967), 134.

5. Maruyama, "Toward Cultural Symbiosis," 200.

6. William J. Lederer and Don D. Jackson, M.D., *The Mirages of Marriage* (New York: W. W. Norton and Co., 1968), 96.

7. Draper L. Kauffman, Jr., *Systems One: An Introduction to Systems Thinking* (St. Paul, Minn.: Future Systems/TLH Associates, 1980), 24.

8. Watzlawick et al., *Pragmatics of Human Communication*, 146.

9. See *Evolution and Consciousness: Human Systems in Transition*, ed. Erich Jantsch and Conrad H. Waddington (Reading, Mass.: Addison-Wesley Publishing Co., 1976).

10. Erich Jantsch, *The Self-Organizing Universe: Scientific and Human Implications of the Emerging Paradigm of Evolution* (Oxford: Pergamon Press, 1980), 19.

11. Martha Crampton, "Organismic Process: A Paradigm for Freeing Human Creativity," *The American Theosophist* 68, no. 5 (May 1980): 133.

12. Ibid.

13. Jantsch and Waddington, *Evolution and Consciousness*, 9-10.

14. Jantsch, *Self-Organizing Universe*, 18.

15. Doran McCarty, *Teilhard de Chardin* (Waco, Tex.: Word Books, 1977), 41.

16. Pierre Teilhard de Chardin, *The Phenomenon of Man* (New York: Harper and Row, 1959), 258.

17. Ibid., 262.

18. J. C. Smuts, *Holism and Evolution* (Westport, Conn.: Greenwood Press, 1973), 318.

19. Swami Prabhavananda, *The Spiritual Heritage of India* (Hollywood, Calif.: Vedanta Press, 1969), 48.

20. *CW* 14, 759.

21. *CW* 16, 400.

22. See Franklin Merrell-Wolff, *The Philosophy of Consciousness Without an Object* (New York: Julian Press, 1973).

23. Klaus F. Riegel, "Dialectic Operations: The Final Period of Cognitive Development," *Human Development* 16:346-70.

24. Ibid., 348.

25. Herb Koplowitz, "A Projection Beyond Piaget's Formal Operations Stage: General System Theory and Unitary Thought," unpublished manuscript, 3. A revised version of this manuscript appears in *Beyond Formal Operations: Late Adolescent and Adult Cognitive Development*, ed. M. Commons, R. Richards, and C. Armon (New York: Praeger Publishers, 1983).

26. Koplowitz, "Projection Beyond Piaget," 16-17.

27. Gerald R. Weeks and Luciano L'Abate, *Paradoxical Psychotherapy: Theory and Practice with Individuals, Couples, and Families* (New York: Brunner/Mazel, 1982), 5.

28. Kauffman, *Systems One*, 38.

29. Ibid., 18-19.

30. Koplowitz, "Projection Beyond Piaget," 11.

31. Weeks and L'Abate, *Paradoxical Psychotherapy*, 121-22.

32. Koplowitz, "Projection Beyond Piaget," 23.

33. Cited in Koplowitz, "Projection Beyond Piaget," 23.

34. Ibid., 25.

35. Gary Zukav, *The Dancing Wu Li Masters* (New York: William Morrow and Co., 1979), 219.

36. Koplowitz, "Projection Beyond Piaget," 38-39.

Chapter 6. FROM EGO TO SELF

1. The development and expansion of one's self-concept is treated in more depth in Swami Rama and Swami Ajaya, *Emotion to Enlightenment* (Honesdale, Pa.: Himalayan Institute, 1976). See especially chs. 1-3.

2. *CW* 10, 304.

3. Erich Fromm, *To Have or to Be?* ed. Ruth Nanda Anshen (New York: Harper and Row, 1976), 6.

4. Ibid., 171.

5. R. Bruce Masterton, "The Nervous System and Behavior," in *Principles of General Psychology*, 5th ed., Gregory A. Kimble, Norman Garmezy, and Edward Zigler (New York: John Wiley and Sons, 1980), 35.

6. C. G. Jung, *Memories, Dreams, Reflections* (New York: Random House, Vintage Books, 1963), 17.

7. *CW* 13, 10.

8. *CW* 11, 833.

9. *CW* 11, 778.

10. *CW* 11, 184.

11. Jung, *Memories, Dreams, Reflections*, 177.

12. Ibid., 276.

13. *CW* 11, 774.

14. *CW* 11, 817.

15. *CW* 11, 783.

16. *CW* 16, 474.

17. *CW* 16, 219.

18. *CW* 16, 366.

19. *CW* 7, 274.

20. *CW* 9, part 2, 45.

21. Srimat Swami Saradanandaji Maharaj, *Sri Ramakrishna: The Great Master*, trans. Swami Jagadananda (Mylapore, India: Sri Ramakrishna Math, 1952), 251. Material in brackets has been added.

22. Shankara, *Crest-Jewel of Discrimination*, 3d ed., trans. Swami Prabhavananda and Christopher Isherwood (Hollywood, Calif.: Vedanta Press, 1978), 83.

23. See Swami Rama, *Enlightenment Without God: Mandukya Upanishad* (Honesdale, Pa.: Himalayan Institute, 1982), 85-99.

24. Ibid., 61, 69-70.

25. Franklin Merrell-Wolff, *The Philosophy of Consciousness Without an Object* (New York: Julian Press, 1973), 164-65.

26. Ibid., 233.

27. Ibid., 219.

28. Swami Prabhavananda and Frederick Manchester, *The Upanishads: Breath of the Eternal* (New York: New American Library, Mentor Books, 1969), 89, 98.

29. Shankara, *Crest-Jewel,* 22.

30. Ibid., 104.

31. Merrell-Wolff, *Philosophy of Consciousness,* 158-59.

32. Franklin Merrell-Wolff, *Pathways through to Space: A Personal Record of Transformation in Consciousness* (New York: Julian Press, 1973), 122.

33. Shankara, *Crest-Jewel,* 122-23.

Chapter 7. TURNING OUTSIDE IN

1. See *CW* 8, 749-95, and Roberto Assagioli, *Psychosyntheses: A Manual of Principles and Techniques* (New York: Viking Press, 1965), 54-55.

2. *CW* 16, 75.

3. Jolande Jacobi, *The Psychology of C. G. Jung* (New Haven, Conn.: Yale University Press, 1973), 108.

4. C. G. Jung, *Modern Man in Search of a Soul* (New York: Harcourt, Brace and World, Harvest Books, 1955), 229.

5. Swami Nikhilananda, Introduction to Shankara, *Self-Knowledge,* trans. Swami Nikhilananda (New York: Ramakrishna-Vivekananda Center, 1970), 20.

6. *CW* 8, 785.

7. Heinrich Zimmer, *The King and the Corpse: Tales of the Soul's Conquest of Evil* (Princeton, N.J.: Princeton University Press, 1971), 241-47.

8. Madhu Khanna, *Yantra: The Tantric Symbol of Cosmic Unity* (London: Thames and Hudson, 1979), 80.

9. *CW* 11, 141.

10. *CW* 16, 504.

11. For further discussion of the way the unconscious mind is dealt with in yoga, see Swami Rama, *Enlightenment Without God: Mandukya Upanishad* (Honesdale, Pa.: Himalayan Institute, 1982), 87-109.

12. Nikhilananda, Introduction to Shankara, *Self-Knowledge,* 57.

13. Shankara, *Crest-Jewel of Discrimination,* 3d ed., trans. Swami Prabhavananda and Christopher Isherwood (Hollywood, Calif.: Vedanta Press, 1978), 103.

14. Roberto Assagioli, *The Balancing and Synthesis of the Opposites* (Montreal: Quebec Center for Psychosynthesis, 1974), 6.

15. Ibid., 9.

16. Paul Watzlawick, John H. Weakland, and Richard Fisch, *Change: Principles of Problem Formation and Problem Resolution* (New York: W. W. Norton and Co., 1974), 10-11.

17. *CW* 13, 17.

18. *The Bhagavad Gita,* trans. Juan Mascaró (Hammondsworth, England: Penguin Books, 1962), 2:69.

19. For a more complete discussion of this process, see Franklin Merrell-Wolff,

The Philosophy of Consciousness Without an Object (New York: Julian Press, 1973).

20. R. D. Laing, *The Politics of the Family and Other Essays* (New York: Random House, Vintage Books, 1972), 82, 78-80.

21. Ibid., 82.

22. Shankara, *Crest-Jewel,* 74.

23. Ibid., 56.

24. *CW* 16, 469.

25. C. G. Jung, *Memories, Dreams, Reflections* (New York: Random House, Vintage Books, 1963), 296-97.

26. *CW* 13, 55.

27. *CW* 16, 400.

28. Cited in *CW* 11, 890.

29. *Meister Eckhart: A Modern Translation,* trans. Raymond Bernard Blakney (New York: Harper Torchbooks, 1941), 85.

30. *CW* 13, 20.

31. Shankara, *Crest-Jewel,* 119.

PART II
APPLICATIONS OF YOGA THERAPY

Introduction to Part II.

1. Richard H. Svihus, M.D., "The Dimensions of Wellness: The Holistic Viewpoint," *American Holistic Medicine* 1, no. 1 (February 1979): 19.

2. Ibid. Quoted from the Apostle Paul in 1 Thess. 5:23.

Chapter 8. BODY AND BEHAVIORAL TECHNIQUES

1. The book *Diet and Nutrition: A Holistic Approach* by Rudolph Ballentine, M.D. (Honesdale, Pa.: Himalayan Institute, 1978), discusses this aspect of yoga therapy in depth and is recommended for all those who wish further knowledge of the relation between food and consciousness.

2. W. Edward Mann, *Orgone, Reich and Eros: Wilhelm Reich's Theory of Life Energy* (New York: Simon and Schuster, Touchstone Books, 1973), 62.

3. Swami Vivekananda, *Raja-Yoga,* rev. ed. (New York: Ramakrishna-Vivekananda Center, 1955), 29.

4. Alexander Lowen, *Pleasure: A Creative Approach to Life* (New York: Penguin Books, 1975), 39-40.

5. Magda Proskauer, "Breathing Therapy," in *Ways of Growth,* ed. H. Otto and J. Mann (New York: Viking Press, 1968), 26.

6. Lowen, *Pleasure,* 38.

7. Ibid., 40.

8. See L. C. Lum, "The Syndrome of Habitual Chronic Hyperventilation," *Modern Trends in Psychosomatic Medicine* 13 (1976): 196-230.

9. Ibid., 226-27.

10. The therapeutic use of breathing techniques has been discussed further in Swami

Rama, Rudolph Ballentine, M.D., and Alan Hymes, M.D., *Science of Breath: A Practical Guide* (Honesdale, Pa.: Himalayan Institute, 1979) and in ch. 6 of Phil Nuernberger, *Freedom from Stress: A Holistic Approach* (Honesdale, Pa.: Himalayan Institute, 1981).

11. *The Bhagavad Gita,* trans. Juan Mascaró (Hammondsworth, England: Penguin Books, 1962), 2:47, 49.

12. *CW* 11, 522.

13. These ten principles are discussed further in ch. 2 of Swami Rama, *Lectures on Yoga* (Honesdale, Pa.: Himalayan Institute, 1979).

14. Hellmuth Kaiser, *Effective Psychotherapy* (New York: Free Press, 1965), 36.

15. Virginia Satir, *Peoplemaking* (Palo Alto, Calif.: Science and Behavior Books, 1972), 60.

16. Ibid., 73-74.

17. Palo Alto, Calif.: Science and Behavior Books, 1975.

Chapter 9. THE RELATIONSHIP BETWEEN THERAPIST AND CLIENT

1. See, for example, Thomas S. Szasz, *The Myth of Mental Illness* (New York: Dell Publishing Co., Delta Books, 1961).

2. See, for example, Swami Rama, *A Practical Guide to Holistic Health* (Honesdale, Pa.: Himalayan Institute, 1980) and *Lectures on Yoga* (Honesdale, Pa.: Himalayan Institute, 1979).

3. Hellmuth Kaiser, *Effective Psychotherapy* (New York: Free Press, 1965), 3-4.

4. *CW* 16:168, 170.

5. *The Bhagavad Gita,* trans. Juan Mascaró (Hammondsworth, England: Penguin Books, 1962), 3:21-24.

6. Lawrence M. Brammer and Everett L. Shostrom, *Therapeutic Psychology: Fundamentals of Counseling and Psychotherapy* (Englewood Cliffs, N.J.: Prentice-Hall, 1960), 230.

7. Judah C. Safier, "Hasidism, Faith, and the Therapeutic Paradox," in *Mystics and Medics: A Comparison of Mystical and Psychotherapeutic Encounters,* ed. Reuven P. Bulka (New York: Human Sciences Press, 1979), 57.

8. Elie Wiesel, *Souls on Fire: Portraits and Legends of Hasidic Masters,* trans. Marion Wiesel (New York: Random House, Vintage Books, 1973), 51.

9. Safier, "Hasidism, Faith, and the Therapeutic Paradox," 58.

10. Paul Watzlawick, *The Language of Change: Elements of Therapeutic Communication* (New York: Basic Books, 1978), 96.

Chapter 10. THE COLLECTIVE UNCONSCIOUS FROM THE YOGIC PERSPECTIVE

1. Additional material on the relation between the chakras and one's functioning may be found in ch. 7 of Swami Rama, Rudolph Ballentine, M.D., and Swami Ajaya, *Yoga and Psychotherapy: The Evolution of Consciousness* (Honesdale, Pa.: Himalayan Institute, 1976).

2. C. G. Jung, "Psychological Commentary on Kundalini Yoga, Lecture IV," *Spring: An Annual of Archetypal Psychology and Jungian Thought* 1976: 21, 27.

3. *CW* 9, part 1, 467 n. 12.

4. Jung, "Psychological Commentary on Kundalini Yoga, Lecture II," *Spring* 1975: 23.

5. Jung, "Psychological Commentary on Kundalini Yoga, Lecture I," *Spring* 1975: 8.

6. Jung, "Kundalini Yoga, Lecture II," 19-20.

7. Violet S. de Laszlow, Introduction to C. G. Jung, *Psyche and Symbol* (Garden City, New York: Doubleday and Co., Anchor Books, 1958), xxxi.

8. C. G. Jung, *Memories, Dreams, Reflections* (New York: Random House, Vintage Books, 1963), 208-9.

9. de Laszlow, Introduction to *Psyche and Symbol*, xxx-xxxi.

10. Jung, "Psychological Commentary on Kundalini Yoga, Lecture III," *Spring* 1976: 27-28.

11. Gerald R. Weeks and Luciano L'Abate, *Paradoxical Psychotherapy: Theory and Practice with Individuals, Couples and Families* (New York: Brunner/Mazel, 1982), 19.

12. Jung, "Kundalini Yoga, Lecture II," 22.

13. See Swami Rama, *Enlightenment Without God: Mandukya Upanishad* (Honesdale, Pa.: Himalayan Institute, 1982), 55-65.

14. *The Bhagavad Gita,* trans. Juan Mascaró (Hammondsworth, England: Penguin Books, 1962), 2:62-66.

15. Jolande Jacobi, *The Psychology of C. G. Jung* (New Haven, Conn.: Yale University Press, 1973), 47n.

16. Alexander Lowen, *Pleasure: A Creative Approach to Life* (New York: Penguin Books, 1975), 15.

17. Erich Fromm, *To Have or to Be?* ed. Ruth Nanda Anshen (New York: Harper and Row, 1976), 170-71.

18. Bob Dylan, "Gotta Serve Somebody," *Slow Train Coming,* Columbia FCT 36120.

19. For an extensive discussion of karma yoga, see ch. 4 of Swami Rama, *Choosing a Path* (Honesdale, Pa.: Himalayan Institute, 1982).

20. *Bhagavad Gita,* trans. Mascaró, 2:48; 3:25.

Chapter 11. SPIRITUAL ASPECTS OF PSYCHOTHERAPY

1. Jung, "Psychological Commentary on Kundalini Yoga, Lecture III," *Spring: An Annual of Archetypal Psychology and Jungian Thought* 1976: 6.

2. Jung, "Psychological Commentary on Kundalini Yoga, Lecture II," *Spring* 1975: 22.

3. Psalm 23.

4. *CW* 11, 854.

5. *CW* 13, 36.

6. Jolande Jacobi, *The Psychology of C. G. Jung* (New Haven, Conn.: Yale University Press, 1973), 139.

7. Jung, "Psychological Commentary on Kundalini Yoga, Lecture IV," *Spring* 1976: 28.

8. Heinrich Zimmer, "The Chakras of Kundalini Yoga," *Spring* 1975: 34.

9. Ibid.

10. For a presentation of the major divisions of yogic practice, see *Choosing a Path* by Sri Swami Rama (Honesdale, Pa.: Himalayan Institute, 1982).

11. Peter Suedfeld, *Restricted Environmental Stimulation: Research and Clinical Applications* (New York: John Wiley and Sons, 1980), 218.

Index

The main building of the national headquarters, Honesdale, Pa.

The Himalayan Institute

Since its establishment in 1971, the Himalayan Institute has been dedicated to helping individuals develop themselves physically, mentally, and spiritually, as well as contributing to the transformation of society. All the Institute programs—educational, therapeutic, research—emphasize holistic health, yoga, and meditation as tools to help achieve those goals. Institute programs combine the best of ancient wisdom and modern science, of Eastern teachings and Western technologies. We invite you to join with us in this ongoing process of personal growth and development.

Our beautiful national headquarters, on a wooded 400-acre campus in the Pocono Mountains of northeastern Pennsylvania, provides a peaceful, healthy setting for our seminars, classes, and training programs in the principles and practices of holistic living. Students from around the world have joined us here for the past fifteen years to attend programs in such diverse areas as biofeedback and stress reduction, hatha yoga, meditation, diet and nutrition, philosophy and metaphysics, and practical psychology for better living. We see the realization of our human potentials as a lifelong quest, leading to increased health, creativity, and happiness.

The Institute is a nonprofit organization. Your membership in the Institute helps to support its programs. Please call or write for information on becoming a member.

Institute Programs, Services, and Facilities

All Institute programs share an emphasis on conscious, holistic living and personal self-development. You may enjoy any of a number of diverse programs, including:

- Special weekend or extended seminars to teach skills and techniques for increasing your ability to be healthy and enjoy life

- Holistic health services

- Professional training for health professionals

- Meditation retreats and advanced meditation instruction

- Cooking and nutritional training

- Hatha yoga and exercise workshops

- Residential programs for self-development

The Himalayan Institute Charitable Hospital

A major aspect of the Institute's work around the world is its construction and management of a modern, comprehensive hospital and holistic health facility in the mountain area of Dehra Dun, India. Outpatient facilities are already providing medical care to those in need, and also mobile units have been equipped to visit outlying villages. Construction work on the main hospital building is progressing as scheduled.

We welcome financial support to help with construction and the provision of services. We also welcome donations of medical supplies, equipment, or professional expertise. If you would like further information on the Hospital, please contact us.

Himalayan Institute Publications

Art of Joyful Living	Swami Rama
Book of Wisdom (Ishopanishad)	Swami Rama
A Call to Humanity	Swami Rama
Celestial Song/Gobind Geet	Swami Rama
Choosing a Path	Swami Rama
The Cosmic Drama: Bichitra Natak	Swami Rama
Enlightenment Without God	Swami Rama
Exercise Without Movement	Swami Rama
Freedom from the Bondage of Karma	Swami Rama
Indian Music, Volume I	Swami Rama
Inspired Thoughts of Swami Rama	Swami Rama
Japji: Meditation in Sikhism	Swami Rama
Lectures on Yoga	Swami Rama
Life Here and Hereafter	Swami Rama
Living with the Himalayan Masters	Swami Rama
Love Whispers	Swami Rama
Marriage, Parenthood, and Enlightenment	Swami Rama
Meditation and Its Practice	Swami Rama
Path of Fire and Light, Vol. I	Swami Rama
Path of Fire and Light, Vol. II	Swami Rama
Perennial Psychology of the Bhagavad Gita	Swami Rama
A Practical Guide to Holistic Health	Swami Rama
Sukhamani Sahib: Fountain of Eternal Joy	Swami Rama
Wisdom of the Ancient Sages	Swami Rama
Creative Use of Emotion	Swami Rama, Swami Ajaya
Science of Breath	Swami Rama, Rudolph Ballentine, M.D., Alan Hymes, M.D.
Yoga and Psychotherapy	Swami Rama, Rudolph Ballentine, M.D., Swami Ajaya
The Mystical Poems of Kabir	Swami Rama, Robert Regli
Yoga-sutras of Patanjali	Usharbudh Arya, D.Litt.
Superconscious Meditation	Usharbudh Arya, D.Litt.
Mantra and Meditation	Usharbudh Arya, D.Litt.
Philosophy of Hatha Yoga	Usharbudh Arya, D.Litt.
Meditation and the Art of Dying	Usharbudh Arya, D.Litt.
God	Usharbudh Arya, D.Litt.

Psychotherapy East and West: A Unifying Paradigm	Swami Ajaya, Ph.D.
Yoga Psychology	Swami Ajaya, Ph.D.
Diet and Nutrition	Rudolph Ballentine, M.D.
Joints and Glands Exercises	Rudolph Ballentine, M.D. (ed.)
Transition to Vegetarianism	Rudolph Ballentine, M.D.
Theory and Practice of Meditation	Rudolph Ballentine, M.D. (ed.)
Freedom from Stress	Phil Nuernberger, Ph.D.
Homeopathic Remedies	Buegel, Chernin, Lewis
Hatha Yoga Manual I	Samskrti and Veda
Hatha Yoga Manual II	Samskrti and Judith Franks
Seven Systems of Indian Philosophy	Rajmani Tigunait, Ph.D.
Yoga on War and Peace	Rajmani Tigunait, Ph.D.
Swami Rama of the Himalayas	L. K. Misra, Ph.D. (ed.)
Sikh Gurus	K.S. Duggal
Philosophy and Faith of Sikhism	K.S. Duggal
The Quiet Mind	John Harvey, Ph.D. (ed.)
Himalayan Mountain Cookery	Martha Ballentine
The Yoga Way Cookbook	Himalayan Institute
Meditation in Christianity	Himalayan Institute
Chants from Eternity	Himalayan Institute
Spiritual Diary	Himalayan Institute
Blank Books	Himalayan Institute

To order or to request a free mail order catalog call or write
The Himalayan Publishers
RR 1, Box 400
Honesdale, PA 18431
Toll-Free 1-800-822-4547